EARL
ISRAELITES:
TWO PEOPLES,
ONE HISTORY

REDISCOVERY OF THE ORIGINS OF ANCIENT ISRAEL

IGOR P. LIPOVSKY

American Academy Press
Washington, D.C.

AMERICAN ACADEMY PRESS

Scripture quotations are taken from the Holy Bible New International Version, copyright 1984, 2011. International Bible Society.

Printed and bound in the United States of America

SECOND REVISED EDITION. Originally published in 2012

Library of Congress Cataloging-in-Publication Data

Lipovsky, Igor P., 1950-
Early Israelites: two peoples, one history / Igor P. Lipovsky – 2nd ed.
p. cm.
Includes bibliographical references and index.
1. Jews-History-2000-1000 B.C.E.-Historiography. 2. Bible O.T. Exodus-Criticism, interpretation, etc. 3. Palestine-Ethnology. 4. Canaanites-History. 5. Jews-Origin. I. Title.

ON THE COVER: Semi-nomadic Western Semites from Beni Hasan tomb painting. 19th century B.C.E. (Egypt)

ISBN: 978-0-578-53630-9

Library of Congress Control Number: 2019910210

American Academy Press

For my wife, Helen Lipovsky (Muldt),
with love and gratitude.
Here is the book I promised you so long ago.

Acknowledgments

I WOULD LIKE TO thank my friends and colleagues from the faculty of Judaic Studies at Yale and Princeton Universities, who read a good part of the book and made many valuable criticisms and helpful suggestions.

I owe thanks to the Harvard Divinity School for the encouraging support and generous contribution to the publication of this book.

I am truly grateful to the British translator and writer, John Nicolson, who helped me with translating part of my book from Russian.

My profound thanks also go to my family, above all to my son Daniel, whose support and help made this book possible. My thanks to him are both richly deserved and most sincerely intended.

Contents

Contents

Introduction

Where did the Ancient Semites come from?

The ancient Near East was a world dominated by Semitic peoples. Akkad, Assyria, Babylonia, Phoenicia, Israel, and the Syrian kingdoms were all results of the Semites' activities. Although Sumer, the very first state in the world, was not of Semitic origin, its inhabitants had been fully assimilated by the Semites in the earliest times and had become an integral part of their world. Egypt resisted the supremacy of the Semitic peoples for considerably longer, but it too eventually adopted their language and culture. The Indo-Europeans appeared on the scene at a later stage. More importantly, their first states, including the Hittite Empire, remained on the periphery, on the northern and eastern boundaries of the Near East. The same was true of the Hurrians, an ancient non-Semitic people whose ethnic origin remains unclear to the present day.

Today, there are few who doubt that the original homeland of the ancient Semites should be sought in the Near East. But where exactly? In the 20th century, the established view was that the most probable, original homeland for all the Semitic tribes was northern Arabia. The geographic position of this area, in the center of today's Semitic world, provides an easy explanation for both these peoples' distribution in the Near East and the dispersion of Semitic languages. Further support for this view is to be found in the considerable water reserves in the North Arabian aquifer, without which the nomadic pastoralists would have had no wells. There is reason to suppose that in ancient times the climate of this region, and indeed of the Near East as a whole, was significantly more humid. Archaeological excavations have shown that approximately 8000-9000 years ago, so much rain fell that today's deserts in the Negev and in northern Sinai had rich vegetation and were home to entire settlements. Only with the passing of time, as the climate became drier, did northern Arabia become a desert; and this was the main reason why the Semitic tribes left their original homeland. But this seemingly convenient and convincing version has one very serious flaw: northern Arabia had already become a desert at least 7000 years ago, i.e. long before the Semites started migrating en masse. Archaeological data confirm that by the 5th millennium B.C.E. the climate in the Near East had become drier and people were gradually leaving their settlements in northern Sinai and in the Negev. The life of the Bedouin in today's Arabia would not have been possible without the camel and this animal was domesticated only in the 11th century B.C.E. Thus, the climatic conditions in northern Arabia did not meet the living conditions needed by a large group of tribes.

However, there is also other, indirect evidence against looking for the Semites' original homeland in northern Arabia. All the ancient Egyptian frescos depict the Semites as people with relatively light skin, as compared to the Egyptians themselves. Consequently, they must have come from regions located much further to the north, where the sun's radiation was considerably less than in Egypt or northern Arabia.

People have also searched for the Semites' original native land in Palestine, Syria, and central Mesopotamia, but the absence of continuity in the succession of cultural strata in these places renders these assumptions doubtful. A more eccentric theory locates the homeland in the territory of today's Sahara. This theory's steadiest supporters have been linguists who have thus been able to explain the relationship of the Semitic languages with Berber, Cushitic, Chadic, and the ancient Egyptian languages. Indeed, the Sahara has not always been a barren desert, but the problem lies in the fact that it became one before northern Arabia did. Moreover, all known migrations by the Semites took place during a period in which the climate of the Near East hardly differed from today's. The most important of these migrations, e.g. those of the Amorites and the Arameans, happened in the historical period, when literacy existed. Although the evidence showing where the Semites came from is not yet clear, we may nevertheless, on the basis of written sources and archaeological evidence, state with absolute certainty that the Semites came to central Mesopotamia, Syria, and Canaan not from the south (Arabia), but from the north – from northwestern Mesopotamia and the upper courses of the two largest rivers in Western Asia, the Tigris and the Euphrates.

The Bible specifically names the original homeland of the Jewish patriarchs as the region surrounding the city of Haran, which was situated approximately 20 miles southwest of today's Turkish city of Şanlıurfa (ancient Edessa), not far from the border with Syria. The biblical texts clearly show that the city of Ur in Sumer, from which Abraham came into Canaan, was not his birthplace. Furthermore, on the way to Canaan, the family of Abraham and his father Terah stopped for a long time in Haran, their place of birth (Genesis 11:31-32). This is where Terah died and where leadership of the clan was transferred to his son, Abraham. Later, the Bible again reminds us that the native land of the Hebrew forefathers was not Canaan, but Haran, in northwestern Mesopotamia. The Book of Genesis gives two other names for this region: Aram-Naharaim and Padan-Aram (Genesis 24:10; 25:20). These names clearly came to be associated with the region of Haran after the arrival of the Arameans. It was here that Abraham sent his trusted servant to find a wife for his son Isaac, since he did not want to intermarry with the local peoples in Canaan (Genesis 24:2-4,10). And it was here – to their relatives back in their homeland – that Jacob's mother Rebekah sent her beloved son, wishing to save him from the revenge of his brother Esau (Genesis 27:42-43). Like Abraham, Isaac too did not wish to enter into family relations with the Canaanites (Genesis 28:1-2). What's more, the Bible does not hide the disappointment and pain felt by Esau's parents as a result of his marriage to a local woman (Genesis 26:34-35).

The prolonged archaeological excavations in Israel and Jordan have unearthed sufficient proof that the Canaanites, a West Semitic people, likewise came from the north in the 4th and 3rd millennia B.C.E. Their predecessors, who belonged to the so-called Ghassulian culture and appeared in Canaan in approximately 4000 B.C.E., were most likely Western Semites too, having come to Southern Levant from the north as well.

At the end of the 3rd millennium B.C.E., large groups of West Semitic peoples – the Amorites – began settling all together in Mesopotamia, Syria, and Canaan, and took control over the majority of cities, forming their own Amorite states. One of these, for example, was Babylon during the reign of the infamous ruler Hammurapi in the 18th century B.C.E. Written and material evidence gathered over recent decades suggests that the Amorites did not come from northern Arabia or the Syrian Desert region, as had previously been thought, but instead from the north, from northwestern Mesopotamia.

The second mass wave of Western Semites, the Arameans, came to Syria and central and southern Mesopotamia much later, in the 12th and 11th centuries B.C.E. Judging from the directions taken by their migrations, their place of exodus was again northwestern Mesopotamia.

It is well known that Akkad, the first Semitic state, was established in central Mesopotamia not by Western, but by Eastern Semites. Subsequently, it was they who subjugated their southern neighbor, Sumer. The history of the relations between these two states testifies that the Akkadians came not from the south, but from the north, as did all the Western Semites.

What did northwestern Mesopotamia, the original homeland of the Semites, actually consist of, in terms of natural habitat? This large area is separated from the rest of Anatolia by imposing mountain ranges – the mountains of south-eastern Taurus in the north and east and the Nur Mountains in the west. This three-sided natural shelter had an important influence on people's lives during this troubled period. Even today, the semicircle of mountains surrounding northwestern Mesopotamia protect it from the cold northerly winds, making the local climate substantially milder and warmer than in the interior regions of Anatolia. This region is only exposed on its south side, where the Syrian lowlands are situated. The upper courses of the Tigris and Euphrates rivers and their tributaries supply this region abundantly with water. The sufficient precipitation, in combination with the relatively flat landscape and fertile soil, makes it possible to engage in agriculture and cattle-farming even at a significant distance from the rivers. This was a country that was ideally suited to the lives of the ancient people from all points of view. It is no coincidence that cotton, a warmth-loving crop that requires a great deal of water and good soil, is today tilled in the area.

What was once the homeland of the ancient Semites is now located almost entirely in modern-day Turkey. The Turkish cities Gaziantep and Kilis are located in its western part, Şanlıurfa and Mardin in the south, and Batman, Diyarbakır, and Adıyaman in the north. As fate would have it, the Semites' native land has turned out to be located on what is now the very northern edge of the Semitic world. It was precisely from this area that the ancient Semites began to descend south, along the river valleys of the Tigris and Euphrates, continuing along the eastern shore of the Mediterranean Sea. But what forced them to abandon their well-favored land? After all, the new lands with their hotter, more difficult climate, hemmed in by the enormous Syrian Desert, suffered from a chronic shortage of rainfall. Most likely, the move was the result of two factors: natural population growth and the advance of the Indo-Europeans and the Hurrians from the north. Here we come up against another problem, this time to do with the native land of the Indo-European peoples.

The search for the original birthplace of the Indo-Europeans is a more complex affair than finding the native land of the Semites. Various researchers have located it in different places at a great distance from one another. Some have placed it on the territory of today's Poland; others in the Balkans; and still others in Iran or Central Asia. Such a spread of opinion is not accidental. It has been at least one and a half to two thousand years since the speakers of the Indo-European languages had scattered over vast areas in Europe and Asia – from Spain in the west to the borders of Tibet in the east, and from the Arctic Ocean in the north to the Indian Ocean in the south. But where did these people's ancestors start out from and what forced them to abandon their original land? Roman and ancient Greek authors have left us a good deal of information about the movements of the Germanic and Slavic peoples, – the Scythians and Sarmatians – while ancient Egyptian sources contain information on the Hittites and the 'Sea Peoples'. The Babylonians and Assyrians were in contact with the Medes, Iranians, Cimmerians, and the peoples of Urartu. Indeed, the history of the ancient Greeks and Romans is itself only a part of Indo-European history. From the wealth of this disparate and fragmentary information provided by different authors from different periods it follows that the starting point for all the migrations of the Indo-Europeans, their original homeland, was located somewhere in the region near the Black Sea; to be more precise, on its northern and western shores. The principal region where the Indo-Europeans lived in prehistoric times was likely the area that is occupied today by the waters of the Black Sea. Approximately 8000 years ago, what are now the Black and Azov Seas did not exist at all. Their place was occupied by a large depression lying substantially below sea level. Admittedly, there was a large fresh-water lake in the area at the time, but it was much smaller than today's Black Sea. Great rivers flowed into this lake, including the Danube, Dniester, Bug, Dnieper, Don, Kuban, and Kızılırmak. The plentiful fresh water, mild climate, and conveniently flat lands obviously made this area just as suited to human habitation as the Semites' original homeland in northwestern Mesopotamia. However, seismic processes occurring between the 6th and 4th millennia B.C.E. resulted in the collapse of the land level in the region of the modern-day Bosporus Strait, and water from the Mediterranean Sea began to flood into the Black Sea depression. The geological cataclysm resulted in an ecological catastrophe: the former fresh-water lake turned into a salty sea and gradually flooded the regions where many Indo-Europeans lived. Granted, it did take decades – perhaps even hundreds of years – to fill up the Black Sea; so while the rising water could not have led to people's deaths, it did necessitate them to migrate in whatever direction they could. The newly-formed sea literally forced the Indo-Europeans out of the places where they were living – particularly the tribes occupying the region to the north and the west of the Black Sea, where the largest area of land was covered by water.

Based on what we know from history about the Indo-European migrations, the Celts and Germans lived in the northwest of the Black Sea area; the Balts and Slavs in the north; the ancestors of the Cimmerians, Sarmatians, and Scythians in the northeast; and the Indo-Iranian tribes in the south-east. It is probable that the ancestors of the Italics and the Greeks lived in the northern portion of the Balkan Peninsula to the southwest of the Celts and the Germans. The Hittites, Luwians, Palaics, and all those whom we classify as belonging to the Anatolian group of Indo-European speakers occupied the southernmost regions of the Black Sea depression and were forced out by the advancing sea into Anatolia and the north of Asia Minor. Subsequently, the Celts and, after them, the Germans gradually occupied the northwest of Europe while the Slavs and Balts spread into northern and eastern Europe, which was already occupied by the Finno-Ugric peoples. The speakers of the Indo-Iranian languages invaded Iran, Central Asia, and northern India. This model of the Indo-Europeans' migration in all directions away from the advancing Black Sea is given indirect support by ancient historians' testimonies regarding the life of the Ostrogoths' Germanic tribes in Crimea, during the first centuries C.E. – namely that an East Slavic people, the Drevlians, was a neighbor of a Germanic tribe that had 'lost its way' in the area of what is now Ukraine, and that there were Baltic Letts living in the Upper Volga region.

The migration of the Indo-Europeans southwards and eastwards resulted in the Semites being displaced from their original homeland in the northwest of Mesopotamia. But they were not the only ones whom the Indo-Europeans forced to abandon their native regions. A similar fate befell the Hurrians in eastern Anatolia, who were forced southwards and settled in northern Syria and Mesopotamia, where they considerably crowded the Semites living there. Hurrian names appeared relatively early – at the end of the 3rd millennium B.C.E. – in northern Mesopotamia. This ethnic group created several of its own states, the strongest of which was Mitanni. The language and ethnic origins of the Hurrians remain a mystery to this day. Many historians consider them to be of Indo-European origin, like the Hittites; however, linguistic analysis of their language has been unable to confirm this. The Hurrians were probably one of the indigenous peoples of southern Trans-Caucasia and eastern Anatolia, related to the ethnic groups that later constituted the state of Urartu. It may also be the case that they, like other peoples who were native to Trans-Caucasia, had already assimilated the culture and language of the advancing Indo-Iranians. It is most likely that the Armenians are their descendants in the modern world.

The interior regions of Anatolia were settled by another indigenous people, the Hatti, who gave their name to a newly arrived group of Indo-Europeans, the Hittites. Unfortunately, we know very little about the Hatti. We may suppose that they completely merged with the newcomers from the north. It is probable that there were many native peoples living in Asia Minor, Anatolia, Trans-Caucasia, and Iran who were, like the Hatti and the Hurrians, unrelated to either the Semites or the Indo-Europeans. But the stronger and more numerous Indo-European tribes either subdued and assimilated them or forced them out into other regions. We may suppose that the same happened to the Sumerians: the arrival of the Indo-Iranians pushed them out of their homeland in the area of ancient Elam and forced them into southern Mesopotamia. There is no trace of these peoples today; they were fully assimilated in ancient times by either the Indo-Europeans or the Semites. For this reason, we are unable to decipher their languages by trying to identify them only on the basis of the language groups that are known to us.

Even when they were still in their original homeland, the ancient Semites, like the Indo-Europeans, were far from homogeneous. Judging by the times and directions of their migrations, we may suppose that as early as the 4th millennium B.C.E., there was a distinct division between Western Semites (Amorites and Arameans) and Eastern Semites (Akkadians and Assyrians). The former were concentrated in the upper Euphrates and the area near its tributaries, while the latter occupied the upper course of the valley of the Tigris River. There was also a geographic division among the Western Semites themselves: the southwest belonged to the Amorites, the north to the Arameans. The Canaanites were a part of the Amorites who had left for Syria, Phoenicia, and Canaan earlier than the other Western Semites. All the cultural and linguistic differences among them arose as the result of living separately from each other for almost a thousand years. The bearers of the Ghassulian culture who had arrived in Canaan even earlier were, from an ethnic point of view, also Canaanites – specifically, their vanguard. There the Western Semites were probably forced out from their original, native land due to different causes at different times.

The Gassulian Star, a mysterious 6,000-year-old
mural from Jordan Valley

The gradual departure of the Ghassulians and the Canaanites was most likely caused by population growth and internal clashes in their homeland, in northwestern Mesopotamia. However, the mass southward migrations of the Amorites, and later of the Arameans, were a result of the pressure applied by the Indo-Europeans from the north. The beginning of the Amorites' exodus coincided with the arrival in Anatolia of the Hittites and related peoples, while the wave of Aramean migrations coincided chronologically with the invasion of the Sea Peoples.

Thus, the exodus of the Semites from their original homeland in the upper courses of the Tigris and Euphrates was a response to a migration of Indo-Europeans and Indo-Arians, who were gradually 'squeezed out' from their own native land in the Black Sea area by an ecological catastrophe. Eventually, the migrations also involved the Hurrians – the indigenous population of Trans-Caucasia and northeastern Anatolia. Leaving the Black Sea area, the Indo-Arians 'pushed' the Hurrians to the south – to northern Mesopotamia, where they clashed with the Semites living there. The invasion of the Hurrians into the upper courses of the Tigris and Euphrates resulted in mass migrations southwards – first by the Eastern Semites (the Akkadians) and then by the Western Semites (the Amorites). The area evacuated by the Amorites was occupied by the Hurrians and the Arameans, a West Semitic ethnic group who were related to the Amorites. Thus, the Arameans – among whom are mistakenly placed the patriarch Abraham and his relatives by certain biblical texts – appeared in the Haran region. On their way to the southeast, several Indo-Aryan tribes did not only displace the Hurrians, but also partially intermarried with them. As a result, Indo-Aryan groups such as the Maryannu became part of the Hurrian community.

The second mass migration of Western Semites from their original homeland began in approximately the 12th century B.C.E. and was likewise a response to migrations by Indo-European tribes. This time, it was the Arameans who left, practically retracing the path of their predecessors, the Amorites. For instance, one of these peoples, the Chaldeans, descended the river valleys of the Tigris and the Euphrates into southern

Mesopotamia. Others went southwestwards, into Syria, where they founded their own kingdoms. However, a significant Aramean population remained in the homeland of the Semites for a long time, even though they were pressured by the Luwians (a group related to the Hittites) and the Iranians, who advanced from the east. Despite the subsequent waves of Hellenization, Christianization, and then Islamization, the local population as a whole preserved its Semitic roots. The ethnic situation changed substantially only following the arrival of the Turkic tribes at the end of the 11th century C.E. In the next several centuries, the population became completely Turkish and Islamic. Today, the entire territory of this vast region is primarily occupied by Turks and Kurds, and nothing remains to remind us of the ancient Semites' native land.

CHAPTER ONE

The beginning of Jewish history

The origins of biblical patriarchs

Jewish history begins with the biblical patriarch Abraham who lived in Ur, one of the most ancient cities of the world, in legendary Sumer. At the time, he was called by the slightly simpler-sounding name of 'Abram'. The Bible does not say how long Abram lived in Ur; however, it does make clear that neither Ur nor southern Mesopotamia as a whole were the patriarch's native land. His family had come from an entirely different area, the region of Haran, which is very far away in northwestern Mesopotamia. But Sumer was not fated to become Abram's new homeland. Maybe there was not enough unoccupied pastureland for the West Semitic nomads or perhaps conflicts arose with the local rulers; we shall probably never know the truth. But in any case the head of the family, Abram's father, Terah, decided to set off for the land of Canaan. But Mesopotamia and Canaan were separated by the vast Syrian Desert, which became traversable only an entire millennium after Abram's death, when the "desert ship" – the camel – was domesticated. In Abram's time, the main beast of burden was the donkey and for this reason even the hereditary nomads did not dare to venture far into the desert. At that time, the journey from Sumer to Canaan involved a round-about route through northwestern Mesopotamia and Haran, the area from which Abram's family originally came. There, in their initial homeland, they were forced to delay their travel for a considerable time. Terah died and authority over the family passed to his eldest son, Abram. In fulfillment of his father's wishes, Abram led his family to the southwest, through Syria and into Canaan. His first stopping place was in the central part of the country, in the area between Shechem in the north and Bethel in the south. But for some reason he did not remain in central Canaan, where water and fertile land were most abundant, but instead gradually pushed southwards, into the hottest and driest regions bordering the Negev Desert. Here, in the south, in the triangle formed by Hebron, Beersheba, and Gerar (near Gaza), Abram and his family lived as semi-nomads. This concluded the Jewish patriarch's first period of traveling. It is a time that raises many questions.

In religious literature, the decision to migrate to Canaan has traditionally been attributed to Abram and has been linked with his new, monotheistic faith. In truth, the fateful decision to leave Ur to go to Canaan was made not by Abram, but by his father, Terah, who did not worship the one God and had no personal relationship with Him. The Bible makes this completely clear: "Terah took his son Abram, his grandson Lot son of Haran, and his daughter-in-law Sarai, the wife of his son Abram, and together they set out from Ur of the Chaldeans to go to Canaan. But when they came to Haran, they settled there" (Genesis 11:31). Thus it was not Abram who took his family, but Terah. And it could not have been otherwise: according to the laws and traditions of the time, Abram's father, as the senior member of the family, was the one who was supposed to make decisions while the rest of his family was required to obey him. But why was Canaan chosen as the destination? After all, it was not close, being located a long way from both Ur and southern Mesopotamia in general; in fact, one could say that it lay at the other end of the ancient Near East. How could Terah have known that his family and tribe would find unoccupied land and available water there? All of these questions have one answer: Terah had received exhaustive information from his kinsmen who had already settled in Canaan. These kinsmen were Western Semites, just as he was, and had already left their common homeland in northwestern Mesopotamia; however, unlike Terah and his family, they had gone not to Sumer, but to Canaan. The journey across such large distances and with such a large quantity of livestock involved many difficulties and much risk. The decision to set out could only have been taken upon knowing that the family would find a place and security in this new land. And Terah likely did receive such guarantees: it is significant that, following his father's death, Abram set out not for Canaan in general, but for the southern part of the country specifically. The Bible itself says nothing of the reasons for departing for Canaan, confining itself to reference to God's will: "The Lord had said to Abram, 'Leave your country, your people and your father's household and go to the land I will show you'" (Genesis 12:1). However, the land for which Abram was heading was not unoccupied; the Bible reminds us that, "At that time the Canaanites were in the land" (Genesis 12:6). Having been the first of the Western Semites to arrive in Canaan, the Canaanites were in Abram's time a settled agricultural people. A later wave of Western Semites, the Amorites, had also settled nearby. They had already occupied the best areas of the land that was vacant, in north and central Canaan; in the arid south, however, there still remained large areas of unoccupied pastureland. By agreement among the West Semitic nomads, this southern part was given to Abram and his people. In those times, of course, southern Canaan was more pleasant than it is today. Above all, the Dead Sea had not yet formed. In its place was the Jordan River Valley, of which the Bible says: "the whole plain of the Jordan was well watered, like the garden of the Lord, like the land of Egypt, toward Zoar. (This was before the Lord destroyed Sodom and Gomorrah)" (Genesis 13:10). According to the Bible, the land that became the bottom of the Dead Sea was previously called the Valley of Siddim (Genesis 14:3) and the Jordan River supplied it with water in abundance. Later, seismic processes resulted in an ecological catastrophe: a significant part of the Jordan valley was transformed into a lifeless, salty sea; flourishing cities perished; and any survivors abandoned this disaster area. As time went on, the climate became increasingly arid and hostile to agriculture; southern Canaan gradually became the undisputed ancestral property of the West Semitic nomads.

In biblical literature, you may encounter the mistaken view that Abram's monotheistic faith had already taken root before he came to Canaan, and that the Lord who prompted him to set out for a new homeland was the same God to whom Abram's descendants prayed. However, the Bible makes no distinction between the god of Terah and the God of Abram. The break with the old deities in fact happened much later, when Abram was already in Canaan. In recent years, it has become common to hypothesize that Ur and Haran were both centers of worship of the god Sin (the moon-god) and that Abram's family were priests in this cult. Certainly, the Moon cult was popular in both cities, but this by no means implies that members of the patriarch's family were priests in the cult and left Ur for Haran because of this reason.

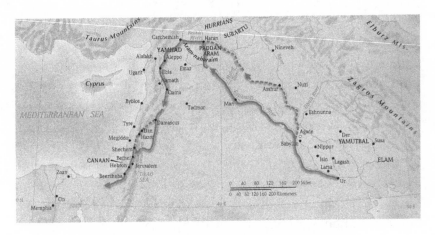

Wanderings of Abraham. 20th century B.C.E.
Holman Bible Atlas.

Who was Abram in reality and to which people did he and his family belong? The names of the biblical family members and the time at which they appeared in Mesopotamia, Canaan, and later Egypt, are signs not only of their West Semitic origin, but also of the fact that they belonged to the Amorites or a related people. We have no information on the ethnic origins of Abram's family up until his arrival in Canaan. It is only in the episode involving the captivity of Lot, his nephew, that the Bible identifies the patriarch himself for the first time: "One who had escaped came and reported this to Abram the Hebrew [Ivri]." (Genesis 14:13). Today the word 'Hebrew' (Ivri) is translated from the biblical Hebrew as 'Jew'. But 4000 years ago, this word had a different meaning and was pronounced differently – 'Habiru' or 'Apiru'. It was the name for semi-nomadic, West Semitic people who did not have their own permanent tribal territory. Even if we assume that the Habiru were not actually Amorites, they were certainly their close relatives. To begin with, this term was more social than ethnic; it signified semi-nomads who were freshly arrived. From an ethnic and linguistic point of view, the Habiru hardly differed from the settled West Semitic peoples of Syria and Canaan who surrounded them. They all had common roots and the same origin; in terms of life style, however, there were important differences. The Habiru remained semi-nomads and did not settle on the land until the 12th century B.C.E. In Abram's time, the Habiru were a large group of tribes scattered throughout Syria, Canaan, and Mesopotamia. They were to be found in all corners of the Semitic world of that time, but especially in Canaan and southern Syria, where they were a serious military and political power.

From the beginning of the 2nd millennium B.C.E., southern and central Canaan was already considered to be the land of the West Semitic semi-nomads. It is important to mention that when Joseph found himself in Egypt, he said of himself: "For I was forcibly carried off from the land of the Hebrews" (Genesis 40:15). Today this phrase means 'from the land of the Jews'. But at the time it sounded and was understood differently, namely as 'from the land of the Semitic semi-nomads'. The Habiru were warriors; dignitaries among the local rulers; artisans; and hired hands. But most lived a pastoral life, wandering nomadically with their herds over the entire territory of the Fertile Crescent. Relations between the Habiru and the settled agricultural population were very much reminiscent of the relations between Bedouin and fellahin (peasants) in Arab countries. Each side distrusted the other; however, periods of hostility alternated with peaceful and even friendly coexistence – and all the more so, since both sides needed to barter foodstuffs and goods. From the cultural point of view, the Habiru very quickly assimilated with the environment in which they lived, adopting the traditions, customs, religious beliefs, and professional skills of the local peoples. The Hebrews constituted only a small part of the Habiru who were in Canaan and southern Syria. As time went by, the term 'Habiru' increasingly took on an ethnic meaning and finally came to signify two groups of Hebrew tribes – the northern and south-ern. Thus Abram and his family were semi-nomadic Western Semites or Habiru.

Family or tribal group?

The Bible speaks only of Abram's family; however, the episode describing the liberation of Abram's nephew Lot makes clear that the patriarch was leading, at the very least, his entire tribe. "When Abram heard that his relative had been taken captive, he called out the 318 trained men born in his household and went in pursuit as far as Dan. During the night Abram divided his men to attack them and he routed them, pursuing them as far as Hobah, north of Damascus. He recovered all the goods and brought back his relative Lot and his possessions, together with the women and the other people" (Genesis 14:14-16). In order to assemble a force of 318 warriors, Abram's family must have numbered at least 6000 - 7000, which made them not a clan, but a rather large tribe. Now according to estimates by archeologists, the entire population of Canaan at the time amounted to no more than 150,000 people. Given that, Abram's tribe was a force of no small strength – and that is in spite of the fact that on the eve of these events, some of their number left to follow Lot to the east. In order to pursue the enemy from today's Dead Sea to Damas-cus, you would have needed not just a large number of people, but also well-trained and experienced warriors. From the bibli-cal narrative, it follows that the local Amorites – Aner, Eshkol, and Mamre – entered into an alliance with Abram. As a rule, families did not conclude alliances among themselves, so what we have here, evidently, is an alliance between the local Amor-ite rulers and Abram as the head of one of the Habiru tribes. Granted, one should treat the numbers given in the Bible, espe-cially in its earliest texts, with utmost caution. And yet, even if the number 318 is for some reason unreliable, it still remains an eloquent fact that Abram and his allies were able to achieve the retreat of the entire coalition of southern Syrian rulers who had invaded Canaan. This testifies to the fact that Abram's 'family' was in fact an entire semi-nomadic tribe or tribes – an alliance with whom would have been a desirable objective for many rulers in the southern part of the country.

At the very beginning of the biblical narrative concerning Abram's stay in the land of Canaan, we encounter a new fact confirming the supposition that 'Abram's family' was in fact not only a tribe, but a group of tribes:

> Now Lot, who was moving about with Abram, also had flocks and herds and tents. But the land could not support them while they stayed together, for their possessions were so great that they were not able to stay together. And quarrelling arose between Abram's herdsmen and the herdsmen of Lot... So Abram said to Lot, 'Let's not have any quarrelling between you and me, or between your herdsmen and mine, for we are brothers. Is not the whole land before you? Let's part company. If you go to the left, I'll go to the right; if you go to the right, I'll go to the left'...So Lot chose for himself the whole plain of the Jordan and set out toward the east. The two men parted company: Abram lived in the land of Canaan, while Lot lived among the cities of the plain and pitched his tents near Sodom (Genesis 13: 5-9, 11-12).

The very description of the places where Lot settled – a region extending for more than 70 miles – is evidence that what we have here is not families, but tribes. Lot's separation from Abram was only the first division among the numerous tribes of West Semitic nomads of Amorite origin who had come to southern Canaan. Those who went east with Lot came to be known as the 'Sutu' ('Sutians'). Some scholars suppose that the ethnonym 'Sutu' derived from 'Sutum', the name for the biblical Sheth, son of the primogenitor Adam. Sheth was thought to be the ancestor of all the West Semitic nomadic tribes covering the area from Canaan to Mesopotamia. It is possible that 'Habiru' was established as the name for the Hebrews later, when they were already in Canaan, and that, when they lived in Mesopotamia and up until their arrival in Canaan, they had been known as Sutu. Be that as it may, those who remained with Abram to the west of the Jordan River became known as Habiru and those who left for the east of the Jordan River were called Sutu, even though during Abram's time there was almost no difference between the former and the latter. However, the Habiru were even then drawn to the settled population and lived right in their midst, while the Sutu preserved a purely nomadic way of life. The Egyptians were very familiar with the nomadic Sutu and had their own name for them – 'Shasu'. Later, the Sutu who lived in Transjordan experienced further divisions, with some of their number forming the origins of peoples, such as the Moabites and the Ammonites.

Adoption of the cult of El

Not only was Abram the leader of the group of Habiru tribes, but he was also their high priest. Upon his arrival in Canaan, he built sacrificial altars and conducted services at Elon-More near Shechem, at Bethel, and at Elonei Mamre near Hebron. "...'You are a mighty prince [of God] among us,'" the Hittite men of Hebron told him" (Genesis 23:6). It was quite common in Canaan in those times for a leader to assume both functions (of supreme ruler and of high priest). The Bible tells of Melchizedek, king of the city of Shalem (Jerusalem), who was simultaneously a priest of the Almighty God (Genesis 14:18). Thus there was nothing surprising in Abram initiating the adoption of a new religious faith within his family and tribe. The famous covenant between Abram and the Lord was concluded in the tribal sanctuary of Elonei Mamre, in the region of Hebron:

"I am God Almighty; walk before me and be blameless... You will be the father of many nations. No longer will you be called Abram; your name will be Abraham...I will establish my covenant as an everlasting covenant between me and you and your descendants after you for the generations to come...The whole land of Canaan, where you are now an alien, I will give as an everlasting possession to you and your descendants after you...Every male among you shall be circumcised...and it will be the sign of the covenant between me and you...As for Sarai your wife, you are no longer to call her Sarai; her name will be Sarah. I...will surely give you a son by her...kings of peoples will come from her" (Genesis 17:1, 4-5, 7-8, 10-11, 15-16).

The change of names and the rite of circumcision were signs not of the religious reform of an already existing cult, but of the adoption of a new faith and a union with a new God. At Elonei Mamre, a true revolution occurred in the religious beliefs of Abraham and his tribe. Abraham rejected the old gods whom he and his tribe had worshipped in both their homeland of Haran and in Ur. Their new homeland brought a new god – most likely, the supreme Canaanite god El. It is also possible that this was the cult of the Most High God (El Elyon), the lord of heaven and earth who ruled in the neighboring city of Shalem and whose king/high-priest, Melchizedek, was an ally of Abraham. It is interesting to compare how each called their god. Melchizedek "blessed Abraham, saying, 'Blessed be Abraham by God Most High, Creator of heaven and earth'" (Genesis 14:19). However, Abraham turned to the king of Sodom and named his God: "But Abraham said to the king of Sodom, 'I have raised my hand to the Lord, God Most High, Creator of heaven and earth...'" (Genesis 14:22). The similarity in the way that this god is characterized is striking. It is fair to assume that the similarity was not confined to external characteristics; it was also a matter of the nature of the religious cult itself. Clearly, the new religion already comprised elements of spontaneous monotheism and became the foundation on which Moses later built his monotheistic faith. It is very difficult today to reconstruct the prototype of the faith that Abraham professed given that all events from this period were recorded only 1000 years later and were subsequently heavily edited by the compilers of the Pentateuch. Naturally, the biblical writers would have tried to impart to Abraham's new religion a distinctly monotheistic character that would have been true of a much later period, thereby creating the appearance of complete continuity from Abraham to Moses.

The family tree of Hebrews and their relatives

The land to which Abraham led his group of tribes differed substantially from both Ur and Haran. Here there were no significant rivers like the Tigris and Euphrates, and there was not as much rain as in northwest Mesopotamia. Life in Canaan completely depended on the amount of rainfall. There were years when rainfall was almost non-existent and the whole country was thus seized by severe droughts, which in turn led to famine. The nearest place where there was always water in abundance was the Nile Delta in Egypt. And it was to the Nile Delta that the nomadic Amorites went when dry periods occurred in Canaan. We have sufficient evidence to suggest that as early as the 18th century B.C.E., there were large communities of Western Semites who had come from Canaan and were living permanently in the eastern part of the Nile Delta. Most likely, they were the same semi-nomadic Amorites who had occupied Canaan; in dry periods they saved themselves from hunger by leaving for the Nile Delta. It may be supposed that the Amorites appeared in the Nile Delta even earlier, in the 20th-19th centuries B.C.E. The greatest obstacle impeding their migration was the fact that Egypt was such a powerful military force. However, as Egypt gradually weakened, the stream of Amorite nomads evidently increased. The migrants no longer returned to Canaan, preferring to stay in the Nile Delta, where there was always sufficient water and pastureland. When the great drought took place in Abraham's time, he, like many West Semitic nomads and semi-nomads, left southern Canaan for the Nile Delta: "Now there was a famine in the land, and Abraham went down to Egypt to live there for a while because the famine was severe" (Genesis 12:10). In fact, it was not only Abraham's tribal group that left for Egypt, but also their closest kinsmen, the tribes of Lot – ancestors of the Moabites and the Ammonites who were also living as nomads in southern Canaan. The Bible calls those who met Abraham there 'Egyptians'. In truth, they were Western Semites who had come to Canaan, and then to Egypt, much earlier than Abraham and had had time to establish themselves. Most likely, the slave woman Hagar was not Egyptian at all, but a woman from those semi-nomadic Amorites who had settled in the Nile Delta. The same applies to the wife of her son Ishmael. The enormous interval – 1000 years – that elapsed between the moment these events occurred and the time they were set down turned everyone who was from Egypt into Egyptians, when in fact, from an ethnic point of view, they were the same Western Semites as Abraham and his fellow tribesmen.

The line of Hagar and her son Ishmael was evidently suppressed by the biblical writers, who were interested in emphasizing their own branch of Isaac and Jacob. Possibly, this line linked Abraham's tribes with the even larger tribal group of Amorites in the Nile Delta. The significance of Ishmael increases if we remember that in concluding the covenant with God, Abraham was primarily thinking of Ishmael's well-being: "And Abraham said to God, 'If only Ishmael might live under your blessing!'" (Genesis 17:18) The Bible underlines another fact: only Isaac and Ishmael, of all Abraham's sons, buried their father. Like Jacob, Ishmael also had twelve sons; they became the fathers of their tribes and lived a nomadic way of life, moving between

24

Egypt and northern Mesopotamia (Genesis 25:16, 18). The authors and redactors of the Bible relegated the line of Hagar/ Ishmael to second place, after the Sarah/Isaac branch. This was a result of the fact that they themselves were derived from the Sarah/Isaac line; another reason is the more important role that Sarah had played in Abraham's family. After all, she was the daughter of his father Terah (admittedly from another woman), while Hagar was unrelated, even though she was from a stronger and more numerous tribal group. Yet it should not be forgotten that there was also a third official line of kinship – the sons of Keturah, who was Abraham's principal wife after Sarah's death. Many tribes of nomadic Amorites traced their origins to this line – including the Midianites, who played an important part in the early stages of Israel's history. Finally, there were also less important lines such as the sons of Abraham's concubines; they were the leaders of lower-ranking tribes. Fearing civil strife after his death, Abraham prudently sent all these tribes further to the east. The biblical account of this event is an example of extreme understatement: "Abraham left everything he owned to Isaac. But while he was still living, he gave gifts to the sons of his concubines and sent them away from his son Isaac to the land of the east" (Genesis 25:5-6). Somewhat later, the Bible clarifies which geographic region was signified by the 'the land of the East' – it was northwest Mesopotamia and northeast Syria (Genesis 29:1).

Thus there were three major branches – Sarah, Hagar, and Keturah – as well as divisions of lesser importance deriving from the concubines; together, they made up the hierarchy of Amorite nomadic tribes whom Abraham brought from Haran. The names of Abraham's sons are, without a doubt, patronymics and represent the legendary fathers of all these tribes and clans. Most of these nomadic Amorites who stayed in Canaan came to be known as Habiru, while others who left for the east and north became increasingly recognized as Sutu. In short, Abraham's family history is actually the family history of the Habiru and Sutu tribes.

The role of the Sarah/Isaac branch was emphasized only because the biblical writers belonged to this line. The forefather Abraham was not only the leader and high-priest of his own tribe, but was the nominal supreme head of several tribal groups of nomadic Amorites. In addition to their own tribal leaders, the Habiru and Sutu evidently also had supreme leaders in each region to whom they could turn for arbitration in the event of conflict and disagreements among the pastoral nomads. These leaders also acted as coordinators when action had to be taken in order to deal with a serious external threat. It is likely that Abraham was just such a supreme leader of the Habiru in southern Canaan, although his power usually extended no further than the territory of his own tribe. His place of residence – if such a thing exists for a semi-nomadic tribe – was Elonei Mamre, near Hebron. Until they left for Egypt, each West Semitic tribe set up its nomadic tents in a strictly defined area and tried not to violate the borders of its relatives. It was precisely this system of distributing unoccupied land between the nomadic and semi-nomadic Amorites that allowed the tribal group headed by Abraham to come to Canaan; however, the same system limited these tribes to the south only. The northern and central parts of Canaan were occupied by other West Semitic nomads who had arrived earlier than Abraham. Probably, it was from these people that Terah found out about the unoccupied pastures in the south, prompting his decision to migrate to southern Canaan (though it was only his son who succeeded in realizing this plan). Judging by the Habiru narrative reflected in the history of Abraham's family, the Jewish patriarch had such great influence on the nomadic Amorites that many of them started considering him their ancestral forefather. At the same time, we should not forget that the nomadic Amorites constituted only a part of Canaan's population – something the Bible constantly reminds us of. The remainder was made up of Canaanites and settled Amorites, who had occupied the parts of the country that were most convenient for living and farming.

Many questions are raised by those places in the Bible where it talks about Abraham's principal wife, Sarah. In Egypt and Gerar, the patriarch passed off his aged wife as his own sister so that the local rulers, seduced by her beauty, would not actually kill him. From non-biblical sources, we know that in the ancient Near East it was indeed the practice for powerful rulers to take into their harems the daughters, sisters, and wives of tribal leaders who were dependent vassals. Their husbands frequently met an unenviable fate. One does not need to look far for examples. Even the legendary King David, of whom the Bible only speaks in superlatives, could not resist the temptation to send to his death the husband of the woman to whom he had taken a fancy. But this custom, as a rule, only concerned young and attractive women, while Sarah, according to the biblical text, was not of the age at which she could have attracted this sort of attention. Even more inexplicable is the report that at 90 years old, the patriarch's wife gave birth to their son Isaac. Why did the compilers of the Pentateuch include such absurd tales in the canonical text? Just to show the omnipotence of God? Are not the improbable tales about Sarah's being put into the harems of local rulers and about her extremely late childbearing a penalty that the compilers have been forced to pay as a result of favoring Sarah's branch? Possibly, in the initial versions of the Habiru tribes' account, Sarah's place was taken by a young and beautiful woman, one of Abraham's other wives. Maybe there were a number of different oral legends concerning the patriarch's wives; or perhaps the same narrative about Abraham featured various different women. Regardless, many centuries later, the keepers of tradition made their ancestor Sarah the main heroine of the narrative about Abraham, writing her into all the episodes in his life. What we probably have here is a redaction dictated by political considerations. For the first compilers of the biblical texts, the fight for 'primogeniture' and status of principal heir to the common patriarch obviously outweighed logic and historical truth. As for later editors of the Pentateuch

– although they were no longer burdened by the considerations that bound the first compilers, they simply did not dare to change the ancient texts. Thus Sarah remained the main heroine of all the various events that had occurred and pertained to numerous women at different times.

A similar problem exists regarding the patriarchs' ages. Their unusual longevity – Abraham is recorded as living to the age of 175 and Sarah to 127 – leads us to think that their names conceal the lives of not one, but two or even several people. Possibly, there were several famous rulers with the name 'Abraham', but in an oral tradition formed over many centuries, they fused those leaders into one legendary patriarch credited with extreme longevity. In just the same way, had there been no written documentary records, the rule of the several Louis in France might have been taken, many centuries later, as the uninterrupted reign of a single person. Or the reigns of the three Russian emperors called Alexander might have been understood, 1000 years later, as the life of only one of them. Moreover, after such a long interval, oral tradition would almost certainly have forgotten that between the reigns of Alexander I and Alexander II came Nicholas I. Unfortunately, the story of the Habiru tribes was set down in the earliest biblical texts too late – at least 1000 years after it had occurred. Even though writing was already known in Canaan, the nomadic Western Semites made no use of it at the time. Another possibility, at least as far as one of the patriarchs is concerned, is that the change of name from Abram to Abraham ('father of the peoples') led to the name 'Abraham' being established as the title for the supreme leader of the Habiru in Canaan, and that for a period of time this title was handed down from each leader to his heir. Whatever the case may be, there is no doubt that the name of each long-living patriarch in reality stands for the names of several people.

The most enigmatic of all the patriarchs is Isaac. Strangely, we know hardly anything about him, although in length of life (180 years) he surpassed the other Jewish forefathers. We have far more information about his father, Abraham, and his sons, Jacob and Esau. Though he is mentioned many times, Isaac never acts independently. Everything written about him is merely a repetition of the stories from Abraham's life. Evidently, the northern and southern Habiru tribes in Canaan had two versions of the same legend about their patriarch's stay in Gerar, in southwest Palestine. According to this legend, the local ruler, Abimelech, King of Gerar, took the patriarch's wife into his harem. Fearing for his life, the patriarch had passed her off as his sister. One night, the Most High came to Abimelech in a dream and warned him that he and those close to him would die because the woman he had taken into his harem was married. Frightened to death, the ruler immediately returned the woman to the patriarch and asked him to beg for God's forgiveness. Subsequently, despite their disagreement about the wells, Abimelech and his commander Phichol concluded a sworn alliance with the patriarch in the region of Beersheba. The two versions of this legend are almost identical, but the first features Abraham and his wife Sarah, while the second – Isaac and his wife Rebekah. Incidentally, both versions of the biblical narrative provide indirect confirmation that the patriarchs were leaders of not a single family or clan, but entire tribes who inculcated fear in the local ruler, forcing the latter to enter into an alliance with the newly arrived pastoralists. But the likeness between Abraham and Isaac does not end here. Rebekah's protracted inability to bear children and her late childbearing are almost a copy of the legend about Sarah. Finally, the Lord's promise to return the land of Canaan to Isaac's descendants is reminiscent of what was promised to Abraham. In summary, everything that the Bible tells us about Isaac merely replicates the stories about Abraham. From what it seems, the significance of patriarch Isaac has been deliberately minimized and he is mentioned only out of necessity, as an intermediary link between Abraham and Jacob.

What reasons did the compilers of the earliest portions of the Pentateuch have for opting to mention Isaac without actually telling us anything about the man himself? After all, nowhere does Isaac figure as the initiator of action; on the contrary, only as the object of acts by other people. Perhaps the more humble place given to Isaac is due to the fact that his favorite son was Esau, the forefather of the Edomites, and not Jacob, the ancestor of the Hebrews. The Bible does not conceal the fact that Isaac openly preferred Esau – and not so much because Esau was his first-born, but because he found him emotionally more to his liking. Had considerable attention been paid to Isaac, this would have inevitably led to a strong focus on Esau's role among the sons and to Jacob being reprimanded for breaching his father's will. Jacob's flight to his relatives in Haran was due not just to his fear of Esau taking revenge, but also to his father's condemnation of his behavior. Had Isaac taken the side of his younger son by Rebekah, Esau would not have dared to threaten Jacob. But Isaac was not fond of Jacob and did not wish to defend him, so the writers of the Bible – descendants of Jacob – did everything they could to suppress Isaac's role in the genealogy of their forefathers. On the other hand, they gave his wife Rebekah, who was zealous in defending the interests of her beloved son Jacob, incomparably more attention, even though this went clearly against the traditions of the time.

While all the nomadic Western Semites of southern Canaan, Sinai, and Midian considered Abraham to be their patriarch, only two of these groups, namely the Hebrews and the Edomites (Idumeans), traced their family tree through Isaac. Jacob is considered the ancestor of the former and Esau of the latter. It is at this stage in the Habiru's tribal hierarchy that the earliest compilers of the Bible had to make substantial changes in the narrative they had inherited. The first difficulty concerned Esau's birthright. The law of the time stipulated that the eldest son or the first son of the principal wife should receive almost all

30

the father's property, particularly his land. The remaining sons had to find themselves a new place. This is the reason for the battle between Jacob and Esau over their birthright. Although the brothers were twins born from the same mother, Esau was considered the eldest and, furthermore, was Isaac's favorite son. However, the idea that the Edomites had seniority over the Jews was completely unacceptable to the compilers of the Bible – and all the more so, since they were working on the biblical text at the time when Edom was a vassal state and a tributary of the United Monarchy. Therefore, the compilers included in the biblical canon two narratives whose purpose was to establish Jacob's birthright. The first of these was the legend that Esau had sold his birthright for lentil soup; the second was that Jacob obtained the blessing of his father, which was intended for Esau, by an act of deception. Neither story offers a flattering picture of cunning Jacob, though both were clearly trying to put the blame on his mother, Rebekah, and her eagerness to do well by him. If Isaac's seniority over Ishmael seems completely acceptable, given that his mother, Sarah, was the principal wife and a relative of Abraham, then the birthright obtained by Jacob looks unconvincing. But such was the price of competing for the leadership; after all, the authors of the Bible themselves belonged to this branch.

Of all the tribes led by Abraham from the upper courses of the Euphrates River, it was the 'house of Jacob' that received the best land, suitable not only for cattle breeding, but for arable farming as well. Jacob's fellow brothers from this large tribal union – the Edomites, Moabites, Ammonites, Ishmaelites, and Midianites – had to content themselves with land that was of significantly inferior quality. With a few exceptions, they settled on the extensive but semi-desert lands of southern and eastern Canaan, northwest Arabia, Sinai, and the regions bordering the Syrian Desert – a place where nomadic cattle-breeding was the only real possibility. Abraham led these tribes into Canaan too late; all the more fertile and well-irrigated lands located in the northern and central parts of the country were already occupied either by local settled peoples or by other nomadic Western Semites – like the ancestors of the northern Hebrew tribes who had arrived earlier. It is true, though, that the houses of Jacob and Edom also had luck on their side: their founders derived from Isaac, the son of Abraham's principal wife, Sarah, and in accordance with the laws of the time, their father thus had the right to the best part of the inheritance. But of the two twin sons born to Isaac, Esau (Edom) was considered the elder and therefore his tribal group was supposed to inherit the land that subsequently came to be called Judah. The rivalry between Jacob and Esau mirrored the real battle between the closely-related West Semitic tribes for southern Canaan, a territory that was becoming increasingly cramped. Esau's line, later to be called the Edomites, won the first stage in this battle. They ousted some of the Hebrew clans – most likely, the future Judahites – from their habitual places in southern Canaan. The episode recounting Jacob's escape to his mother's relatives in Haran may be indirect evidence of the temporary departure of several southern Habiru clans for their old native-land in Haran. It is possible that these were the ancestors of the southern tribes of Judah, Reuben, Simeon, and Levi. But there, in northwestern Mesopotamia, Abraham's fear – from the time he was unwilling to send his son Isaac back to Haran – was realized: namely a conflict of interests between returning and local Habiru tribes. The land belonging to those who had left for Canaan had long since been occupied by their kinsmen. And though the latter took the fugitives in, they evidently placed them in a position of dependence. Jacob's fourteen-year service to his uncle Laban testifies to the difficult life of the Hebrews upon their return. Inevitably, there were conflicts and disagreements, and these were reflected in the dispute between Jacob and Laban. In the end, the southern Hebrews decided to leave for Canaan once again. This choice was made upon hearing the news that the semi-nomadic Amorites from northern and central

Canaan had gone to the Nile Delta in Egypt; their land, which had formerly been inaccessible to the southern Hebrews, was now available for occupation. So Jacob led his tribes back into Canaan. The warm meeting with his brother Esau in northern Canaan was by no means a surprise: the Amorite tribes' departure for Egypt had made continued hostility over territory absolutely pointless, since there was now land in abundance. Moreover, the departure of a large number of nomadic Western Semites weakened Esau's position in Canaan and thus made the return of his kinsmen from northwestern Mesopotamia extremely desirable. This explains why the chiefs of the two southern tribal groups now met amicably. Admittedly, in contrast to the canonical biblical text, the apocryphal Book of Jubilees asserts that peace between the two brothers was short-lived and that after the death of their father, Isaac, their dispute over the inheritance led to a war between them. This war was won by the 'house of Jacob'.

The Bible tells us that Jacob decided not to hurry to the south and instead delay for a considerable amount of time in the central part of Canaan. He lived nomadically for a long period in the Shechem region and his sons pastured livestock in the Dothan Valley – something that had never occurred earlier in the time of Abraham and Isaac. This is unquestionable confirmation of the fact that pastureland in central and northern Canaan, which had previously been occupied when Jacob left for Haran, had now become available for the nomads (the area nomadically farmed by the 'family' of Abraham-Isaac-Jacob did not, as a rule, extend beyond the borders of Judah's tribe). Here we encounter further evidence that Jacob's tribes were inferior in strength to the Edomites' ancestors; Jacob was frightened by the fact that Esau had so many warriors (Genesis 32:6-7). Indeed, in order to field 400 warriors, Esau's tribes must have contained at least 8000 to 9000 people, which once again renders flawed the idea that Abraham-Isaac-Jacob was a 'family' of patriarchs. However, it should be noted that after the numerous divisions of the Habiru

and Sutu tribes during Abraham's time and the following seces-
sion of the Edomites, Jacob's tribes were small in size. This is
confirmed by the slaughter in Shechem, when Jacob, indignant
at the behavior of his sons Simon and Levi, reproached them:
"You have brought trouble on me by making me a stench to the
Canaanites and Perizzites, the people living in this land. We are
few in number, and if they join forces against me and attack me,
I and my household will be destroyed'" (Genesis 34:30).

Thus the patriarchs were leaders of entire tribal unions and
the biblical family was nothing less than a group of closely-related
peoples. Abraham was not only the head of his family, but the
leader of a large group of tribes which divided up over time into
separate and independent peoples. The biblical family's move
from Ur to Haran and from Haran to Canaan, as well as its temporary departure for Egypt, were, in fact, migrations of the West
Semitic pastoralists. Behind the complex personal lives of Abraham, Lot, Isaac, Ishmael, Jacob, and Esau lies the history of their
peoples – who, at various times, entered into conflict with each
other and united together against common enemies. The separations from one another of Abraham and Lot, then of Isaac and
Ishmael, and finally of Jacob and Esau were not the 'splitting up
of relatives', but rather the separations of related tribes that had
gradually become sufficiently large and numerous to function as
separate and independent peoples. Nomadic cattle breeding, the
principal occupation of these pastoralists, did not allow a large
group of fellow tribesmen to come together on any one piece of
territory, but instead forced them to constantly search for new
land with sufficient pasture and sources of water for their cattle.
This was the economic background to the biblical family's divisions. Abraham's departure for the south of Canaan was a result
not of the high population density in the country's central part,
but of the lack of available pasture. There, in southern Canaan,
Jacob and Esau, and their descendants through Isaac, found a
new homeland for themselves and their tribes.

CHAPTER TWO

The Southerners and the Northerners

Jacob and Israel: the two forefathers of the Hebrew tribes

Two particularly important moments in biblical history are connected with Jacob's return from Haran to Canaan. Both incidents deal with the giving of his second name, Israel. The first took place during the night prior to his meeting with Esau and his warriors near a tributary of the Jordan River, the Jabbok. The Bible narrates the incident as follows:

> So Jacob was left alone, and a man wrestled with him till daybreak. When the man saw that he could not overpower him, he touched the socket of Jacob's hip so that his hip was wrenched as he wrestled with the man. Then the man said, 'Let me go, for it is daybreak.' But Jacob replied, 'I will not let you go unless you bless me.' The man asked him, 'What is your name?' 'Jacob,' he answered. Then the man said, 'Your name will no longer be Jacob, but Israel, because you have

struggled with God and with men and have overcome.' Jacob said, 'Please tell me your name.' But he replied, 'Why do you ask my name?' Then he blessed him there. So Jacob called the place Peniel, saying, 'It is because I saw God face to face, and yet my life was spared.' (Genesis 32: 24-30)

The second incident happened later, when Jacob and his people arrived in Bethel – the sanctuary of the Hebrew tribes. Jacob had prayed at the sanctuary when he was on his way to Haran from his brother Esau's. This time, "God said to him, 'Your name is Jacob, but you will no longer be called Jacob; your name will be Israel.' So he named him Israel" (Genesis 35:10).

God also repeated the promise he had previously given to Abraham and Isaac – that he would give the land of Canaan to him and his descendants. In this way, God gave Jacob the new name 'Israel' twice. This giving of the new name, as well as the promise that Jacob would father a great people and that his descendants would receive Canaan are very much reminiscent of the covenant with Abraham at Elonei Mamre. It is possible that the initial point of the episode was to renew the vow made between Jacob and the God of his fathers, which was a traditional ritual that was common in Canaan at the time. But the biblical writers gave the episode an entirely different character. They did not simply change Jacob's personal name, as was the case with Abraham; they gave him a completely different second name as well. Moreover, this did not happen at his birth or when he accepted the new faith, nor did it occur at a time of dramatic military events, but during a normal period of peace. The Hebrew name 'Israel' literally means 'fighter against god'; of course, at the time the gods that were meant were the pagan gods with whom human heroes had to fight. But what we know of Jacob's life from the Bible has nothing at all to do with warfare or religious reform. The Bible tells us of no events that could have justified taking a new name or title. The entirely unexpected episode of the fight with an unknown person (a god or divine messenger) does not clarify anything. Instead, it creates the impression that an event from a different story about a different person was inserted into the oral narrative about Jacob at a later date – in accordance with considerations that were relevant at this later time.

From the moment Abram received his new name (Abraham) from the Lord, it completely ousted the previous version and began to be used everywhere in the biblical texts. Something very different, however, happened with Jacob's second name. In spite of God's word, "'Your name will no longer be Jacob, but Israel...'" (Genesis 32: 28), the biblical texts make equal use of both names. Moreover, the compilers of Genesis emphasize with suspicious frequency the identity of Jacob and Israel, as if wishing to prove that this was a single, common ancestor in lieu of the forefathers of two different tribal groups.

The situation with the patriarchs' wives is similarly interesting. Abraham had only one principal wife, Sarah; Isaac likewise had only Rebekah. But Jacob had two wives simultaneously and both held the same status, something that had never been the case for any of his predecessors. Was this not the link with which the family trees of two groups of Hebrew tribes – the northern and southern Habiru – were artificially united into a single genealogy? Jacob was first given the wife and sons of Israel – the forefather of the northern tribes – and was then given the latter's name as well. Certainly, not every branch of the family descended from Abraham was included in the official biblical canon. Mention is made only of those who did not call into question the primacy of the Abraham-Isaac-Jacob line. It is likely that the oral tradition of the nomadic Western Semites included many legends associated with the history of the northern group of Hebrew tribes that later came to be known as Israel. However, only a few of these legends were woven into the genealogy of the southern group, that of Jacob. Jacob's struggle with God's messenger during the night before his meeting with

Esau was undoubtedly taken from the oral tradition concerning Israel. Jacob's second wife, Rachel, and their sons, Joseph and Benjamin, also belong to the genealogy of the northern tribes. It is most likely that the northern group of Hebrew tribes came to Canaan from northwestern Mesopotamia before Abraham's time, approximately in the 23rd century B.C.E., and occupied land that was vacant in northern and central Palestine. Only later, in about the 20th century B.C.E., did Abraham arrive in Canaan with his group of tribes. Unlike their kinsmen from the northern group, Abraham's tribes – or at least a part of them – had already lived in southern Mesopotamia. So, since they arrived in Canaan later, they were forced to be content with the more arid regions of southern and eastern Palestine. Thus, by the beginning of the second millennium B.C.E., five groups of nomadic Western Semites had settled in Canaan. Two of these settled in the western part of the country, and it was from them that the northern Hebrew tribes of Israel and southern Hebrew tribes of Jacob would later split off. The eastern part of Canaan, the Transjordan, was occupied by two other tribal unions, – Ammon and Moab – who had arrived with the biblical patriarch Abraham. Finally, Edom settled on his own in the southeast. Among the neighboring settled peoples, the first two tribal groups subsequently came to be more commonly known as 'Habiru' and the other three as 'Sutu' or 'Shasu', as the Egyptians called them. They were all closely related, had common ancestors, and spoke the same language. But they had separated at different times and thus had different degrees of closeness to one another.

If we attempt to construct a model of kinship between the five groups of nomadic Western Semites, we get the following picture: the southern group of Edom was the closest of all the groups to Jacob's; next in terms of closeness came the two eastern tribal alliances in Transjordan, Moab and Ammon, who were just as close to each other as both the southern groups. Finally and rather paradoxically, the most distant were the northern tribes who later came to be known as Israel. This model thus complexly inverts traditional ideas of degrees of kinship and closeness among the southern and northern Hebrew tribes. Under the new model, Moab and Ammon, not to mention Edom, turn out to be more closely related to the southern group of Hebrew tribes than the northern tribes.

The southern group of Jacob consisted of only four tribes: Judah, Reuben, Simeon, and Levi. The largest of these was the tribe of Judah, while the smallest was Levi. It would therefore be correct to identify this southern Hebrew group as Jacob-Judah, all the more so since the Southern Kingdom took its name from this largest tribe. Unfortunately, until the 12th century B.C.E., we knew nothing about the northern Hebrew tribes. All the biblical history known to us from before that time was, in fact, only the history of the southern Hebrew group of Jacob-Judah, to which the genealogy of the northern tribes was subsequently added. The combined history of these two groups began only in the 12th century B.C.E., when the southern group returned from Egypt and a part of it joined the already existing tribal union of Israel in central Canaan. The basis of the biblical canon that we have today concerning the family of Abraham-Isaac-Jacob and the twelve sons of Jacob-Israel was most likely written during the United Monarchy, in the reigns of David and Solomon. It was then, following the political interests of the United Monarchy of Israel and Judah, that the keepers of the tradition – namely the Levites and Aaronites – unified the genealogy and history of the two different Hebrew groups. The northern tribes were written retrospectively into the biblical history of the southern group, Jacob-Judah, even though they evidently had an even more interesting and dramatic past than the southern tribes. And it is their history that can help us better understand what happened in Canaan and Egypt in the 18th–13th centuries B.C.E., a period about which the Bible remains largely silent.

The basis of the northern Hebrew tribes consisted of the tribes of Ephraim, Manasseh, and Benjamin. The first two were the larger and stronger, tracing their genealogy directly to the legendary Joseph – which is why they were known as the 'house of Joseph'. The third tribe was significantly smaller and had special relations of kinship with the first two. Given that Joseph himself was considered the favorite son of Israel, the father of the northern tribes, this entire group may be identified as 'Israel-Joseph'. The 'house of Joseph' not only occupied a privileged position within the group of northern tribes, but was also the founder of the Israelite tribal confederation, established in central Canaan in the 13th century B.C.E. Other tribes such as Dan, Naphtali, Gad, and Asher played a secondary and subordinate role – something that is reflected in the biblical canon: these tribes' founding fathers were also considered the sons of the patriarch, but by women of a lower social status. The tribes of Zebulon and Issachar were on an intermediate level, between the first and the second groups. At the same time, all these tribes, including both the 'house of Joseph' and the secondary tribes, traced their origins to a common patriarch, Israel.

Sometime at the end of the 18th century B.C.E. the Israel-Joseph group abandoned northern and central Canaan and left for the Nile Delta in Egypt. This most likely happened in the time of the biblical patriarch Isaac and during a period of drought and famine in Canaan. The Bible says as follows:

> Now there was a famine in the land – besides the earlier famine of Abraham's time – and Isaac went to Abimelech king of the Philistines in Gerar. The Lord appeared to Isaac and said, 'Do not go down to Egypt; live in the land where I tell you to live. Stay in this land for a while, and I will be with you and will bless you. For to you and your descendants I will give all these lands and will confirm the oath I swore to your father Abraham.' (Genesis 26:1-3)

Thus Isaac and his southern tribes did not leave for Egypt. The fact that the biblical writers emphasize this, however, is indirect evidence that the other part of the nomadic Western Semites did leave Canaan for the Nile Delta.

It was usually the southern part of Canaan that suffered most from drought, and it was here that the two related southern groups of Jacob and Edom led a nomadic way of life. However, if they did not leave, then why did the northern tribes? After all, there was more water in central Canaan than in the south. Evidently, the reason for the departure of the northern tribes, or some of them, was not so much drought as civil strife. The narrative about Joseph and his brothers can shed some light on this problem. There is no doubt that the authors of Genesis took this story from the oral history of the northern tribes. However, they considered it necessary to add to it the founding fathers from their own southern group, so that the new version of the narrative would confirm the single genealogy they had created for the two groups. Above all, our attention is drawn by a geographical misunderstanding: the forefather Jacob is situated in the valley of Hebron, i.e. on the ancestral land of the southern Hebrew tribes, but sends his sons to pasture cattle right in the middle of the territory of the northern tribes – in the region of Shechem and the Dothan Valley. Anyone familiar with the geography and natural environment of Palestine would find it difficult to understand why it was necessary to drive the cattle such a distance, even onto land that belonged to other people, if pasture of the same quality existed near Hebron. Secondly, it is striking that only the forefathers of the southern tribes, Reuben and Judah, act as Joseph's saviors. Possibly, this legend is founded on a real historical fact – an internal conflict within the northern group of Israel-Joseph. Such a conflict could have broken out between the 'house of Joseph' and the other northern tribes. Another possibility can be that the Jacob-Judah southern group adopted a neutral position at a key moment and allowed the 'house of

Joseph' safe passage through their territory into Egypt. It would then be clear that the tribes of Ephraim and Manasseh arrived in Egypt first and that the reproaches they directed against their fellow tribesmen might have been well-founded. It may also have been conceivable that it was not drought or famine but the privileged position of the 'house of Joseph' in Egypt in the time of the Hyksos that subsequently led the other northern tribes to come there. By contrast, the southern group of Jacob came to the Nile Delta much later, only in the second half of the 17th century B.C.E., and its life in Egypt took a different course than that of its northern brothers.

There can be no doubt that the biblical narrative about the family of Abraham-Isaac-Jacob is the history of the two semi-nomadic West Semitic peoples – the southern group of Jacob and the northern group of Israel. The authors of the earliest part of the Pentateuch did not simply set down oral legends transmitted over many centuries; they went much further: they wove these narratives together to create a common genealogy. In order to understand to what extent the biblical writers were able to pre-cisely pass on the history of the long-gone days, it is important to know when this past was set down and how much time had elapsed since the events themselves.

When was the story of Abraham-Isaac-Jacob written?

The period between the arrival of Abraham in Canaan and the departure of Jacob for Egypt lies approximately between the 20th and 17th centuries B.C.E. The Bible names Ur of Chaldeans as the city from which Abraham departed. As is well known, the Chaldeans were a large group of Aramean tribes. The Arameans, however, appeared in southern Mesopotamia only after the 11th century B.C.E. So in the 20th century, when Abraham departed, the city could not have been called so. An analogous problem

42

exists with the ruler of the city of Gerar, Abimelech; there are two similar narratives about him – the first concerning Abraham and the second having to do with Isaac. In both legends this ruler and his lands are called 'Philistine'. However, the Philistines appeared in Gerar, in the southwest of Canaan, at the turn of 1200 B.C.E., i.e. 700-800 years after Abraham and Isaac. Therefore, neither Abimelech himself nor his lands could have been Philistine. Moreover, if the biblical writers had already forgotten when the Philistines arrived and regarded them as long-established inhabitants, this means that they set down these events not earlier than the 11th-10th centuries B.C.E.

Other episodes that shed light on the time when the narratives about the patriarchs were written have to do with camels. These animals are mentioned on a number of occasions, namely during Eliezer's arrival in Haran to fetch Rebekah as a bride for Isaac. Camels are also featured as draught animals, including during Jacob's return to Canaan. But the camel was domesticated only in the 11th century B.C.E. and thus there was no way that it could have been used in the 20th-17th centuries B.C.E. Yet this is far from the entire picture.

The forefather Isaac sends his son Jacob to relatives living in the northwest of Mesopotamia, in Haran. But instead of Haran, a new name, 'Paddan-Aram', appears in the text and Rebekah's brother, Laban, is called the 'son of Bethuel the Aramean' (Genesis 28:5). The Arameans are mentioned in both the geographic name and ethnic origin, but they were West Semitic tribes who appeared in those regions only in the 12th century B.C.E. How could it be that Laban, the son of Abraham's nephew, a nomadic Amorite whom the Bible had earlier classified as an 'Ivri' (Hebrew), could become an Aramean? The most logical explanation of all this is to suppose that at the time when this oral narrative was recorded, there were no longer any Amorites in the northwest of Mesopotamia: they had been pushed out by new West Semitic tribes, the Arameans. It cannot be ruled out that the remaining Amorites intermarried with the newcomers, who were closely related to them in terms of ethnic origin.

The latter supposition finds confirmation in the following episode: Kemuel, the son of Nahor, brother of Abraham, was called the forefather of Aram (of all the Arameans). It is questionable that the numerous Aramean tribes derived from one of the nomadic Amorite clans. A more likely interpretation is that the descendants of Kemuel intermarried and merged with the arriving Arameans. Be that as it may, the gratuitous mention of the Arameans testifies that the narrative about the patriarchs was undoubtedly set down later than the 12th century B.C.E. There is other irrefutable evidence that the legend about Abraham-Isaac-Jacob was composed in its final form after the stay in Egypt and return to Canaan. Such evidence includes, for example, Abraham's dream:

> As the sun was setting, Abraham fell into a deep sleep, and a thick and dreadful darkness came over him. Then the Lord said to him, 'Know for certain that your descendants will be strangers in a country not their own, and they will be enslaved and mistreated four hundred years. But I will punish the nation they serve as slaves, and afterward they will come out with great possessions.' (Genesis 15: 12-14)

The same is to be inferred from the prediction received by Rebekah that her eldest son (Esau) would serve the younger (Jacob). This indeed took place, but not earlier than the 10th century B.C.E., during the United Monarchy, when Edom became a tributary of David and Solomon. Just as interesting is the prophecy of Jacob himself before his death in Egypt. He mentions the religious center in Shiloh – a center that was founded only several centuries later – and foretells the destiny of each Hebrew tribe, fates that became common knowledge only in the 10th century B.C.E.

Religious tradition assigns authorship of the entire Pentateuch to Moses, thus placing the compilation of the Pentateuch during the period of the Exodus from Egypt and the wandering through the desert, i.e. in the first half of the 12th century B.C.E. However, historical analysis of the narrative concerning the Abraham-Isaac-Jacob family unquestionably testifies that it was recorded in the first half of the 10th century B.C.E., during the United Monarchy. What's more, the episodes dealing with Abraham's faith and characterization of the God of the fathers were substantially edited at an even later time.

Thus, events from the 20th-17th centuries B.C.E. were only recorded in the 10th century B.C.E. This led the authors of the Pentateuch to subconsciously superimpose the cultural, historical, and ethnic landscape of their own times on the period of Abraham, Isaac, and Jacob, which occurred almost a 1000 years before them. This is the real reason behind the mistakes in peoples' and places' names. The good news is that knowing when the narrative of the patriarchs was created allows us to try to correct other anachronisms.

Who were the biblical Hittites?

The biblical text gives us reason to think that the religious center of the southern group of Jacob and their leaders' places of residence were located in the Hebron region, in Elonei Mamre, which had initially belonged to the Amorite ruler Mamre. Mamre and his brothers, Eshkol and Aner, were allies of Abraham. These were probably the rulers of the settled Amorites who had come to Canaan before Abraham's nomadic tribes arrived. We know that these three Amorite rulers participated with Abraham in the war against the coalition of southern Syrian kings, helping to secure the victory that led to the liberation of Abraham's nephew Lot. This narrative tells us that the region of Hebron was occupied by Western Semites who were Amorites like Abraham, but already settled. However, another legend, which deals with Sarah's burial, paints a completely different ethnic picture. This narrative calls the local population 'Hittites' and gives Hebron itself a new name – Kiriath-Arba. Should we view this as proof of serious ethnic changes in southern Canaan? Could the Indo-European Hittites really have had time, during the course of several decades at most, to replace the Western Semites? And could the Hittites have arrived in southern Canaan during the 20th-19th centuries B.C.E.? Evidently not. Proof of this lies in the clearly Semitic name of the 'Hittite' Ephron, son of Zohar, from whom Abraham buys the well-known Cave of Machpelah. We may assert with reasonable confidence that the Hittites arrived much later, probably in the 12th century B.C.E. when the Hittite Empire was destroyed by the Sea Peoples and a wave of Indo-European peoples came crashing down upon the Semitic regions of the Near East. Perhaps they were not Hittites themselves, but instead émigrés from other Indo-Europeans peoples – for instance, the Luwians, who were generally called 'Hittites'. The Bible brings up the Hittites in another early narrative, the legend about Esau: "When Esau was forty years old, he married Judith daughter of Beeri the Hittite, and also Basemath daughter of Elon the Hittite" (Genesis 26:34). It is true that elsewhere Basemath is called the daughter of Ishmael, but Ada, again the wife of Esau, is mentioned as the daughter of Elon the Hittite. Here, as in the preceding narrative, all the Hittite names are clearly of Semitic origin. Moreover, the Hittites are referred to as the sons and daughters of Canaan, i.e. as natives of Canaan. There is clear inconsistency in both the geographical names and in the ethnonyms given to the peoples. Evidently, this was something that was inevitable when oral narratives from different periods were recorded many hundreds of years later – and not in chronological order, but in accordance with the religious and political considerations of the biblical writers. It is likely that the southern Hebrew tribes from Jacob's group found the

'Hittites' in southern Palestine upon their return from Egypt and conquest of Canaan. Likewise self-evident is that the 'Hittites' very quickly assimilated among the Semitic inhabitants who pre-dominated there and not only lost their own language, but also their own names. The Book of Joshua, which tells of the con-quest of Canaan by the Hebrew tribes, calls the Hittites a people who had lived in Palestine and fought against the Israelites, but says nothing of the Hittites in southern Canaan or in Hebron (Joshua 11:3). Moreover, the book mentions Oam, the ruler of Hebron, as one of the Amorite kings and links the ancient name for Hebron – Kiriath-Arba – not with the Hittites, but with the Anakites (Rephaim), the remnants of the ancient, Neolithic pop-ulation of Canaan (Joshua 15:13-14).

Indeed, we may wonder whether we are dealing with the Hit-tites at all. Perhaps what we actually have here is another people of Amorite or Canaanite origin whose name was very similar to the ethnonym 'Hittite'? If so, then confusion would certainly have ensued since the authors of the biblical texts about the patriarchs created them at a time when the name 'Hittite' was extremely common. Here we need to be reminded of the fact that, according to the Semitic genealogy in the Book of Genesis, the sons of Canaan – the forefather of all the Canaanite peoples – were named 'Hittites' (Genesis 10: 15). If Abraham bought the Cave of Machpelah from these 'Hittites', then indeed they were not a people of Indo-European origin from Anatolia, but from one of the West Semitic peoples of Canaan. It would be hardly surprising if the first biblical writers in the 10th century B.C.E. confused the name of this Canaanite people, mentioned in the ancient narrative about Abraham, with the ethnonym 'Hit-tite' that was well-known in their own time. Another possibil-ity is that the confusion happened much later when the 'Hittite' people were no longer remembered and this ethnonym became associated with the better-known Indo-European Hittites. In any case, the reference to Hittites living in southern Canaan during the period of Abraham and Isaac sounds absurd given that, for the duration of the 20th-18th centuries B.C.E., the Hittites did not leave central and southeastern Anatolia. Theoretically, they could have ended up in southern Canaan, but not earlier than the end of the 17th or beginning of the 16th century B.C.E., when the Hittite king Hattushili I established himself in Northern Syria and his grandson, Murshili I, captured Babylon. It is true, of course, that military campaigns with the aim of looting are one thing and the colonization of captured lands quite another. Furthermore, all this took place at a great distance from Canaan and even further from the south of that country. At the same time, it should not be forgotten that it was not later than the second half of the 17th century B.C.E. that the southern Hebrew tribes (Jacob's group) left for Egypt, where the northern tribes (the house of Joseph) were already living. Consequently, there could not have been any contact between the Hittites as a people and the Hebrew tribes during the 20-17th centuries B.C.E., at least in southern Canaan, which is the area covered by the Bible.

From the 15th until the beginning of the 12th century B.C.E., all of Canaan was under the control of Egypt, the main adversary of the Hittites in the Near East. So it is doubtful that the Egyptians would have allowed any serious colonizing activity in these regions. Finally, there is not a single extra-biblical source that mentions a settlement of Hittites in Canaan. It was only in the 14th-13th centuries B.C.E. that Hittite military detachments appeared in southern Syria and in the country of Amurru (today's Lebanon), but again not in Palestine. The Hebrew tribes settled in Canaan in the 12th century B.C.E., but the Bible only cursorily mentions the 'Hittites', listing them as one of their adversaries. Thus the region over which the Hittites spread (if we're talking about the Indo-European Hittites) in no way intersected with the paths taken by the Hebrew tribes. As for the Hittite mercenaries who served at the courts of the Israelite and

Judahite kings, they can never be considered as proof of this people's presence in Canaan.

So we are left with only one possibility: either what we have here is a people of West Semitic origin whose name was subsequently confused with that of the Indo-European Hittites, or it was indeed the case that some groups of Hittites ran off to Canaan after the downfall of the Hittite Empire – but this could not have happened earlier than the beginning of the 12th century B.C.E. It cannot be ruled out that the Canaanite and Amorite rulers used the Hittite refugees as warrior-mercenaries against the Hebrew tribes. This would explain the minimal mention of the Hittites as a hostile people during the period of Canaan's conquest. In either case, it would be just as senseless to speak of the Hittites' presence in Canaan during the time of Abraham-Isaac-Jacob as it would to talk about that of the Philistines in the same period.

The narrative about the patriarchs demonstrates an unequivocally negative attitude to intermarrying with other peoples, even with those who were considered ethnically close. Abraham has no desire to look for a wife for his son from among the 'foreign' peoples of Canaan, but instead sends his servant to his relatives, in the northwest of Mesopotamia. His son Isaac does the same, sending Jacob once again to the family's relatives in Padan-Aram. Esau's two Hittite wives "...were a source of grief to Isaac and Rebekah" (Genesis 26:34-35) and Isaac himself cautioned Jacob, "Do not marry a Canaanite woman" (Genesis 28:1). It is true that the narrative gives no explanation of this hostility to foreigners. At that time, there could not have been a religious reason. Instead, the primary factor was a sense of kinship and tribal closeness; family and tribe were the best defense and guarantee against all adversities. Even today, Bedouin in the Middle East attempt to maintain the same traditions of blood kinship as the pastoralists in ancient times. This mistrust of foreign peoples was, however, artificially strengthened later by the redactors of the Bible when emphasis was placed on the battle for monotheism against the influences of the surrounding peoples' pagan cults. Despite the redactors' attempts to mark the family of Abraham-Isaac-Jacob as a separate entity, the narrative about the patriarchs actually contains quite a few facts testifying to the contrary, i.e. evidence of the tendency for the nomadic Western Semites to intermarry with the peoples of Canaan. Esau, for example, had at least two Hittite wives and a third of Hivite origin. Although he is traditionally considered the forefather of the Edomites, and not of the Jews, Esau, given that he was regarded as the elder and favored son of the Jewish patriarch Isaac, certainly acted in the same way as the leaders of the Hebrew tribes. The biblical texts give us abundant confirmation of this. For instance, Judah, the forefather of the principal tribe of the southern group of Jacob, had a Canaanite wife; their son, Shelah, was regarded by the leaders of this tribe as their principal ancestor. A similar example is provided by Simeon, the forefather of another southern Hebrew tribe whose son, Shaul, was also the offspring of a Canaanite woman. The northern Hebrew tribes were likewise unafraid of kinship with other peoples. Joseph, the forefather of the strongest of these tribes, was married to Asenath, the daughter of the Egyptian pagan priest Potipherah. It was this Egyptian woman who bore Joseph his sons Manasseh and Ephraim, the founders of the two most well-known northern tribes that played an enormous role in ancient Israel's history. The instances listed above are undoubtedly only the tip of the iceberg in the process by which the Hebrew tribes assimilated with the local peoples of Canaan. Their inclusion in the biblical canon is only due to the fact that they concerned the forefathers of the Hebrews. It is likely that the intentions of Abraham and Isaac to find brides for their sons in their former homeland of Haran were a result not so much of hostility towards the 'daughters of Canaan', but of a desire to preserve family ties and union with the other closely related group of nomadic Western Semites, whose leader and founder was considered to be Nahor.

Creation of common genealogy and history

When recording the narrative about the patriarchs, the first authors of the Bible were forced to find a solution for two serious problems of that time. The first concerned the birthright or right of primacy both among the nomadic Amorites in Canaan and among the Hebrew tribes themselves. The second problem pertained to the necessity of unifying the family trees of the two related tribal groups – the northern (Israel) and the southern (Jacob) – which came to be joined together in a single kingdom. The problem of Isaac's seniority proved simplest to solve since his mother Sarah possessed a higher status among the women and concubines of Abraham, being the daughter of the patriarch's father by another woman. Jacob's primacy over Esau seems somewhat less persuasive despite the inclusion in the biblical canon of both the story about the sale of the birthright for lentil soup and the episode in which Isaac's blessing is obtained by deceit. Despite the efforts of the biblical writers, Esau, the founder of Edom, appears more worthy than Jacob, the forefather of the southern Hebrew tribes. Evidently, relations between the two southern groups of 'Edom' and 'Jacob' were initially so warm and friendly that despite the conflicts that followed later, memory of their former closeness persisted in the oral legends.

No less problematic was the primacy of Judah, the strongest of the southern tribes. After all, Judah stood lower in the line of inheritance than his three elder brothers born to Leah – Reuben, Simeon and Levi. Therefore, for each of these brothers the biblical writers took stories from the oral tradition to cast doubt on their right to lead the southern group. The right to choose belonged only to the forefather Jacob; and it was into his mouth that words were put depriving the elder sons of any claims to primacy. Thus the eldest son, Reuben, was blamed for having had in the past an affair with his father's concubine, Bilhah: "Reuben, you are my firstborn...you will no longer excel, for you went up onto your father's bed, onto my couch and defiled it" (Genesis 49:3-4). Simeon and Levi were found to be at fault for the slaughter in Shechem, which they perpetrated in revenge for their sister Dinah, who had been dishonored by the son of the ruler of the city: "Simeon and Levi are brothers – their swords are weapons of violence. Let me not enter their council, let me not join their assembly, for they have killed men in their anger and hamstrung oxen as they pleased. Cursed be their anger, so fierce, and their fury, so cruel! I will scatter them in Jacob and disperse them in Israel" (Genesis 49:5-7).

After his elder brothers' claims to primacy had been dismissed, Judah's right to power could be established: "Judah, your brothers will praise you; your hand will be on the neck of your enemies; your father's sons will bow down to you...The scepter will not depart from Judah, nor the ruler's staff from between his feet...and the obedience of the nations is his" (Genesis 49:8, 10). It stands to reason that the inclusion of such words in the biblical canon was possible not earlier than the first half of the 10th century B.C.E., when all power was transferred into the hands of the dynasty of David, a descendant of the tribe of Judah. However, the redactors of the Bible found themselves in an extremely tricky situation when evaluating the 'house of Joseph'. They could not withhold from Joseph what was due to him as the main partner in the union, but they tried to avoid, wherever possible, mentioning his right to power:

> Joseph is a fruitful vine, a fruitful vine near a spring, whose branches climb over a wall. With bitterness archers attacked him; they shot at him with hostility. But his bow remained steady, his strong arms stayed limber, because of the hand of the Mighty One of Jacob, because of the Shepherd, the Rock

of Israel...Your father's blessings are greater than the blessings of the ancient mountains, than the bounty of the age-old
hills. Let all these rest on the head of Joseph, on the brow of
the prince among his brothers. (Genesis 49: 22-24, 26)

It was necessary to distinguish the 'house of Joseph' from
the other tribes – firstly as the main power among the northern
tribes and secondly, for its special, privileged position in Egypt
– but without providing justification for Joseph's claims to primacy among the Hebrew tribes. So elsewhere his father turns to
Joseph and reminds him, "And to you, as one who is over your
brothers, I give the ridge of land I took from the Amorites with
my sword and my bow" (Genesis 48:22).

Admittedly, with regards to providing proof of the primacy of
the Isaac-Jacob-Judah line, i.e. of the dynasty of King David, the
authors of Genesis fulfilled their objective only partially. Their
arguments in favor of Jacob's primacy over Esau and of Judah
over his elder brothers seem unconvincing. Yet this can also be
taken as proof that the biblical writers may be trusted. Obviously,
their creative freedom was highly limited; they were only enti-
tled to make a compilation from the existing oral stories rather
than to create a new narrative. Consequently, we are dealing not
with creative invention, but with genuine legends that reflected
the actual history of the nomadic Western Semites in Canaan.
Guided by the political interests of both the United Monarchy
and the dynasty of David itself, the compilers of Genesis were
only able to make a compilation from the oral stories that were
known at the time. The most they could do was to do this in
such a way as to legitimize the supreme power of David's line
and the latter's claims to ruling not only over their own southern
tribes, but over the northern tribes as well. If the authors of the
Old Testament had been allowed to do more than merely edit
the oral narrative of the Hebrew tribes, then they could have
found even more convincing and weighty 'proof' in favor of the

primacy of the line of Jacob and Judah. Thus the existing biblical text about the patriarchs is merely a skillful interweaving of various stories taken from the narratives of both the southern and northern Hebrew tribes, but it is by no means a fabrication.

As for the second objective, – unifying the family trees of the southern and northern tribes – the writers of the Pentateuch fared much better. They succeeded so well in intertwining the various pieces of narratives about Jacob and Israel, the forefathers of the southern and northern tribes, that all subsequent generations of the Jewish people considered Jacob and Israel to be a single forefather with a double name, Jacob-Israel.

Genesis, the first book of the Pentateuch, ends with the death of Jacob in Egypt, where the southern tribes had come to escape the drought and famine in Canaan. In accordance with the patriarch's last wish, his body was brought from Egypt to Canaan and buried there in the famous Cave of Machpelah near Hebron, where the remains of Abraham and Isaac had already been laid to rest. Thus all three patriarchs, the forefathers of the southern Hebrew tribes, found their final resting place in the area where they had primarily lived, the Hebron region. Their wives were also buried there: Sarah, Rebekah, and Leah, but not Rachel. Rachel was buried in Bethlehem, which was called Ephrat at the time. But why? After all, Bethlehem was located only several miles from Hebron and the Cave of Machpelah. If it was possible to bring Jacob's body all the way from Egypt, then why did his wife Rachel (who died giving birth to their son Benjamin) not receive the same treatment? How did Leah, though not Jacob's favorite wife, as the Bible itself admits, come to lie next to her husband upon her death, while his dearly beloved Rachel, who was also his legal spouse and the mother of his beloved sons, end up outside the family burial-vault? There is another aspect that is also of interest. Joseph, the beloved son of Jacob-Israel, was the only person who, according to the Bible, received the honor of having his bones brought from Egypt when the exodus took place. But, like Rachel, he too was not buried in the Cave of Machpelah near Hebron; his tomb is in central Palestine, near Shechem – the principal place of residence of the northern Hebrew tribes. The answer to this enigma is clear: both Rachel and Joseph were historical characters from the narrative of the northern tribes. Perhaps Rachel was the principal wife of the legendary forefather of the northern tribes, Israel, while Joseph would have been considered his eldest son. From the biblical episode about Rachel's death, we know that it took place as she was heading southwards from Bethel, the religious center of the northern tribes, and that her death took everyone by surprise during some kind of mass move; thus it was necessary to bury her quickly in the spot where she had died. In their effort to compose a single family tree for the two groups, the authors of Genesis found an interesting compromise regarding the wives of Jacob and Israel. Leah, Jacob's principal wife, was given senior status, but is presented as unloved while Rachel, principal spouse of Israel, became the second, but only beloved wife of the common patriarch.

In this way the writers of the Pentateuch managed to preserve the primacy of the southern tribes as legal heirs, while giving the northern tribes love and acknowledgment of their own special merits. The compilers of Genesis felt the need to merge not only the patriarchs of the two tribal groups, but also their sons – the forefathers of the specific Hebrew tribes. In this respect, we should note the words of the forefather Jacob to Joseph: "Now then, your two sons born to you in Egypt before I came to you here will be reckoned as mine; Ephraim and Manasseh will be mine, just as Reuben and Simeon are mine. Any children born to you after them will be yours" (Genesis 48:5-6). It is significant that Jacob 'appropriated' only Joseph's eldest children, but did not lay claim to any of the children of his other sons. Such echoes of the original existence of two separate tribal groups with different family trees have survived in many biblical sources. For example, one of the psalms of gratitude to God clearly states, "With your mighty arm you redeemed your people, the descendants of Jacob and Joseph" (Psalm 77:15). Despite the fact that, according to the biblical version, the 'house of Joseph' was only part of the 'house of Jacob' – or, to be more exact, one of Jacob's sons, – the ancient tradition puts him on an independent and equal footing with the entire 'house of Jacob'.

There is yet another interesting fact that attracts our attention: it was not only the tribal group of Jacob-Israel that was composed of twelve sons and twelve tribes; other nomadic West Semitic groups – for example, Esau (Edom), Ishmael, and Nahor – had the same number of descendant tribes. Evidently, the number 12 had symbolic significance in the mythology of the nomadic Amorites and thus the number of tribes in each of the independent large groups had to equal this number. In actuality, the real number of the Hebrew tribes was probably less than twelve. But the main point was something else: all twelve Hebrew tribes – the 'family' of which the Book of Genesis speaks – only came together to form a union during the time of the United Monarchy.

Thus the stories of the biblical patriarchs indicate that the ancestors of the Hebrews were semi-nomadic Western Semites who came to Canaan from their native land near the upper courses of the Euphrates River. From the very beginning, they were two different tribal groups who appeared in Canaan at different times. The first to come were the ancestors of the northern Hebrew tribes, who settled on land in central and northern Palestine. Later, a new and large tribal alliance that was headed by the biblical patriarch Abraham came to Canaan. His alliance included the ancestors of closely-related peoples who later became known as the southern Hebrew tribes – the Edomites, Moabites, Ammonites, Ishmaelites, Midianites, Kenites, and Amalekites. The sons, grandsons, and great-grandsons of Abraham enumerated in the Bible were the forefathers of the tribes and clans. The Abraham-Isaac-Jacob family tree is only a small part of the genealogy of the rulers of the nomadic and semi-nomadic Western Semites (the Sutu and Habiru). Many centuries later, when the southern Hebrew tribes had already returned from Egypt, a new branch was woven into their family tree – the northern tribes with whom they united in a common kingdom. Thus Jacob became simultaneously Israel; the number of his sons (tribes) increased to 12; and the remarkable legend about Joseph and his brothers became the shared property of the northern and southern tribes. What could have united two different groups of semi-nomadic Western Semites (of Amorite origin)? It was Egypt – or rather, what had occurred to them there.

CHAPTER THREE

In the Egypt
of the Hyksos

What does the Bible hide?

The narrative of the Hebrews' stay in Egypt is the most mysterious and obscure part of the Old Testament. In comparison, even the more ancient stories about the Hebrew patriarchs are a much richer source of information. Amazingly, the Bible tells us hardly anything about the four centuries that the Hebrew tribes spent in Egypt. While the book that comes before it, the Book of Genesis, is full of names of individuals, peoples, cities, and countries, the Book of Exodus, which deals with the Hebrews' stay in Egypt, is enigmatically silent on the four centuries the Hebrews lived in this country. And yet the Egyptian period lasted longer than the time that Abraham, Isaac, and Jacob had spent in Canaan. Moreover, the theme of slavery in Egypt is so important that it subsequently becomes a leitmotif of all the biblical books, being mentioned more than 100 times. This complete silence ends only with the birth of Moses, after which all the information we have about the Hebrews in Egypt relates exclusively to the exodus. We even have incomparably more information about the 40 years of wandering through the desert than the 430-year stay in Egypt. Is this a matter of chance? Of course not. The silence that the Bible keeps regarding life in Egypt is deliberate and testifies to the fact that the first writers of the Pentateuch intentionally avoided including in the biblical canon any oral narratives that would have contradicted their official version of the Israelite people's origin. This silence was an attempt to hide the fact that the Hebrews initially comprised two ethnically close, but distinct tribal groups – the northern of Israel-Joseph and the southern of Jacob-Judah; and that these two peoples arrived in and, more importantly, left Egypt at different centuries. Thus we have two dates for the Hebrews' arrival in Egypt and two dates for their departure from the country. Moreover, the Northerners and Southerners lived in the Nile Delta for different periods of time and evidently played dissimilar roles in Egypt's political history.

The biblical account of the Hebrews' arrival in the Nile Delta, the peaceful life they lived there, and their enslavement by the pharaohs and dramatic exodus under the leadership of Moses relate only to the southern group of Jacob-Judah. The northern group of Israel-Joseph had a completely different experience, which was not, and could not have been, properly reflected in the Bible. The Northerners and the 'house of Joseph' in particular, were an integral part of the people that conquered Egypt – the so-called Hyksos – and shared their rise and fall. The 'house of Joseph's' stay in Egypt was substantially shorter: this tribal group was forced to leave Egypt for Canaan not later than the middle of the 15th century B.C.E., while their southern brothers from the tribal group of Jacob-Judah continued to live in the Nile Delta right up until the start of the 12th century B.C.E.

The different arrival and departure times, as well as the very different lengths of time that the two groups of Hebrew tribes lived in Egypt, made it impossible to combine the oral narratives of both groups into a single version like in the earlier Book of

Genesis. It was for this reason that the authors of Exodus thought it best to keep silent about the very extensive time period that the Hebrews spent in Egypt. All names and events that could have helped identify the locations, key moments, or active participants of this period were excised. It was only this kind of unified version of the 'Egyptian enslavement' that could join together the narratives of the two tribal groups. Here we find the biblical writers using the working methods that we saw in the previous chapter: it was not that they fabricated or invented anything; they just skillfully combined the well-known stories of the time, while endeavoring to fashion them into a common genealogy and history for the Northerners and Southerners, who were brought together in the same country by the hand of fate.

The arrival of the northern Hebrew tribes in Egypt dates to the period of the Middle Kingdom, which existed 1938-1630 B.C.E. Historians consider the Middle Kingdom to have started with the 12th Dynasty, which ruled Egypt for almost 200 years. The pharaohs of the 12th Dynasty were mainly interested in Nubia and Libya, so most Egyptian war campaigns of this period were directed to the south and west. Canaan, the country closest to Egypt in the east, was not particularly attractive to the Egyptian pharaohs of the Middle Kingdom. Maybe the pharaohs were deterred by the difficulty of laying siege to the Canaanite cities or perhaps the prospects of loot in Nubia and Libya seemed more attractive to them. For whatever reason, Canaan remained independent of Egypt, despite its proximity. Admittedly, several pharaohs from the 12th Dynasty did launch individual campaigns into Canaan and Syria, but their objective was to plunder, not to subordinate the country. Senusret III, one of the best-known pharaohs of this dynasty, carried out at least one large-scale campaign against Canaan.

The end of the 12th Dynasty came with the reign of Sebeknefru, the first female pharaoh in Egyptian history. The fact that a woman was forced to take the throne was evidence that this dynasty's end was near – and indeed it came in 1756 B.C.E. Evaluating as a whole Egypt's position during the rule of the 12th Dynasty, we see neither a weakening of military power nor an economic decline. However, the situation completely changed with the coming of the 13th Dynasty, which ruled from 1756 to 1630 B.C.E. During this period of about 100 years, there were 70 different pharaohs. Various parts of the country periodically had their own pharaohs, who competed with one another, each proclaiming himself the only legitimate ruler. Many reigned for only a few months. It was during this period that there appeared yet another dynasty, the so-called 14th, the center of which was the city of Xois in the north of the Nile Delta. The internal disputes and weakening of central power led to the loss of conquered territories in Nubia and Libya and to the abandonment of any idea of conducting military campaigns into Canaan.

Instead, Canaan itself came to Egypt: Western Semites (Amorites) gradually penetrated into the Nile Delta. Today we possess convincing archaeological evidence of the fact that from at least the 18th century B.C.E., the Nile Delta was settled by Western Semites whose material culture unmistakably demonstrates their Canaanite origins. The infiltration of the Western Semites evidently began much earlier, but at the time it was limited and controlled by the Egyptian authorities. It is improbable that the newcomers were settled inhabitants from Canaanite city states. Most likely, semi-nomadic Amorites moved to the Nile Delta to escape the drought and famine that periodically forced them out of Canaan. It was these tribes that Abraham encountered when, fleeing the drought, he was compelled to go to Egypt. The fact that the Bible calls the local ruler 'pharaoh' does not necessarily mean that he was not of West Semitic origin; Abraham probably encountered not Egyptians, but semi-nomadic Amorites, just like himself. It appears that his concubine Hagar, the mother of his son Ishmael, was also descended from these same Amorites, who had settled in the Nile Delta.

West Semitic nomads settle the Nile Delta

The Western Semites began settling the Nile Delta while the pharaohs of the 12th Dynasty were still ruling, but at that time central Egyptian power was still strong enough to keep this process under control. An entire system of fortresses existed along the eastern border of Egypt, giving the Egyptians effective control of the roads and limiting the nomads' access to Egypt from Asia. We know of three written documents that directly or indirectly confirm the Western Semites' penetration into the Nile Delta by the 21st-20th centuries B.C.E., i.e. during the First Intermediate Period (2130-1938) and the beginning of the Middle Kingdom. These documents are: 'the Admonition of Ipuver', 'the Instructions for King Meri-ka-Re' and 'the Prophecy of Neferty'. All three documents unambiguously testify to the pressure the nomadic Amorites put on the eastern border of Egypt as well as to their starting to settle in the Nile Delta. They confirm the statement in the Book of Genesis that drought and famine forced the people to leave for Egypt. These documents confirm that what we have here is not a settled population, but nomadic tribes. But the same written sources show that the Egyptians behaved with hostility and even cruelty to Western Semites affected by a lack of water and were trying to minimize their access to the Nile Delta. However, an internal battle for power resulted in an overall weakening of Egypt during the 13th Dynasty; as a result, border controls ceased to function. From this time onwards, tribes of nomadic and semi-nomadic Amorites driven from Canaan by periodic droughts began entering Egypt and living in the Nile Delta without impediment. It cannot be said that the Egyptian pharaohs did not realize the scale of the threat that the newcomers from Asia posed, but internal strife prevented them from closing their eastern border. Moreover, this was something that by no means all the rulers would have even wanted to do. It is highly probable that many of the

70 pharaohs of the 13th Dynasty, particularly at the end of the dynasty's rule, were no longer Egyptians themselves, but originated from the Amorite tribal leaders and were ruling under Egyptian names. But even those who originated from distinguished Egyptian families increasingly depended on help from the Western Semites. Thus, in beginning to back candidates for the Egyptian throne, the newcomers from Canaan gradually became the decisive military in Egypt.

The Egyptians' growing military dependence on the Western Semites soon led the rulers of the Amorite tribes to decide to no longer remain camouflaged, but to instead rule Egypt themselves. 1630 B.C.E. was the last year in the history of the 13th Dynasty and the first in the reign of the new 15th (West Semitic) Dynasty. Historians consider this year to be the end of the Middle Kingdom and the beginning of the Second Intermediate Period (1630-1523 B.C.E.), when all control of Egypt fell into the hands of the Western Semites/Amorites – the so-called Hyksos.

Who were the Hyksos?

The name 'Hyksos' was first used by Manetho, an Egyptian priest and historian who lived in the 3rd century B.C.E. and wrote a history of Egypt in Greek. Unfortunately, his manuscripts have not survived; all that we have are extensive excerpts from his works compiled by ancient authors. Manetho was cited most frequently by the Jewish historian Josephus Flavius, who lived in the second half of the first century C.E.

Manetho speaks of the subjugation of Egypt by the Hyksos, an unknown people who had come from Asia. He writes:

> ...For what cause I know not, a blast of God smote us; and unexpectedly, from the regions of the East, invaders of obscure race marched in confidence of victory against our land. By main force they easily overpowered the rulers of

the land, they then burned our cities ruthlessly, razed to the ground the temples of the gods, and treated all the natives with a cruel hostility, massacring some and leading into slavery the wives and children of others. Finally, they appointed as king one of their number whose name was Salitis. He had his seat at Memphis, levying tribute from Upper and Lower Egypt, and leaving garrisons behind in the most advantageous positions. Above all, he fortified the district to the east, foreseeing that the Assyrians, as they grew stronger, would one day covet and attack his kingdom. In the Saite [Sethroite] nome, he found a city very favorably situated on the east of the Bubastite branch of the Nile, and called Avaris after an ancient religious tradition. This place he rebuilt and fortified with massive walls, planting there a garrison of as many as 240,000 heavy-armed men to guard his frontier. Here he would come in summer time, partly to serve out rations and pay his troops, partly to train them carefully in manoeuvres and so strike terror into foreign tribes. (Manetho, Aegyptiaca, frag. 42, 1.75-79.2).

Since the citations from Manetho were written in Greek, the term 'Hyksos' is a Greek variant of the Egyptian words 'hekau khasut' – meaning 'foreign rulers' or, to be more precise, 'foreign Asiatic rulers'. Unfortunately, the quotes from Manetho's manuscript give us very little historical information, apart from confirmation of the fundamental fact that the Hyksos ruled over Egypt. Manetho was describing events that had happened almost 1500 years before, so the picture he paints actually reflects the conquest of Egypt not so much by the Hyksos, as by the Assyrians, Babylonians, or Persians, who were much closer to him in time than the Hyksos. Manetho was as removed in time from the Hyksos period as we are today from the Huns' invasion of Rome. Archaeological data do not confirm the terrible pictures of destruction depicted by Manetho, whereas mention of the potential threat to the Hyksos from Assyria (in the 17th-16th centuries B.C.E.!!) only adds to the complete confusion regarding the portrayal of the Hyksos in the 3rd century B.C.E. However, even modern historians have been unable to avoid mistakes when trying to explain the origins of the Hyksos. At first, scholars tried to associate the Hyksos with the Hittites, then with the Hurrians, and finally, they identified them as Indo-European nomadic tribes. They saw evidence of an Indo-European origin in the fact that it was the Hyksos who familiarized the Egyptians with horses and war chariots and taught them more effective methods of obtaining metals – in other words, introduced them to innovations that were considered to have been brought to the Near East by Indo-Europeans. But archaeological excavations conducted in recent decades have dispelled all doubt: the so-called Hyksos were in truth semi-nomadic Western Semites who came not from just anywhere in Asia, but specifically from Canaan. Unfortunately, these West Semitic nomads left us no written testimonies; they probably did not even have their own form of writing. However, linguistic analysis of their names from Egyptian sources provides unmistakable confirmation of their West Semitic and indeed Amorite origin. Could we really think that the Hittites or Hurrians arrived in Egypt en masse in the 18th-16th centuries B.C.E. if the former were sitting tight in Anatolia at the time and the latter were in northeastern Syria? It was only much later when both the Hittites and the Hurrians started clashing with the Egyptians – and then it was not in Egypt itself, but in Syria and the land of the Amurru.

When using the term 'Hyksos', we should not forget that this was what the Egyptians called only the pharaohs and rulers of West Semitic origin. A completely different name – 'a'amu' – was used for commoners from Syria and Canaan. This is consonant with the name of the West Semitic tribes of that time (Amorites) and the name for Phoenicia and southern Syria (Amurru). The Egyptians used the name 'a'amu' for almost 1000 years, from the beginning of the Middle Kingdom until the end of the New Kingdom, i.e. during the entire period when the word 'Amorite' was in use. The Egyptians had met the a'amu long before the rule of the Hyksos began. On the one hand, they were hired workers who came to Egypt for seasonal work, and on the other, they were the numerous slaves and captives taken during the pharaohs' campaigns in Canaan, Phoenicia, and southern Syria. For example, Amenemhet II, a pharaoh from the 12th Dynasty, left us a record of his campaign on the Lebanese coast, which resulted in him taking captive 1554 Asiatics (a'amu). We also know of written administrative documents dating to the 18th-17th centuries B.C.E. that mention Asiatics working in temples and private homes; the absolute majority of these Asiatic names are clearly of Amorite origin. Likewise, of the 77 legible names on the list of workers from a single private estate, at least 48 of them are Amorite. There is another type of written evidence for the arrival of the a'amus in Egypt. This includes the unique fresco in the burial tomb of Khnumhotep II, ruler of the nome of Oryx, (known today as the Beni Hasan tomb painting), which depicts the arrival of the semi-nomadic Amorite clan in Egypt. The inscription on this fresco mentions Abisha, the head of the nomadic Amorite clan, and 37 of his fellow tribesmen. This fresco dates to the beginning of the 19th century B.C.E.

A clan of Western Semites arrives in Egypt from Canaan.
19th century B.C.E.

Thus the Egyptian sources confirm the accounts given in the books of Genesis and Exodus – specifically with regard to the departure of the Amorite nomads for Egypt and their life in that country. Undoubtedly, like the Egyptian 'a'amu' and Manetho's 'Hyksos', the biblical 'Ivri' and the 'Habiru' of Canaan were one large West Semitic ethnos of Amorite origin. In this respect, both the southern and the northern Hebrew tribes were merely a small part of the large ethnos that dominated in Canaan, Phoenicia, southern Syria, and later in the Nile Delta as well.

Hyksos' connections with Canaan

By combining biblical and ancient Egyptian sources and by taking into account the latest archaeological data, we are able to reconstruct an approximate picture of the Hyksos' conquest of Egypt and the arrival of the Hebrew tribes in the Nile Delta. This picture will be incomplete if we leave out Canaan, because those who subordinated Egypt not only came from Canaan, but had also lived there for a lengthy period of time. Here we have in mind the semi-nomadic Amorite tribes who came from northwestern Mesopotamia to southern Syria, Phoenicia, and northern/central Canaan in approximately the 23rd century B.C.E. This large group of tribes also included nomads from the northern Hebrew tribes, who subsequently came to be known as 'Israel'. The arrival of a large mass of nomads led to the collapse of the entire system of Canaanite city states. Some of the cities were destroyed; others were deserted by their inhabitants, who evidently left for regions in the south of Canaan, which had suffered least from the invasion. Archaeological data testify to the quick and violent nature of the destruction of the Early Bronze Age's (3050-2300 B.C.E.) entire urban culture. They also provide evidence that this culture was replaced by an entirely different one.

The new culture of the semi-nomadic tribes predominated in northern and central Canaan for three centuries, from the 23rd to the 20th century B.C.E. Throughout this period, pastoralists and small agricultural communities predominated in Canaan. Similar processes occurred on the Lebanese coast and in southern Syria. Unlike these regions, southern Palestine and Transjordan hardly suffered at all. Archeologists have traced their full continuity with the previous Canaanite city culture. It is likely that the southern and eastern regions served as places of refuge for the former population of Western Canaan. 'The Story of Sinuhe', a well-known ancient Egyptian document from the 20th century B.C.E., fully confirms the domination of the semi-nomadic peoples in northern and central Canaan. Sinuhe was an Egyptian high official at the court of the Pharaoh who ran away from his country during the difficult time of the interregnum. He left us a detailed description of northern and central Canaan, where he lived for many years. From this it follows that pastoralists lived everywhere in Retenu, as the Egyptians called Canaan. Although he lived in these regions for many years, Sinuhe never once mentions seeing or visiting any large city there – which is hardly surprising since, judging by the archaeological data, all large cities had already been long since destroyed or abandoned by their inhabitants.

Some historians put forward an entirely different kind of explanation for the sudden downfall of central and northern Canaan's entire urban culture: they claim that either invasions by the Egyptian army or a change in the climate were responsible. As proof, they refer to inscriptions discovered in the burial tomb of the Egyptian high official and general Uni. The latter served Pharaoh Pepi I (the third pharaoh of the 6th Dynasty) and described a campaign by the Egyptian army into the "country of the sand dwellers", i.e. into northern Sinai and southwest Canaan. Further evidence used in this argument is a bas-relief from Upper Egypt that dates to the end of the 5th Dynasty and depicts the Egyptians besieging a fortified city, most likely in Canaan. However, historians know of campaigns carried out by the Egyptian army both prior to and after the fall of Canaanite city culture, but these military operations did not lead to the wholesale destruction of the entire system of cities. Moreover, during the 23rd-20th centuries B.C.E. – the campaigns took place at the end of the Old Kingdom and the First Intermediate Period – Egypt itself was undergoing decentralization of authority and general decline, resulting in the breaking of traditional links with Canaan and the Lebanese coast. At this time, military raids on Canaan were the exception rather than the rule and Egyptian military activity was minimal. Uni's expedition was probably a response to attacks by the Amorite nomads who were threatening Egypt's eastern border, rather than a campaign to conquer them.

The explanation advancing serious climate change is even less convincing. Firstly, the climate does not change suddenly; and secondly, to the south and east of the Dead Sea, i.e. in those regions that are climatically more 'vulnerable', archaeologists have discovered a consistent continuation of the previous culture in the form of prosperous cities that did not suffer at all during the period when the entire system of Canaanite cities was being destroyed.

The main reason for the destruction of the Canaanite cities of the Early Bronze Age (3050-2300 B.C.E.) was therefore not sporadic military campaigns undertaken by the Egyptians or climate change of any kind, but an invasion from the north by a large mass of semi-nomadic Amorite tribes. The latter came to Canaan from southern Syria and the Lebanese coast, where they had arrived after having traveled from northwest Mesopotamia, the original native land of all the Western Semites. At approximately this time, another powerful wave of Amorite tribes headed in a south-easterly direction along the river valleys of the Tigris and Euphrates. Many Mesopotamian cities experienced the same fate as the cities of Canaan. But in terms of territory and population, Mesopotamia clearly surpassed Canaan and southern Syria, so the Amorites very quickly intermingled with the local population and adopted their culture. Here this period of chaos and ruin turned out to be much shorter, lasting only around 100 years (2230-2130 B.C.E.).

Unlike Mesopotamia, Canaan experienced the arrival of a second wave of Amorite tribes in approximately the 20th century B.C.E. It involved those nomadic Western Semites who for some reason could not live in Mesopotamia and decided to join their fellow tribesmen in Canaan. This group of pastoralists was led by the biblical patriarch Abraham and included not only southern Hebrew tribes, but also their closest relatives – the future Edomites, Moabites, and Ammonites – and the ancestors of the Midianites and of the peoples of the desert who traced their origins to Abraham. In contrast to the first wave of Amorite nomads who came to northern/central Canaan in the 23rd century B.C.E., the second wave of pastoralists took place in regions that remained vacant, i.e. in the south and in Transjordan. Their arrival in Canaan was relatively peaceful or at least involved far less destruction and shock than the first wave. Thus, both chronologically and geographically, the Hebrew tribes were for a long time far removed from each other.

Yet Canaan too did not serve all the nomadic Amorites as their final resting place. Later, the majority of them moved further, to the Nile Delta in the southwest. Evidently, climatic conditions in the Nile Delta – above all, the abundance of water in all seasons – were more suitable for the semi-nomadic cattle breeders than Canaan with its periodic droughts and consequent famines. Significantly, the Book of Genesis compares the Egyptian land to the 'garden of the Lord' (Genesis 13:10). Most likely, the first Amorite pastoralists came to the Nile Delta precisely because of the drought and famine in Canaan. In time, the West

Semitic nomads came more and more frequently to Egypt and stayed for increasingly longer periods of time. This was how the a'amu became a permanent presence in the Nile Delta.

By the 20th century B.C.E., ancient Egyptian sources were already voicing alarm regarding the pressure exerted by the a'amu on the country's eastern border. However, the Western Semites began penetrating into these parts much earlier, at least no later than the so-called First Intermediate Period, which is known as a time of crisis and decline. In essence, the Book of Genesis serves as confirmation that the West Semitic pastoralists moved to the Nile Delta due to the periodic droughts in Canaan. Abraham 'descended' into Egypt. Isaac was planning to head in the same direction, and only the intervention of God kept him back in Canaan. Joseph likewise ended up in Egypt when he was sold into slavery. And finally, Jacob and all his relatives left for the Nile Delta not to avoid yet another drought, but to live there permanently. Hagar, who was Abraham's concubine and the mother of his elder son Ishmael, also originated from Egypt, most likely from the same kind of Western Semites as Abraham. Abraham's return to Canaan is merely evidence that, in that period, i.e. approximately the 20th century B.C.E., the Egyptians still exerted quite effective control over their eastern border and did not allow the pastoralists to live for long in the Nile Delta. At the same time, however, anxiety over the encroachment of the a'amu from the east found expression in many ancient Egyptian documents that are known to us. The Bible indirectly confirms that during the time of Isaac (19th-18th centuries B.C.E.?) some of the West Semitic tribes left for Egypt due to another harsh drought. It may be supposed that these were northern Hebrew tribes from central Canaan or, in particular, the 'house of Joseph'. It is likely that the lifetime of the biblical Isaac – a considerable period (180 years) – coincided with the rule of the 12th Egyptian Dynasty and partially with the 13th combined Dynasty as well. Finally, the lifetime of the biblical Jacob probably coincided with both the rule of the combined 13th and 14th Dynasties and the Second Intermediate Period in the history of Egypt, when power in the country passed decisively into the hands of the West Semitic rulers, the Hyksos.

What did the Egyptian pharaohs conceal?

The period during which the Hyksos ruled is the most obscure and mysterious in the history of ancient Egypt. We still have no written texts, inscriptions, or bas-reliefs deriving from the Hyksos; we know nothing about the pyramids or burial tombs of their pharaohs or their high officials, not to mention wall frescos or sculptures. But the shroud of mystery and darkness covering the period when the West Semitic pharaohs ruled is no accident. The rule of the Amorite foreigners was even in the most ancient times considered by the Egyptians to be disgraceful and humiliating. For this reason, after the Hyksos had been driven out, the Egyptian pharaohs systematically and methodically endeavored to obliterate all traces of the Amorites' rule over Egypt and to erase from memory anything that had to do with the Hyksos. Following orders given by the pharaohs of the New Kingdom, absolutely everything in the country that could have in any way served as a reminder of the Hyksos and their rule was destroyed. For this reason, there is little hope today that a Hyksos written monument, which could shed light on this dark period of history, will ever be discovered. The only thing that remains for archaeologists to do is to study the remains of the Hyksos material culture in the Nile Delta and, above all, in the capital, Avaris. But here too there are considerable difficulties. The vindictive Egyptians completely destroyed the capital, burning it to the ground along with the Hyksos settlements in the Nile Delta. The surviving written and material monuments from this period belong to the enemies of the Hyksos – the pharaohs of the 17th Dynasty from Thebes, who were initially the vassals of the Amorites, but later became their principal adversaries. Indeed, the pharaohs of the 17th and then the 18th Dynasties did everything to ensure that no one among subsequent generations would know anything about the Hyksos or their deeds. It is interesting that the darkest time in Egyptian history, the Hyksos period, chronologically coincided with the most mysterious part of the Bible dealing with the Hebrews' stay in Egypt. In both cases, any memory of events that took place during this time was deliberately erased. The pharaohs of the New Kingdom attempted to consign to oblivion the shame of being ruled over by foreigners; and the biblical writers tried to force their readers to forget the fact that the sons of Jacob and Israel had arrived in and left Egypt at different times and indeed had different histories up until their unification in the 12th century B.C.E.

Unfortunately, all we know about the Hyksos has been extracted either directly or indirectly from the written sources left by their enemies – the Thebes-based pharaohs of the 17th and 18th Dynasties. Not a single written monument has come down to us that could have represented the point of view of the Hyksos themselves. There is no doubt that such records did exist, but they were destroyed by their adversaries from Thebes. However, even the poor and distorted information that we have from the mouths of the Hyksos' enemies can help us put together a picture of what happened in Egypt during the Second Intermediate Period.

Manetho clearly made a mistake when he depicted the arrival of the Hyksos as an 'invasion' that was 'sudden' and 'unexpected' for the Egyptians. What actually happened was completely different: the infiltration of the Amorite pastoralists was gradual and peaceful, occurring over the course of several centuries. Most likely, this process even took place with the agreement of the Egyptian authorities, at least to begin with. The Nile Delta was at that time sparsely populated and contained much unoccupied land that was suitable for breeding and grazing cattle.

The Egyptian officials exacted rather large payments from these Amorite tribes who took refuge from the periodic droughts in Canaan. Moreover, in addition to the financial benefits, the arrival of the Amorites was also a source of cheap labor. Needing money to pay the amounts demanded by the Egyptian officials, the Western Semites willingly went to work as hired laborers for the local landowners; they were widely used as servants in wealthy households, and were well-known for their skill as blacksmiths.

The archaeological data that we have at our disposal show that the Western Semites settled in the Nile Delta no later than the 18th century B.C.E. However, it is extremely likely that the Amorite pastoralists arrived in these parts much earlier, perhaps even at the end of the Old Kingdom, in approximately the 23rd century B.C.E. The above-mentioned military campaign conducted by General Uni in northern Sinai and southern Canaan was a response to the encroachment of semi-nomadic Amorites on Egypt's eastern border. The ensuing First Intermediate Period (2130-1938 B.C.E.) in the history of Egypt was extremely favorable for the infiltration of the West Semitic tribes into the Nile Delta. At this time, the country practically split into separate regions or nomes, which were constantly at war with one another. The eastern border was open and undefended, and the Western Semites began moving into the Nile Delta, which had a better climate than Canaan and Sinai. We know about the arrival of Amorite tribes in the Nile Delta from ancient Egyptian documents of that period. Archaeological excavations can shed little light on the situation since the West Semitic cattle-breeders lived in portable tents and did not build cities, fortifications, or even settlements. Therefore, it would be senseless to search for archaeological proof of their material culture's presence in the Nile Delta at that time. Such searches are extraordinarily difficult and are probably doomed to fail.

Egypt's unification and strengthening during the Middle Kingdom led to some of the Amorite tribes being driven out back to southern Canaan and to the fortification of Egypt's eastern border. Indirect evidence of this is found in the biblical narrative concerning Abraham's stay in Egypt. The episode that tells of Abraham's wife Sarah being put into the 'pharaoh's' harem is only a literary transposition of real migrations made by the semi-nomadic Amorites. Thus the second half of the 20th century and the entire 19th century B.C.E. were an interruption in the Western Semites' settlement of the Nile Delta. The situation changed only towards the middle of the 18th century B.C.E. The new weakening of the central authority in Egypt and decline in the country's military power coincided with the end of the 12th Dynasty. The 13th Dynasty was typified by continual changes of power, with each pharaoh hardly having time to replace his predecessor. Civil wars raged and separatism intensified among the nomes. Guarding the eastern frontier was no longer of interest to anyone. It was during this period that the Amorites once again began settling the Nile Delta in large numbers. In the eastern part of the Nile Delta an enormous fortified city emerged. This was Avaris, which subsequently became the capital of the Western Semites while they were in Egypt. Avaris was three times larger than Hazor, the largest city at the time in Canaan. The city's rapid growth and large size testify to the enormous influx of Amorite tribes into the Nile Delta as well as to the fact that these pastoralists were now beginning to settle. We have reason to suppose that by the 17th century B.C.E., the majority of the semi-nomadic Amorites from Canaan and southern Syria had concentrated in the Nile Delta and that they far outnumbered the local Egyptian population, which evidently quickly intermarried with the Western Semites. On the other hand, those Amorites who settled in the Nile Delta – and in particular, in Avaris – assimilated culturally. Not only did they adopt many elements of Egyptian culture, but they also adapted their West Semitic religious cults to the local Egyptian ones.

During the rule of the numerous pharaohs of the 13th Dynasty, the legal status and political role of the Amorites who had settled in the Nile Delta changed substantially. From being newcomers with no rights who lived in Egypt at the discretion of the Pharaoh, they became full residents of the Delta with an ever-growing influence on the internal politics of Egypt. Without the military support of the Amorite tribes' leaders, no candidate for the position of Pharaoh could count on success. There was rivalry between pharaohs competing for power, but there were also new dynasties that emerged to lay claim to the throne. One of these dynasties was the so-called 14th, which became a force to be reckoned with in the north of the Nile Delta and was clearly West Semitic in origin. By the end of the rule of the 13th Dynasty, several pharaohs were Egyptian by name only, being in actual fact descended from the Amorite rulers. The central power's drastic weakening resulted in Egypt once again disintegrating into separate nomes whose rulers were sole masters of their regions. Eventually, the complete chaos and confusion in Egyptian politics essentially constituted an invitation to the Amorite tribal rulers of the Nile Delta to seize power.

The Amorites: the new rulers of the Nile country

A new and purely West Semitic dynasty of pharaohs thus emerged – the 15th (1630-1523 B.C.E.), usually referred to as the Hyksos dynasty. However, the Amorite rulers – the Hyksos – came to power not as foreign conquerors, but as Egyptians of West Semitic origin who used the symbolism, language, culture, and rituals of Egypt. Moreover, in their foreign and domestic policy, they represented the interests of Egypt and not of any other country. This was the principal difference that distinguished the rule of the Hyksos from the later reigns of the Assyrians, Babylonians, and the Persians.

The Amorite rulers, most of whom had been born in Egypt and were not the first generation of their families to live in the country, considered themselves to be not conquerors of Egypt, but Egyptian pharaohs; they ruled in accordance with the local customs and in the interests of the local population. In short, they identified themselves with Egypt, which they considered their own country. The name 'hekau khasut' – 'foreign Asiatic rulers' ('Hyksos' in Greek) – was conferred upon them by their enemies, the Theban pharaohs of Upper Egypt, who were traditional rivals of the rulers from Lower Egypt. In Lower Egypt itself, where the West Semitic pharaohs ruled, the word 'Hyksos' was probably unknown.

Basing his account solely on written records left by the New Kingdom pharaohs, Manetho was seriously mistaken in his appraisal of the Hyksos, especially when drawing parallels with later Assyrian or Persian conquerors, with whom he was better acquainted. In reality, there was neither a 'sudden invasion' by an 'unknown people' nor 'terrible destruction' or 'cruel treatment' of the Egyptians. Control over Egypt was not seized; rather, it fell, all by itself, into the hands of the Amorite rulers, as over-ripe fruit falls from a tree. The foreignness of the Amorite rule in Egypt was grossly exaggerated by their opponents, the Theban pharaohs, who never abandoned their claim to supreme power and exploited to the full the West Semitic origins of the Hyksos in their propaganda. Should we call the rule of the Amorite king Hammurabi (1792-1750 B.C.E.) in Babylon 'foreign' just because Babylon, just like many other Mesopotamian states of the time, was in the hands of the Amorite tribes? Moreover, until they came to power in Egypt, the semi-nomadic Amorites had lived in the Nile Delta for centuries and were largely no longer an external factor but an internal one. It is also important to remember that relations between the northern (Hyksos) and southern (Theban) pharaohs were shaped not so much by the hostility of the Egyptians towards the Amorites, as by the traditional rivalry between Upper and Lower Egypt. In reality, this was a battle for the right to unify Egypt and for hegemony over the entire country – so the West Semitic origin of the pharaohs of the Lower Kingdom was merely a convenient pretext for, but by no means a cause of, the hostility and fighting.

The 15th Hyksos Dynasty (1630-1523 B.C.E.) mainly had power over northern Egypt (the Lower Kingdom). At the same time, in the southern part of the country, i.e. the Upper Kingdom, another dynasty emerged – the 17th Theban dynasty (1630-1540 B.C.E.). Unlike the 15th Dynasty, the 17th was of Egyptian origin, and this colored the dynasty's propaganda against the pharaohs of the Lower Kingdom. The Hyksos had made Avaris in the Nile Delta their capital. Here, among Amorite tribes that were their kinsmen, they felt more at ease and, more importantly, safer. The capital of the southern pharaohs was the city of Thebes. The border between the territories belonging to Thebes and to Avaris passed through the central part of the country, in the region of the ancient city of Cuzai. Our picture of the division within Egypt would not be complete without mention of yet another dynasty, the 16th. Some Egyptologists consider this dynasty to be Hyksos too and assume that the West Semitic rulers who comprised it submitted to the pharaohs of the 15th Dynasty and ruled over one of the regions of the Nile Delta. Others call this dynasty Theban, supposing it to be the precursor of the 17th. It is remarkable that such different opinions about this dynasty have been expressed not just by Egyptologists today, but also by historians in ancient times. Nevertheless, all agree that the 16th Dynasty was of secondary significance and that its emergence testified to the fragmentation of Egypt. For almost the entire duration of the Second Intermediate Period (approximately 108 years), the Hyksos north enjoyed military superiority while the southern Theban pharaohs acknowledged the Hyksos as their lords and masters. Only at the end of this period did the balance change to favor Thebes and the southerners dared to challenge the Hyksos pharaohs.

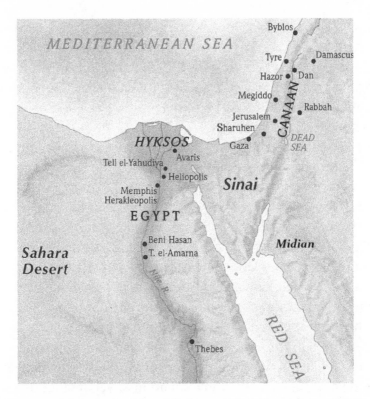

Egypt and Canaan in time of Hyksos. 17th-16th centuries. B.C.E.

Of the few written sources about the Hyksos that we have, the most trustworthy and reliable is the so-called 'Turin Canon Papyrus'. This ancient Egyptian papyrus is the most complete record of all the Egyptian pharaohs from the Old to the New Kingdom and was compiled in the 13th century B.C.E. during the reign of Ramesses II. Unfortunately, the Turin Canon has suffered so badly from the effects of time that only small parts of it can now be read. Despite this, it has provided us with information – backed up by seals and scarabs found in Egypt and Palestine – about the rule of at least six Hyksos pharaohs from the 15th Dynasty. In chronological order, their names are as follows: Sheshi, Ya'acob-har, Khyan, Apepi I, Apepi II, and Hammudi.

Individual seals and scarabs additionally mention two more names of Hyksos rulers: Anathar and Ya'acobaam. Some Egyptologists ascribe these names to the second Hyksos dynasty – the 16th. The Egyptian rendering of the Amorite names made them practically unrecognizable; however, even in their Egyptian forms, names such as Ya'acob-har, Ya'acobaam, or Hammudi undoubtedly appear West Semitic.

The written records left by the southern, Theban pharaohs unambiguously testify to the fact that the foreign policy conducted by the Hyksos was peaceful, while their internal policy was tolerant. We have absolutely no evidence of any kind of Hyksos campaigns of conquest – either towards the east (Canaan and Syria) or towards the west (Libya). At least, in neither Canaan nor Syria has any trace of Hyksos conquest been discovered to date. The seals and scarabs with the names of the Hyksos pharaohs discovered in Palestine most likely found their way there in a peaceful manner. It is no accident that the Hyksos rule in Egypt coincides with the heyday of urban culture in Canaan. The departure of the semi-nomadic Amorites from Canaan and their subsequent seizing of power in Egypt gave Canaan peace and prosperity in two ways. Firstly, the departure of a large mass of Amorite pastoralists in itself secured the Canaanite cities and settlements against clashes with their restless neighbors. The best example of conflict of this kind between a settled population and nomads is the biblical episode of the slaughter of the inhabitants of the city of Shechem by Simon and Levi, the sons of Jacob. This episode from the Hebrew narrative found its way into the Book of Genesis not by chance; it is, in fact, an echo of a real event: the southern Hebrew tribes routed Shechem in revenge for an insult inflicted on the daughter of their leader. Secondly, when the Amorites came to power in northern Egypt, this put an end to the Egyptian army's periodic predatory campaigns into Canaan. Having gained full control not only of the Nile Delta, but of the Lower Kingdom as well, the Amorite rulers were no longer in need of vacant pastureland, food from farmers, or wares made by townspeople. Moreover, had they embarked on distant campaigns to the east or to the west, this could have provoked unexpected attacks from their main enemies, the Theban pharaohs. It certainly cannot be ruled out that the peacefulness of the Hyksos was due to just such a threat from the south, a threat that constantly restrained them from engaging in overseas adventures. But a more likely explanation is that many cities in southern and central Canaan were allies of the Hyksos pharaohs. Data from archaeological excavations testify to the establishment of a new culture in Canaan – the culture of the Middle Bronze Age (2000-1550 B.C.E.), brought from the north by Amorite tribes. The shapes and color of the ceramics reveal a link between this new culture and Syria and northwestern Mesopotamia, from where the Amorite tribes had come. The forms of personal names in use at this time indicate the predominance of the Amorite population in both Syria and Canaan. Thus, the Hyksos pharaohs were dealing in Canaan with their own Amorite brethren.

In Canaan and the Nile Delta, similar processes occurred – regarding the settlement of part of the semi-nomadic Amorites on the land. The inhabitants of the Hyksos capital Avaris and of many cities in Canaan were all Amorite. This ethnic closeness and tribal ties were the key factors in the establishment of alliances between the Hyksos of Egypt and the Amorite population of Canaan. It should not be forgotten that when they were driven out of Egypt, the Hyksos looked for refuge and support in Canaan, in the southern city of Sharuhen, which was one of their allies. It is probable that these alliances were based on tribal kinship. According to the Bible, the Hebrew tribes who came from Egypt into Canaan were forbidden to fight against the Edomites, Moabites, or Ammonites living in Transjordan, since they were all relatives (Deuteronomy 2:4-5, 9, 19); and this prohibition existed in spite of the hostility of the latter peoples towards the

Hebrews and the at least 430 years that had passed since the two groups had last been in regular contact with each other. So while Canaan provided the Hyksos pharaohs with a friendly rear, – and one that was cemented by relations of kinship – the rule of the Hyksos in northern Egypt provided Canaan with a guarantee against Egyptian aggression. The mutually beneficial symbiosis between the Hyksos in Egypt and the Amorites in Canaan helped Palestine grow both economically and culturally.

The Hyksos pharaohs pursued a peaceful foreign policy with regard to their neighbors not only to the east, in Asia, but also to the west. Unlike the pharaohs of the 12th Dynasty, the Hyksos did not attempt to seize Libya and were tolerant towards the Libyan settlers in the western part of the Nile Delta. The main problem for the Hyksos was the southern pharaohs of Thebes. Formally, the latter recognized the supreme authority of the Lower Kingdom and even paid them tribute, but at the same time it was common knowledge that they never, at any point, dropped their claim of hegemony over Egypt. Military confrontation with the pharaohs of the Upper Kingdom was therefore only a question of time. Nevertheless, despite their military superiority, the Hyksos were patient with their potential adversaries. They did not rout the Upper Kingdom, and allowed the southern pharaohs a high degree of autonomy.

The Hyksos' lack of hegemonic and imperialist aspirations can probably be explained by their semi-nomadic Amorite origins. They did not set out to build grand pyramids or temples; they were not intent upon seizing as much foreign land or as many cities as possible; and their court was not noted for its splendor or richness. It is remarkable that even the Theban pharaohs, who depicted themselves as Egypt's defenders, could not accuse the Hyksos of treating Egyptians and captives cruelly. Although the pharaohs of the New Kingdom retrospectively attributed all manner of destruction to the Hyksos, in reality Hyksos policy was not only peaceful and tolerant, but even liberal – if such a term can be applied to any ruler in the 17-16th centuries B.C.E. Perhaps the only area of foreign activity that sparked their keen interest was trading with other countries. We have archaeological evidence that they traded actively not only with Canaan and Syria, but also with Mesopotamia, Asia Minor, and the Cretan and Mycenaean world. The Hyksos even managed to organize trading with Nubia, despite the active opposition of the Theban pharaohs, who controlled all the caravan routes leading in that direction.

The Egypt of the Hyksos was an interesting mixture of two states – one Amorite, the other Egyptian. The Amorite state was located in the Nile Delta, while the Egyptian state was in the Nile Valley; however, supreme power over both states belonged to the Amorite tribal rulers. Why did the Amorite tribes settle only in the Nile Delta and not try to go further up the river along the Nile Valley? Most likely, there was unoccupied and irrigated land only in the Nile Delta and not in the densely-populated valley. If the Hyksos had been the cruel conquerors portrayed by Manetho, then they would have turned the fields of the Egyptian peasants into pastureland for their own cattle. However, no one – not even the Hyksos' adversaries, the Theban pharaohs – ever accused them of this. At the same time, however, the clear division into Amorite and Egyptian territories also had a negative aspect: it made it impossible for the Amorites to merge with the local population in the same way that they did in Syria, Canaan, and Mesopotamia. From documents found in the archives of the cities of Mari and Alalakh we know that from the end of the 3rd millennium B.C.E., the Amorites established full hegemony over Mesopotamia, Syria, and Canaan. Everywhere in these regions Amorite states took shape – for example, Babylon in central Mesopotamia, Larsa and Eshnunna in southern Mesopotamia, Yamhad in northern Syria, Qatna in central Syria, and Hazor in northern Canaan. The Amorites very quickly assimilated the culture of the local inhabitants and merged with them. Over the course of a mere half-millennium, from 2100-1600 B.C.E., they dissolved among the Semitic population, to whom they were related by kin, and to such an extent that they lost all distinctive characteristics. But Egypt under the Hyksos presented a completely different picture. With the exception of the Egyptianized tribal elite, the Amorites in Egypt preserved their own language and culture, which were very different from the local ones. The Theban pharaohs from the Upper Kingdom exploited this to give their wars with the Hyksos a nationalist and liberationist pathos. The same factor contributed to the destruction of the Hyksos rule in the Nile Delta and the expulsion of the Amorite tribes from Egypt – something that had not happened in any of the Amorite states of Mesopotamia, Syria, or Canaan.

The 'house of Joseph' and the 'house of Jacob' in Egypt

The question of the Hebrew tribes' place and role among the Hyksos is of great importance. From the ethnic point of view, the two formed a single whole; both were semi-nomadic Amorite tribes. The main difference between the Amorites in Egypt was the political role played by their tribal leadership; and this role depended, in turn, on the size of the tribes and the time of their arrival in Egypt. Having established themselves in the Nile Delta earlier than their fellow tribesmen, the largest groups of Amorites occupied the top rung in the Hyksos hierarchy, and it was probably these same Amorites from whom the Hyksos pharaohs descended. The less numerous Amorite tribes and particularly those who came to Egypt later, during the rule of the Hyksos, played a lesser role and depended on the protection of their relatives who were part of the Hyksos hierarchy.

This principle extended to the Hebrew tribes as well. The 'house of Joseph', forced to move to Egypt earlier than its fellow tribesmen, was able to assume a privileged position in the

Hyksos kingdom. This is explained by the fact that Ephraim and Manasseh, the principal tribes comprising the 'house of Joseph', arrived in the Nile Delta before the Hyksos themselves came to power, sometime at the beginning of the 13th Dynasty, in the second half of the 18th century B.C.E. The 'house of Joseph' was possibly one of those Amorite rulers who were invited to take power by the pharaohs at the time when the pharaohs were still of Egyptian origin. The other northern tribes who came slightly later reinforced the position of the 'house of Joseph' and helped it secure a privileged position in the Hyksos hierarchy. Thus we may say that the northern (Israelite) tribes were a constituent part of the Hyksos, while their tribal elite were probably part of the entourage of the Hyksos pharaohs. It is likely that before their move to Egypt, Ephraim and Manasseh were one large tribe of semi-nomadic Western Semites, which we can, for convenience, call 'Joseph' after their legendary forefather. They divided once they were in Egypt, after a rapid increase in their numbers. The rulers, and perhaps the entire elite of the 'house of Joseph', adopted the Egyptian culture and language, and took wives from among Egyptian families of priests and high officials. The 'house of Joseph' was made up of typical Hyksos - West Semitic rulers who had embraced the Egyptian way of life and traditions. According to the Bible, the house's legendary forefather, Joseph, led the life of an Egyptian high official, had an Egyptian name, and was married to the daughter of an influential Egyptian priest. Upon his death, he was buried in accordance with the Egyptian, not West Semitic, ceremonial ritual: "after they embalmed him, he was placed in a coffin in Egypt" (Genesis 50:26). As far as we can tell from the biblical description, Joseph occupied the post of supreme vizier (minister) at the court of an Egyptian pharaoh of the 13th Dynasty or at the court of the Hyksos king. We may allege that, like Joseph himself, his descendants also led an Egyptian lifestyle. However, as later events showed, this cultural assimilation affected only the tribal rulers and their families; most commoners in these tribes remained faithful to the West Semitic traditions and language.

It is likely that the 'house of Joseph' owed its special place among the Hebrew tribes not so much to its numerousness as to its privileged position in the Egypt of the Hyksos. It became protector and benefactor to all its fellow tribesmen – at first to the northern tribes and then to the southern ones as well.

The story of the southern tribes, the 'house of Jacob', in Egypt began 100 years later than the experience of the northern tribes, i.e. approximately at the end of the 17th century B.C.E., when the Hyksos were already rulers of the Lower Kingdom. Most likely, their arrival in Egypt occurred precisely as described in the Bible: prolonged drought and famine forced them to abandon Canaan and settle peacefully in the eastern part of the Nile Delta. Furthermore, all this took place with the help and protection of the 'house of Joseph'. The 'house of Jacob' and 'house of Joseph' thus found themselves under a single roof in Egypt. Yet the roles that they played in the Hyksos kingdom were completely different: while the 'house of Joseph' enjoyed a central and privileged position, the southern tribes lived humbly on the periphery of the Lower Kingdom and likely played no active part in Hyksos politics or the confrontation between the Hyksos and the Theban pharaohs. They led a quiet pastoral life under the high protection of the 'house of Joseph', thanks to whom they were able to solve all their problems in Egypt.

The fall of the Hyksos and first exodus of the Western Semites

The end of the Hyksos' rule in Egypt, as was to be expected, came from the south, at the hands of the Theban pharaohs. For approximately 70 years the Theban pharaohs had been the Hyksos' vassals and had punctually paid tribute to the Lower Kingdom. The first to dare to challenge the Hyksos was Seqenenre

Tao. He made thorough and very lengthy preparations for war with the Western Semites. His first move was to seize gold deposits in Nubia as a source of finance for the upcoming war. Then, taking advantage of the internal discord within the Nubian Kingdom of Karmah, he managed to strike an alliance with its rulers. Having secured gold and a reliable rear on his southern boundary, he recruited a large number of Nubian mercenaries to his army. The Nubians were considered good warriors and excellent archers, and their participation substantially boosted the might of the Egyptian army. The military preparations of the Theban vassal greatly alarmed the Hyksos Pharaoh Apepi I (Ausere). A serious crisis began to brew. We know some of its details from an ancient Egyptian papyrus written three and a half centuries later, during the rule of Merneptah, a pharaoh of the 19th Dynasty. Attempting to put the difficult vassal in his place, the Hyksos pharaoh diplomatically hinted that, "the roars of hippopotami from Thebes are preventing him from falling asleep" (Thebes was almost 700 miles from Avaris!) and requested that action be taken to remove the source of anxiety. Instead of carrying out this request, Seqenenre Tao attacked his Hyksos suzerain – but with appalling results for himself. In the decisive battle with the Western Semites his army suffered a crushing defeat and he himself was killed. His mummy has preserved the traces of terrible wounds sustained in battle: his skull was pierced three times by blows from the axes and spears of the Western Semites. The slain Pharaoh's successor, his eldest son Kamose, learned from the defeat of his father. He reorganized the defeated army and hired even more Nubian mercenaries. And then he went even further by borrowing substantially from the military practices and weapons of the Hyksos. It was the Western Semites who acquainted the Egyptians with horses and military chariots, as well as with new and more effective types of military axe and bow. They also taught them more progressive methods of obtaining metals. Thus, after re-equipping his army in the West

Semitic manner, Kamose decided to attack the Hyksos without warning and without declaring war. And he succeeded in catching the Hyksos Pharaoh Apepi unawares, surrounding and laying siege to his capital of Avaris. But this treachery did not help the Theban pharaoh. Recovering their wits, the Hyksos quickly gathered the forces of the loyal Amorite tribes and fought off Kamose's attack. What happened next is not clear. We know only that Kamose left a boasting report about his campaign, but humbly kept quiet as to the reasons for his retreat. In addition, Kamose's rule was suspiciously short – a mere three years. It may be that he met the same fate as his father. Meanwhile, the Hyksos pharaoh Apepi attempted several times to reach an agreement with the Nubians regarding an alliance against Thebes, but was evidently unsuccessful, since the rulers of Karmah continued helping the Hyksos' enemies.

After this, there was a break in the war lasting many years, clearly as a result of the death of both adversaries, Kamose and Apepi. The final stage in the military action involved their successors, Kamose's younger brother Ahmose and the new Hyksos pharaoh, Hammudi. This time, success went to the Theban ruler. Avaris was again surrounded both on dry land and by river. At the decisive moment, many Amorite tribes decided not to support Hammudi, and this proved fateful for the rule of the Western Semites in Egypt. Learning from the defeats of his predecessors, Ahmose cut off in advance all paths by which the Hyksos might have received help. The situation of those besieged in Avaris became hopeless. Yet despite their numerical superiority, the Egyptians could not take Avaris by storm. Manetho, relying on ancient Egyptian sources, wrote as follows: "[The Hyksos] had built a wall surrounding this city, which was large and strong, in order to keep all their possessions and plunder in a place of strength. [The Egyptian pharaoh] attempted to take the city by force and by siege with 480,000 men surrounding it. But he despaired of taking the place by siege, and concluded a treaty with them, that they should leave Egypt, and go, without any harm coming to them, wherever they wished" (Josephus Flavius, *Against Apion*, Book 1, Section 73).

Data gathered from archaeological excavations on the site of the city of Avaris (now called Tell El-Dab'a) in large part confirm Manetho's reports of a mass exodus of the city's inhabitants from Egypt. The material culture characteristic of the Western Semites from Canaan ended abruptly with the fall of Avaris and was, after an interval, replaced with a completely different culture, Egyptian in character. The destruction suffered by Avaris contains no trace of a battle for the city or of the death of its inhabitants. The city was most likely destroyed and burnt after the mass exodus of its population. Thus ended the rule of the 15th Hyksos dynasty in Egypt, after approximately 108 years. The Hyksos escaped to their allies and fellow tribesmen in Canaan. Fearing the restoration of Hyksos rule, Ahmose launched a campaign against southern Canaan and over the course of three years laid siege to the city of Sharuhen, where the former Hyksos rulers had firmly established themselves. The capture of Sharuhen signified an irrevocable end to the influence of the Western Semites over Egypt and the beginning of a new era in the country's history – the period of the New Kingdom. Ahmose founded a new dynasty, the 18th, and served as its first pharaoh.

The defeat of the Hyksos changed the fate of the Amorite tribes in the Nile Delta. Some of these tribes were forced to leave immediately, together with the West Semitic rulers who were in effect their tribal leaders. However, the exodus of the Hyksos was probably not the simultaneous event that Manetho portrays it to be. The first to leave Egypt were those who lived in Avaris or who had sought refuge there during the siege – the army, the Pharaoh's court and their families, and the inhabitants of the Hyksos capital. But most Amorites did not live in the capital or in fortified cities; they were scattered throughout the Nile Delta. Moreover, the semi-nomadic Amorites had, over the course of a lifetime, settled on the land. This is confirmed by the Bible: "Now the Israelites settled in Egypt in the region of Goshen. They acquired property there and were fruitful and increased greatly in number" (Genesis 47:27). The settled Amorite population, scattered over the perimeter of the entire Nile Delta, could never have left Egypt simultaneously, and still less together with the escaping Hyksos army and the court of the Pharaoh. Ahmose and his successors, the pharaohs of the 18th Dynasty, were confronted on many occasions with the question of what to do with the Amorites who remained in the Nile Delta. Most likely, Egyptian policy towards the West Semitic population underwent frequent changes, depending on the specific pharaoh and the circumstances. Initially, when the New Kingdom was still gaining in strength, the Amorites were still too numerous and strong to be collectively enslaved or driven out of the Nile Delta. It is well known that Ahmose and his closest successors – the pharaohs Amenhotep I, Thutmose I, and Thutmose II – were too busy suppressing internal revolts and campaigning in Nubia and Libya to get involved in a serious conflict with the Western Semites in the Nile Delta. However, the Egyptians as a whole were negatively disposed to the continued presence of large numbers of Amorites in their country; they were afraid that the Western Semites could again seize power in Egypt, as had happened during the Hyksos period, or unite with their adversaries in a time of war.

The Bible also notes similar suspicions with regard to the West Semitic population: "Then a new king, who did not know about Joseph, came to power in Egypt. 'Look,' he said to his people, 'the Israelites have become much too numerous for us. Come, we must deal shrewdly with them or they will become even more numerous and, if war breaks out, will join our enemies, fight against us and leave the country' (Exodus 1: 8-10). It was probably for good reason that the Egyptians rejected the idea of driving out all the Western Semites immediately after the flight of the Hyksos. They feared that banishing the Western

Semites would enrage the Amorite rulers and lead them to once again unite in a war for control over Egypt, but that this would happen outside the country and beyond the control of the army. The Egyptian pharaohs preferred a strategy of gradually forcing out the West Semitic populations. But as Egypt's strength grew, the pharaohs pursued a policy that was increasingly hostile and uncompromising towards the remaining Amorites. It was probably during the rule of Thutmose III (1479-1426 B.C.E.) that the majority of the Western Semites were forced to leave the Nile Delta. Their departure stretched over many decades. The first to leave were the Amorite tribes whose rulers were directly linked with the Hyksos pharaohs and were part of their milieu – for instance, the Hyksos 'house of Joseph'. And vice-versa, those Amorites who lived further from Avaris and had not participated in the wars waged by the Hyksos were allowed to stay longer.

At some point in the middle of the 15th century B.C.E. the 'house of Joseph', which consisted of the tribes of Ephraim, Manasseh, and Benjamin, left Egypt and returned to Canaan. It is possible that another northern tribe, Naphtali, left with them as well. As for the 'house of Jacob', which comprised four southern Hebrew tribes, they remained in Egypt for a long time – until the beginning of the 12th century B.C.E. The rulers of the southern tribes probably had little difficulty in proving that they, unlike the 'house of Joseph', had nothing to do with the Hyksos and had not participated in the latter's wars with the Egyptians. For this or perhaps some other reason, the southern group of Jacob-Judah did not share the fate of the majority of the Amorite tribes, who were forced out of the Nile Delta in the 15th century. And it was not only the southern Hebrew tribes that the Egyptians allowed to stay, but also other groups of Amorites who were not connected with the Hyksos. Most likely, these were the very same Amorite tribes who much later participated, together with the 'house of Jacob', in the biblical Exodus led by Moses.

CHAPTER 4

The 'House of Joseph' in Canaan. 15th-13th centuries B.C.E.

BUT WHERE DID THE Amorites go from Egypt? They headed for whence they had originally come, i.e. Canaan, southern Syria, and the Lebanese coast. The 'house of Joseph' returned to the region of Shechem, its former tribal lands. However, not everything was straightforward. During these tribes' absence from Canaan over the course of two and a half centuries, substantial changes had taken place. For example, by the middle of the 15th century B.C.E. most of the population of this country had become settled. Those Amorite tribes who had not left to go to the Nile Delta settled on the land in Canaan itself and adopted Canaanite urban and agricultural culture. But the most important thing was that the tribal territories of the Amorites who had left for Egypt, including the Hebrews, were now largely occupied and had been divided up among the Canaanites and the Amorite city states. Several Israelite tribes were practically homeless upon their return to Canaan.

It was at this moment that 'Habiru/Apiru' became established as a name for all Western Semites who had returned from the Nile Delta, including the Hebrews. This name was used not for semi-nomadic Amorites in general, but only for those Amorites who had lost their own tribal territory and thus became, though not by their own choice, homeless wanderers. It has to be remembered that in the Nile Delta the West Semitic population had adopted a settled lifestyle; their return to a nomadic way of life was forced and incomplete. From the biblical texts dealing with the exodus of the Hebrew tribes from Egypt we know how difficult and painful they found the process of returning to the nomadic life and how they strove to re-establish their previous, more comfortable and secure, settled lifestyle.

If at the beginning of the 2nd millennium B.C.E., the term 'Habiru' applied to semi-nomadic, non-settled Amorites, by the 15th century its meaning had clearly narrowed: it now pertained only to homeless Western Semites who had lost their tribal territory. In addition to the Amorites-Habiru who found themselves without a home through no choice of their own, there were also other nomadic Amorites who had retained their tribal territories because they had not gone to Egypt. This was true, for instance, of the close relatives of the southern Hebrew tribes – the Edomites, Moabites, and Ammonites. These tribes were give another name, 'Sutu', which was also the name given to more distant relatives of the Hebrews – the Midianites, Kenites, Ishmaelites, and Amalekites, desert peoples who traced their genealogy to the patriarch Abraham. Unlike the 'Sutu', who were voluntary nomads on land that was their own, the 'Habiru' were forced wanderers who had lost their tribal lands and were keen not only to repossess these lands, but to resume their settled way of life there once again.

Evidently, the majority of these Habiru in Canaan comprised the three northern tribes related to the 'house of Joseph' – Ephraim, Manasseh, and Benjamin. It is possible that they were joined by another, fourth tribe, Naphtali. Still more Amorites found themselves in the position of Habiru in southern Syria and on the Lebanese coast. Like the Israelite tribes, they too became homeless when they found their lands occupied upon their return from Egypt. The position of the Habiru was made much more difficult by the fact that the rulers of the local city states who had 'seized' their tribal territories were vassals of the Pharaoh and under the protection of Egypt. Conquering Canaan would have been impossible due to Egypt's indisputable military superiority in the 15th-13th centuries B.C.E. While Egypt's hold over Canaan and southern Syria remained intact, the most the Habiru could do was to engage in partisan warfare and to lay siege to particular cities. These actions were keenly felt by the local rulers, but were on a scale insufficient to merit a response from the Egyptian army.

You can try looking in the Bible for the history of the northern Hebrew tribes in Canaan prior to their unification with the southern tribes in the 12th century B.C.E., but it will be in vain. This history, just like any account of their stay in Egypt, was purposely omitted by the biblical writers. Any mention of it would have contradicted the official version, which insisted on a common origin and history for the Northerners and Southerners and according to which both tribal groups left Egypt at the same time under the leadership of their ruler and lawgiver, Moses. Moreover, given that the authors of the Old Testament themselves, i.e. the Aaronites and the Levites, came exclusively from the southern tribes, it was natural that they should present the history of their Jacob-Judah group as the common past of all the Hebrew tribes until the United Monarchy split in approximately 928 B.C.E. The early history of the northern group of Israel-Joseph is therefore entirely missing from the Bible. This gaping omission covers three periods: 1) the northern tribes' stay in Canaan from the 23rd to 18th centuries B.C.E.; 2) their life in Egypt from the 18th to 15th centuries B.C.E.; 3) the period spent by several northern tribes in Canaan in the 15th to 13th centuries B.C.E. Although many narratives concerning the 'house of Joseph' were woven into the version of a unified past, we know almost nothing about the first two stages of the northern tribes' history.

The Amarna letters on Habiru and Sutu

However, we also have at our disposal non-biblical written documents that shed some light on the 3rd period – the 15th to 13th centuries B.C.E., – during which several northern tribes lived in Canaan. The most important collection of such documents is the Amarna letters, an archive whose name derives from the El-Amarna Valley, which is situated 190 miles from Cairo on the eastern bank of the Nile. This was the site of the capital of Egypt, Akhetaten, which was founded by the reformer pharaoh Amenhotep IV, more commonly known as Akhenaten. Amenhotep's archive was discovered long ago, in 1887, but it is only during recent decades that we have been able to read it in full. At the present time it consists of 382 clay tablets, although originally there may have been many more. The majority of the tablets were written in the 'international' language of the time, Akkadian, but there are also tablets in Hittite, Hurrian, and Assyrian.

The entire archive can be divided into three parts. The first contains letters from the kings of sovereign states (Babylonia, Mitanni, Assyria, the Hittite Empire, Alashia (Cyprus) and Arzawaza). The second consists of correspondence from vassals in Syria and the land of the Amurru (the Lebanese coast and part of southern Syria). Only the third part is made up of letters from the Canaanite city rulers to their suzerain, the Egyptian pharaoh. The latter two parts deal almost entirely with internal feuds between the rulers of Canaan and the land of the Amurru. The three parts are roughly equal in terms of volume of text, if not in numbers of tablets. Chronologically, the Amarna letters cover a very short period of time (20-30 years) and most likely date to 1350-1330 B.C.E. We are, of course, most interested in the second and third parts, which allow us to reconstruct the political situation in Canaan and southern Syria. Given that in ancient times life changed at an incomparably slower pace than it does today, we may suppose that everything that was typical for the second half of the 14th century B.C.E. in Canaan and in southern Syria was likewise characteristic of the entire period of 15-13th B.C.E.

It is the frequent references to the Habiru that have sparked the greatest interest in the letters of the rulers of Canaan and Amurru. These Habiru must have included the northern (Israelite) tribes. Admittedly, many historians deny any link between the Habiru and the Hebrews. Their arguments can mainly be reduced to two objections. First, the Habiru were scattered across various corners of the ancient Near East; they are mentioned in written sources from Mesopotamia, Syria, and Canaan. And, wherever they lived, they were under the influence of local languages and cultures that differed greatly from one another. So, the argument goes, there is no reason to suppose that the Habiru from Syria, Mesopotamia, and Canaan were at one time an ethnic group with their own language and culture. Secondly, in denying the Habiru the status of an ethnos, these scholars regard them as a social group among the local population which was for some reason deprived of its land and houses and whose members became mercenaries and robbers. Some authors go even further, asserting that the word 'Habiru' itself is not West Semitic, but Akkadian in origin and means 'robber' or 'brigand'. As evidence for this point of view, they usually cite excerpts from the letters of the rulers of Canaan and Amurru, in which the latter accuse their enemies, the Habiru, of pillaging and robbery. Unfortunately, we do not know the opinion of the Habiru themselves concerning the Canaanite and Syrian kings with whom they were at war, but it could hardly have been better than that which their adversaries had of them. The fact that the Habiru spoke the languages of the surrounding peoples can hardly be considered a serious argument against their existence as a separate ethnic group. After all, nomads and semi-nomads throughout the Near East quickly adopted the culture of the Semitic peoples with whom they were related and among whom they lived. As for Canaan and the Lebanese coast (Amurru), here there could have been no linguistic problems between the local Canaanite-Amorite population and the Habiru because both groups were practically one and the same, ethnically. Admittedly, in some respects the opponents of identifying the Habiru as Hebrews are right. We cannot equate the 'Habiru' with the 'Ibri/Ivri'. The Hebrews made up only a very small part of the numerous Habiru tribes. The latter, having been squeezed out of the Nile Delta, spread out over the entire territory of Canaan, Amurru, and Syria. It would be naïve to assume that the Habiru who fought against the local kings in northern Lebanon belonged to the Israelite tribes. On the other hand, there can be almost no doubt that those who were known as Habiru in the region of Shechem were directly related to the 'house of Joseph', in the same way that central and northern Canaan was the field of activity of the northern (Israelite) tribes. The name 'Habiru' probably applied to all the semi-nomadic Amorites who had previously lived in the Nile Delta. At first, they were known as Asiatic newcomers – 'a'amu'; then as foreign rulers – 'Hyksos'; and finally, after they were driven out of Egypt, they became homeless mercenaries, 'Habiru'.

In history, a large mass of people cannot disappear without trace. Subduing a country as big as Egypt and ruling it for more than 100 years would have been possible only for Amorite tribes who were sufficiently numerous: only a great number of tribes would have been in a position to successfully oppose the strong armies of the burgeoning New Kingdom. Numerous West Semitic populations could not have disappeared all at once, so it is not surprising that they appeared once again, but in a different place and under a new name. The Hebrews, and the 'house of Joseph' in particular, were only a small part of these Western Semites and shared their fate. Scattering over Canaan, Amurru, and Syria, the Habiru were unified not only ethnically and linguistically, but also socially. These West Semitic tribes of Amorite origin had been stripped of their own territory and houses; they were forced to return to a semi-nomadic lifestyle and to become mercenaries in the service of local rulers. In this respect, we cannot but agree with those historians who emphasize the social coloring of the name 'Habiru' and the fact that the Habiru were homeless and found themselves forced into mercenary activity. However, it would be wrong to transform an entire ethnos into a marginal social group, especially since the Amarna letters – the main source for the history of Canaan in this period – do not provide any basis for such a conclusion.

Those biblical scholars who deny any link between the names 'Ibri/Ivri' and 'Habiru/Apiru' often propose their own alternative versions for the origin of the ethnonym 'Ibri/Ivri'. According to one of these versions, 'Ibri/Ivri derived from the name 'Eber', the great-great grandfather of Abraham. But why would it come from Eber, whom the Bible does not single out in any way among the ancestors of Abraham? It is a question that no supporter of this hypothesis has been able to answer intelligibly, apart from reference to the fact that the name 'Eber' has a close resemblance to 'Ibri'. Another version is based on an attempt to interpret 'Ibri' as 'eber ha-nahar', i.e. 'beyond the river' – meaning the Euphrates River and indicating that the Hebrew tribes came to Canaan from Mesopotamia. But this historical-linguistic construction linking the Euphrates River and distant Canaan is so artificial that even its adherents consider it unsatisfactory.

Canaan and Amurru in 15th-13th centuries BCE.
W. Moran. The Amarna Letters.

It has to be admitted that none of the Amarna letters gives the slightest hint as to who the Habiru were and how they appeared in Canaan and on the Lebanese coast. However, judging by the letters' character and tone, the identity of the Habiru was so well known to the Egyptian pharaoh that the local rulers deemed any explanation unnecessary. It is absolutely obvious that the Habiru did not appear in the middle of the 14th century B.C.E., but considerably earlier and that their arrival was somehow connected with events in Egypt. Common to all the letters from the rulers of both Canaan and Amurru is the deep conviction that the Habiru represented a power that was hostile to Egypt. Moreover, their anti-Egyptian character was considered self-evident and long established. For this reason, wishing to discredit their adversaries in the eyes of the Egyptians, each ruler considered it sufficient to report that these adversaries were linked with, and had the support of, the Habiru (there was no more serious accusation implying disloyalty to Egypt). Meanwhile, the Habiru themselves, at least during the time of the Amarna letters, claimed to be loyal to Egypt and outwardly displayed no hostility. Evidently, a serious conflict between the Habiru and Egypt had taken place much earlier and this was something of which the rulers of Canaan and Amurru knew very well. If, as some scholars claim, the Habiru had only been a local social group of homeless mercenaries and robbers, then how did they acquire their reputation as sworn enemies of Egypt? After all, the Egyptians, as is clear from the Amarna letters, had not appeared in Canaan and Amurru for a long time and the local rulers were already losing hope of receiving any help from them. The hypothesis that the Habiru were a social group finds no support in the texts of the Amarna archive. No ruler of Canaan, Amurru, or Syria makes any mention of the Habiru – or any part of them – being landless peasants or bankrupt townsmen. Likewise, there are no references to insurrections among the local population as a result of social causes. The information that we have from correspondence sent by local rulers is, in fact, more likely to provide evidence of the opposite. For instance, in one of his numerous letters Rib-Hadda, ruler of the city of Gubla (Biblos), complains that his peasants have been ruined by war, are starving, and are leaving for other cities where it is possible to make a living. And there is not a word about peasant uprisings or any ties between these impoverished peasants or townsmen and the Habiru.

In another letter to the Egyptian pharaoh Rib-Hadda makes an eloquent admission: it transpires that his ruined and hungry peasants have helped him beat off attacks by the Habiru. They would hardly have done so if the Habiru had comprised the same kind of people as themselves. In yet another letter to the pharaoh, Rib-Hadda mournfully exclaims, "What can I say to my peasants? Their sons, daughters, and everything of value in their houses have been sold into the land of Yarimuta just so that we can have food to eat." (EA 85, text: VAT 1626, 6-15). Thus, despite the fact that they were completely ruined, the peasants did not desert to the Habiru, but instead continued supporting their ruler in his battle with the latter. Moreover, in their letters, neither Rib-Hadda nor any other ruler ever draw any parallel or analogy between the homeless, ruined people and the Habiru. This again calls into question the social explanation for the emergence of the Habiru.

The Amarna letters contain numerous pieces of evidence of the Habiru entering into alliances with certain local rulers against others. Again, this does not fit very well with claims that the Habiru were robbers and brigands. As far as the Habiru were concerned, such alliances were possible only if they followed political and not class considerations. Likewise, the local rulers would have hardly risked including the Habiru in their armies had they been mutineers or robbers. From this point of view, a letter from the southern Syrian ruler Biryawaza is significant. Biryawaza writes that he, together with his "brothers, the Habiru and Sutu, bows down to the Pharaoh." If 'Habiru' really did mean 'robber' and 'brigand' or something of this sort, as certain scholars claim, then for a vassal to write to his suzerain on behalf of 'robbers and brigands' would have been an inconceivable insult – and all the more so since Biryawaza had previously sent the Pharaoh the following fawning letter: "Say to the king, my lord: Message of Biryawaza, your servant, the dirt of your feet and the ground you tread on, the chair you sit on and the footstool at your feet. I fall at the feet of the king, my lord, the Sun of the dawn (over peoples), 7 times plus 7 times. My lord is the Sun in the sky, and like the coming forth of the Sun in the sky (your) servants await the coming forth of the words from the mouth of their lord." (EA 195, text: C 4761, 16-32). All the rulers of Canaan and Amurru who complained of the Habiru in their letters note their large numbers and military strength. The above-mentioned Rib-Hadda on several occasions reminded the Pharaoh of how mighty the Habiru were and how difficult it would be to wage war against them (EA 68, text: VAT 1239, 12-32). Judging by his letters, the Habiru and their allies were gradually depriving him of all the villages and towns in his power. "Do not you yourself know that the land of Amurru always follows the stronger party?" Rib-Hadda asked one of the Egyptian high officials. In the absence of the Egyptians, the Habiru were perceived as the main military power in Canaan and Amurru. "What am I, who live among Habiru, to do?" asked Rib-Hadda and desperately begged the Pharaoh to send troops and save him from the Habiru. (EA 130, text: VAT 1624, 32-42). "If the king, my lord, does [not give heed] to the words of [his] servant," he warned the Pharaoh, "then... all the lands of the king, as far as Egypt, will be joined to the Habiru." (EA 88, text: BM 29800, 28-39). Because he could not send an army, the Pharaoh directed the rulers of Sidon, Tyre, and Beirut to help Rib-Hadda with their forces, but they ignored his orders.

The fact that the Habiru were a serious military power and enjoyed the support of several local rulers emerges from a letter written by another Egyptian vassal, Mayarzana, ruler of the city of Hasi. "The Habiru captured Mahzibtu, a city of the king, my lord, and plundered it, sent it up in flames, and then the Habiru took refuge with Amanhatpe (ruler of the city of Tushultu). And the Habiru captured Gilunu, a city of the king, my lord, plundered it, sent it up in flames, and hardly one family escaped from Gilunu. Then the Habiru took refuge with Amanhatpe. And the Habiru captured Magdallu, a city of the king, my lord, my god, my Sun, plundered it, sent it up in flames, and hardly one family escaped from Magdallu. Then the Habiru took refuge with Amanhatpe. And Ushtu, a city of the king, my lord, the Habiru captured, plundered it, and sent it up in flames. Then the Habiru took refuge with Amanhatpe. And then the Habiru having raided Hasi, a city of the king, my lord, we did battle with the Habiru, and we defeated them." (EA 185, text: VAT 1725, 16-75). In his lengthy letter, Mayarzana talks in detail about the fact that Amanhatpe, ruler of the city of Tushultu, was defeated and, being an ally of the Habiru, found asylum with them. In conclusion, Mayarzana asks the Pharaoh to punish the betrayer Amanhatpe as an example to all.

Canaanite ruler receives captives brought in under guard.
Ivory carving from Megiddo, 14th-12th centuries B.C.E.

The Habiru were active not only in Amurru (the Lebanese coast and Southern Syria), but also in Canaan itself. The Amarna archive contains several letters from Biridiya, ruler of the Canaanite city of Megiddo, who, like Rib-Hadda, complained of the difficulties of fighting against the Habiru. He sent the Pharaoh a complaint against the sons of Labayu, ruler of the city of Shakmu (Shechem), accusing them of hiring the Habiru and the Sutu to wage war against him (EA 246, text: VAT 1649, 1-11). Another Canaanite ruler, Milk-ilu from the city of Gazru (Gezer), found himself in an incomparably poorer position: he asked the Pharaoh to save him and Shuwardatu, the ruler of the city of Quiltu, from the Habiru (EA 246, text: VAT 1649, 1-11). A different Canaanite ruler, whose name on the tablet is illegible, wrote as follows: "May the king, my lord, know that the mayors that were in the major cities of my lord are gone, and the entire land of the king, my lord, has deserted to the Habiru" (EA 272, text: BM 29863, 1-17). This is echoed by the ruler of Jerusalem, Abdi-Heba, who warns the Pharaoh that "the king has no lands. That Habiru has plundered all the lands of the king. If there are archers this year, the lands of the king, my lord, will remain. But if there are no archers, lost are the lands of my king, my lord" (EA 286, text: VAT 1642, 53-60). For his part, Abdi-Heba accused Milk-ilu and the sons of Labayu of giving land belonging to the king to the Habiru (EA 287, text: VAT 1644, 4-32). Labayu himself was also accused of ceding the land of Shechem to the Habiru (EA 289, text: VAT 1645, 18-24). Most likely, this kind of accusation was due to the fact that the ruler of Jerusalem was in the midst of a war with these Canaanite kings. At the same time – providing indirect confirmation of the Habiru's anti-Egyptian reputation, – in one of his letters Abdi-Heba expresses indignation that at the court of the Pharaoh he is treated like a Habiru (EA 288, text: VAT 1643, 29-33).

The letters of the Canaanite rulers make it clear that from a military point of view, the Habiru were markedly superior to them and that, had it not been for the threat of interference by Egypt, all of Canaan would have been in their hands. For instance, Yapahu, the new governor of the city of Gazru, openly confessed his military weakness: "May the king, my lord, the Sun from the sky," he wrote to the Pharaoh, "take thought for his land. Since the Habiru are stronger than we, may the king, my lord, give me his help, and may the king, my lord, get me away from the Habiru lest the Habiru destroy us" (EA 299, text: BM 29832, 12-21). The same was confirmed by a different Canaanite ruler, Shub-Andu: "As the Habiru are more powerful than we, may the king take cognizance of his lands" (EA 305, text: C 4780, 15-24). And yet another Canaanite or southern Syrian king, Dagan-takala, simply implored the Pharaoh to save him: "Save me from the powerful enemies, from the hand of the Habiru, robbers, and Sutu. And save me, Great King, my lord! And behold! I have written to you! Moreover, you Great King, my lord, save me or I will be lost to the Great King, my lord!" (EA 318, text: BM 29857). It is significant that Dagan-takala, who was a contemporary of these events, distinguished – unlike some of today's scholars – between the two terms 'robbers' and 'Habiru'. It is interesting that those rulers of Canaan and Amurru who accused the Habiru of robbery in reality described their acts not as robbery, but as the actions of a hostile army. However, when one takes into account the moral norms of the times, it is difficult to draw a line between actions carried out by an enemy army and common pillaging. A better example of the latter is the military campaigns of the Egyptian army in Canaan – campaigns which in effect amounted to legitimized robbery.

One of the letters in the Amarna archive contains a very important definition of the Habiru – a definition that appears nowhere else. An unidentified author, probably one of the rulers of the country of Amurru, writes of his rival, comparing him with the Habiru and calling him 'a runaway dog'. Note that he does not call him a stray dog, which would have been a hint at the unsettled, homeless character of the Habiru, but precisely a 'runaway', i.e. a dog that has run away from its master. This was probably a veiled reference to the circumstances in which the Habiru had arrived in Canaan and in the land of the Amurru, and to their enforced flight from Egypt (EA 67, text: VAT 1591, 13-18).

There is another fact that is made clear by the Amarna letters: the Habiru did not have a single leadership or ruler, nor were they united in a tribal alliance or alliances –this made the position of the local rulers easier. In one of his letters, Rib-Hadda, ruler of the city of Gubla, expresses his fear at the mere thought that the Habiru could unite. It is probable that after the Hyksos pharaohs had been driven out of Egypt, the Amorites that had remained in the Nile Delta found themselves without either authoritative rulers or the system of tribal organization that had existed until then. It is significant that the founder of the New Kingdom, the Egyptian pharaoh Ahmose, was willing to spend three years besieging the southern Canaanite city of Sharuhen in order to 'finish off' the Hyksos and their tribal elite, thereby depriving the Amorites, who were hostile towards him, of leadership. After the loss of the Hyksos leaders and in an atmosphere of growing pressure from the Egyptians, the Western Semites from the Nile Delta were unable to find new leaders to replace them and so, in different tribal groups departing at different times, they abandoned inhospitable Egypt. As subsequent events showed, outstanding rulers once again appeared among the Western Semites, but this time their power was limited solely to their own tribal groups and the territory of Canaan.

To what extent do the Amarna letters reflect the history of the northern Hebrew tribes in Canaan during the 15th-13th centuries B.C.E.? After all, the letters do not mention any of the Israelite tribes or any character from the Bible. But the archive can be of help in three respects. Firstly, wherever mention is made of the Habiru in central and northern Canaan, there is a high probability that it is precisely the Israelite tribes that are meant. Secondly, the letters sent by local rulers give us an idea of the political situation in which these tribes were living, up until their conquest of Canaan one and a half to two centuries later. Finally, the archive provides a certain amount of information on the Habiru as a whole and hypothetically on the Hebrews' place among them. Having been forced out of the Nile Delta, the Amorite tribes scattered under the name 'Habiru' across Canaan, Syria, and Mesopotamia. However, they settled in the largest numbers in Canaan, on the Lebanese coast, and in southern Syria, i.e. in the places from where they had originally come to Egypt. Here they comprised a significant part of the population and therefore had a decisive influence on the future of this region. In other regions, e.g. in northern Syria and Mesopotamia, the Habiru were only a small part of the local population and accordingly played no role of any importance.

Certain biblical scholars look for the ancestors of the Hebrews not among the Habiru, but among the Sutu. According to written sources at our disposal, the Sutu were West Semitic tribes of Amorite origin who lived as pastoral nomads on the semi-arid lands from southern Transjordan to northern Syria. The Egyptians termed them – or at least those of them who had led a nomadic way of life in southern Transjordan – 'Shasu'. The Amarna letters often mention the Sutu alongside the Habiru; however, all the rulers of Canaan, Amurru, Syria, and Mesopotamia made a clear distinction between the Sutu and the Habiru – but without explaining why. The main difference seems to have been that the Sutu/Shasu did not go to Egypt, did not lead a settled life in the Nile Delta, and had nothing to do with the Hyksos. Unlike the Habiru, they were not homeless, since they had managed to keep their tribal territories in Transjordan and Syria. Despite clashes with Egypt, the Sutu did not have such a deep 'historical' conflict with this country as the Habiru and were consequently not considered an anti-Egyptian power in the region. Moreover, several Sutu/Shasu tribes were even in the service of the Egyptians. It is significant that none of the rulers of Canaan or Amurru complained to the Pharaoh about contact between their rivals and the Sutu, and yet they often accused one another of alliance with the Habiru.

Another important difference was way of life. The Sutu continued their nomadic way of life, while the Habiru, who had already settled before they were driven out of the Nile Delta, were keen to return to their former lifestyle as soon as possible. It cannot be ruled out that by the 14th century B.C.E. they were already leading a semi-settled lifestyle as both cattle breeders and arable farmers. However, it was Egypt's hold over Canaan and Amurru that kept them from settling on the land completely. As soon as Egyptian rule came to an end, the Habiru quickly conquered these countries and settled.

In the letters of the rulers of Canaan, Syria, and Mesopotamia, the Sutu were usually depicted as nomads and brigands who robbed trading caravans passing through their territory. They rarely respected the local or even Egyptian authorities and, like all pastoralists, were difficult to manage and control. The settled population treated them with distrust. The local rulers and Egyptian authorities periodically took them into their service as mercenaries on the one hand, but on the other were forced to arrange military expeditions to suppress the most aggressive tribes. In this respect, the Habiru were considered more predictable in their behavior and closer in way of life to the settled peoples around them, so the local Canaanite-Amorite population trusted the Habiru more than the Sutu. The latter had such a dubious reputation that even such an obedient Egyptian vassal as Rib-Hadda, ruler of Biblos, did not hesitate to send two letters to the Pharaoh openly expressing indignation about the conduct of an Egyptian high official. He wrote: "Pahura has committed

an enormity against me. He sent Sutu
and they killed shirdanu-people. And he
brought 3 men into Egypt. How long has
the city been enraged at me! And indeed
the city keeps saying, 'A deed that has
not been done since time immemorial
has been done to us!'" (EA 122, text: VAT
1625, 31-49). The Assyrian king Ashur-
uballit likewise complained about an
attack – in this case an attack by the Sutu
on the Pharaoh's envoys. He reported that
the nomadic Sutu were exposing the lives
of the kings' couriers to mortal danger
(EA 16, text: C 4746, 37-55). Nevertheless, the Sutu/Shasu were mentioned not
so much as nomadic brigands, but rather
as mercenaries in the armies of the rulers of Canaan and Amurru. They served
both those who supported Egypt and
those who tried to free themselves from
Egyptian power. For example, the son of
Aziru, ruler of the city of Shumur, in an
attempt to extricate his father from Egypt,
where he had been detained against his
will, wrote to one of the Egyptian high
officials: "All the country and all the
Sutu forces said to me, also to that point,
'Aziru is not going to get out of Egypt.'
And now the Sutu are deserting the country and I am repeatedly informed, 'Your
father is staying in Egypt, and so we are
going to wage war against you'" (EA 169,
text: VAT 1660, 16-39). This threat was

Shasu (Sutu), the
closest relatives of
the Hebrews

effective and Aziru, who was suspected of disloyalty to Egypt, was sent home.

Despite the considerable differences between the Sutu and the Habiru, the two groups were originally a single large ethnos comprising the West Semitic peoples of Amorite origin who came to Canaan and the Lebanese coast in the 23rd-20th centuries B.C.E. Most likely, the nomadic Amorites who were subsequently called Sutu or Shasu arrived in Canaan in the 20th century B.C.E. as part of the tribal alliance led by the biblical patriarch Abraham. Many of them, indeed, traced their genealogy to Abraham. The Book of Genesis provides a very short digression on the genealogy of these desert peoples, treating them as descendants of Abraham from his 'Egyptian woman' Hagar, his second wife Keturah, and from unnamed concubines. In the Amorite tribal hierarchy, the ancestors of these peoples occupied a secondary and subordinate position, which is why they inherited semi-arid lands of inferior quality that were suited to a primarily nomadic way of life. The Sutu comprised not only secondary descendants of Abraham, but also tribes who traced their ancestry to his nephew Lot, e.g. the Moabites and Ammonites in Transjordan and those who considered themselves to be descendants of Abraham's brother Nahor, a nomad in northern Syria. The Sutu or Shasu also included the most closely related relatives of the 'house of Jacob', the Edomites. In contrast to the Hebrew tribes, the Edomites did not leave for Egypt, but stayed on their tribal lands in the southern part of Transjordan. Most likely, the Sutu who were active in Canaan during the 15-13th centuries B.C.E. were related to the ancestors of the Moabites, Ammonites, and Edomites. On the other hand, the Sutu who were mercenaries on the northern Lebanese coast, e.g. in the city of Shumur, in the service of Aziru, were either from the desert tribes who traced their origins to secondary branches of Abraham or were from the nomadic Amorites who believed they belonged to the tribal group of Nahor.

Warriors from Shasu tribes taken by Seti I. Karnak temple,
Luxor. 13th century B.C.E.

Egyptian rule and Hurrian presence in Canaan

Having left Egypt, the 'house of Joseph' could not escape
the power of the pharaohs over them. Canaan, whither they
returned in the middle of the 15th century B.C.E., was already
under Egyptian rule. From the reign of Thutmose III to the time
of Merneptah, i.e. over the course of approximately two and a
half centuries, the Egyptians controlled Palestine, the Lebanese
coast, and southern Syria. Admittedly, this control varied greatly
over time. It was at its most severe during the reign of Thutmose III, who almost every year led military expeditions into
Canaan and Syria, and during the period when the might of the
New Kingdom was at its greatest, under the pharaohs Seti I and
Ramesses II of the 19th Dynasty, each of whom organized a number of campaigns into Palestine and Syria.

On the other hand, Egyptian power in Canaan during the
second half of the 14th century B.C.E. was purely nominal, if it
existed at all. Egyptian interest in Palestine and the Lebanese
coast noticeably diminished in the reign of Pharaoh Amenhotep
III. Thanks to his alliance with the Hurrian kingdom of Mitanni,
Amenhotep III was little concerned with Asiatic affairs, being
more involved in military expeditions into Nubia and in internal
politics. However, it was only during the reign of the reformer-
pharaoh Akhenaten (Amenhotep IV) that Egyptian interest in

Seti I engages in battle with the Shasu.Karnak temple.

Canaan and Syria was completely extinguished. Preoccupied with religious reform and internal problems, Akhenaten paid almost no attention to the catastrophic situation of his vassals in Canaan and Amurru and to the advances made by the Hittites in Syria. In this respect, correspondence between Akizzi, ruler of the kingdom of Qatna in Central Syria, and the court of the Pharaoh is revealing. Reporting the intrigues of the Hittites and the transfer of southern and central Syria into the hands of the Hittites' allies, this Egyptian vassal asked the Pharaoh to send troops. But Egyptian help never arrived. Instead, the Egyptian emissaries advised Akizzi to turn to the kings of Mitanni, the enemies of the Hittites, for support (EA 55, text: BM 29819, 38-66; EA 56, text: VAT 1714, 36-42).

The Amarna letters contain considerable evidence that the envoys of Babylon, Assyria, and Mitanni, as well as the Pharaoh's own couriers were on a number of occasions robbed and murdered on Canaan territory – and in many cases not by the Habiru or Sutu, but by rulers who were Egypt's local vassals. For example, in his letter to the Pharaoh, the Babylonian king Burra-Buriyash wrote in indignation that his merchants and envoys had been robbed and killed in Canaan on their way to Egypt, and reproached the Pharaoh that this was the work not of some robbers, but of the Pharaoh's own vassals – the local rulers Shum-Adda, son of Balume, and Shutatna, son of Sharatum; moreover, Shutatna, ruler of the city of Akka, had forced the envoy of the Babylonian king to serve him (EA 8, text: VAT 152, 8-42). It is unclear whether the Pharaoh satisfied the Babylonians' demands for compensation, but we do know that up until the beginning of the 13th century B.C.E., Egypt was unable to send its troops into Canaan and establish order there. Lack of interest and, even more importantly, of the resources needed to carry out an active policy in Asia was also characteristic of Akhenaten's successors, the last pharaohs of the 18th Dynasty. For approximately 50-70 years, until the pharaohs of the 19th Dynasty came to power, Canaan was now free of the Egyptians' severe attentions. It was during this period that the northern Hebrew tribes tried to gain control over part of Canaan. The Amarna letters make it perfectly clear that the Habiru, as the Israelite tribes were known at the time, went on the offensive against the Egyptian vassals in Canaan. But the same texts also make it evident that the Habiru were not united and did not have a common ruler. Moreover, the Hebrew tribes did not yet stand out from the Habiru as a whole and the Israelite tribes had not yet formed an alliance. This internal reason, which implied the lack of a unified tribal organization, made the conquest of Canaan impossible during the weakening of Egyptian power. In the second half of the 14th century B.C.E., the Habiru were not yet independent; rather, they acted in alliance with several local rulers. The Amorites-Habiru were unable to unite as they had done previously in the Nile Delta since they were too scattered over the enormous territory of Canaan, Amurru, and Syria and, furthermore, were disorganized due to constant pressure and reprisals from Egypt.

In contrast to the Hyksos, the pharaohs of the New Kingdom brought Canaan neither peace nor prosperity. The Amarna letters unambiguously prove that Egyptian rule did not unite Canaan and did not rid it of internal rifts and wars. It is clear that Egypt was merely extracting material and human resources from Canaan while ruining its economy. All the wars with Mitanni and the Hittites were carried out with the forced use of Canaanite military power. The Egyptians particularly used soldier-mercenaries from the Habiru and Sutu. Moreover, they deliberately encouraged the Canaanite rulers to fight one another in order to ensure that they did not unite against Egypt.

The envoys from Canaan and Amurru bring gifts for Thutmose IV (1400-1390 B.C.E.). A painting from the Theban tomb of Sobekhotep

A similar situation took shape on the Lebanese coast, in Amurru. Canaan and Amurru were in every respect almost one and the same and possessed populations that were identical ethnically and linguistically. Both were fragmented into a great number of city states that were constantly scrapping with one another while being dependent on Egypt. Reminders came from both countries that the Habiru were anti-Egyptian and that the Sutu were nomadic brigands. Admittedly, the Lebanese coast was economically and culturally more developed than Palestine. Furthermore, the political situation in Amurru was influenced by the fact that the Hittite army was nearby in northern Syria and the Hittites were fighting for control of central and southern Syria, using a mixture of diplomacy and brute force. In both Canaan and Amurru a battle was waged between two local parties – the pro-Egyptians and the anti-Egyptians. The former were represented in Amurru by the governor of Biblos, Rib-Hadda, while the latter by the rulers of the city of Shumur, Abdi-Ashirta and his son Aziru. It was this second group that attempted to subjugate the cities of the Lebanese coast and, with the help of the Habiru and the Hittites, to throw off the Egyptian yoke.

In Canaan the situation was more complex. The main battle was between two cities – Shechem, which dominated in central Palestine, and Jerusalem, which prevailed in the south of the country. Labayu and his sons, the rulers of Shechem, staked their future on alliance with the Habiru, while the King of Jerusalem, Abdi-Heba, chose to support the Egyptians. In Canaan, however, the adversaries of Egypt were in a worse position than in Amurru. Canaan was the country closest to Egypt and most distant from the Hittites. While Aziru could count on the help of the Hittite army, Labayu's chances of securing such aid were negligible. This proved to be the deciding factor. Allied with the Habiru, Aziru succeeded in enlisting the support of the Hittites and in seizing his country from the hands of the Egyptians.

Labayu and his sons fell victim to an Egyptian conspiracy and failed to achieve what they had planned.

We have reason to suppose that the Habiru who helped Labayu and his sons were related to the 'house of Joseph'. It is likely that in exchange for their support, the ruler of Shechem gave them back part of the tribal territory that had belonged to them prior to their departure for Egypt. At any rate, he was accused exactly of this by Abdi-Heba, the ruler of Jerusalem.

The Amarna letters provide evidence of an interesting phenomenon: the names of many rulers of Canaanite and Syrian cities were clearly of Indo-Aryan or Hurrian origin despite the fact that their bearers represented the West Semitic culture and language. This reminds us that in the reign of Amenhotep II, the Egyptians called Canaan 'Haru' – the very same name that they used for the Hurrian people and their lands. It is remarkable that a tablet with Hurrian names was found even in the southern Canaanite city of Gezer. Unfortunately, we have no written sources that could explain the arrival of the Hurrians or their role in Canaan and southern Syria. But from what we already know, we may conclude that rather large groups of Hurrians penetrated Palestine and southern Syria, thereby changing to some extent the ethnic balance there. Their number also included Indo-Aryans, from whom the ruling elite of the newcomers, the so-called Maryannu, derived. Yet admittedly, the frequency of Hurrian and Indo-Aryan names in the written documents provides insufficient evidence for judging the extent to which the population of Canaan was Hurrianized or Arianized. After all, literacy was, as a rule, the property of the political and economic elite, most of whom had merged with the conquerors from outside and who, in fact, consisted largely of them.

The most likely time for the Hurrians' arrival in Canaan is from the second half of the 16th until the beginning of the 15th century B.C.E. This period saw the zenith of the military might of

Mitanni, the principal Hurrian state, when its borders stretched as far as southern Syria. Later, Canaan fell under the control of the Egyptians for an extensive period. The Egyptians would hardly have tolerated Hurrian invasions, or, at any rate, would at least have mentioned them in their steles and bas-reliefs. On the other hand, the Hurrians could not have appeared in Canaan earlier than the 16th century, since at the time their southern borders extended only to northern Syria. Indeed, it was during the second half of the 16th century B.C.E., when Mitanni was at its largest, that many cities in southern Syria and Canaan were destroyed. Some historians try to attribute this wave of devastation to Egyptian military campaigns, asserting that the Egyptians wanted to finish off the Hyksos and their allies in Palestine once and for all. The Canadian Egyptologist Donald Redford, however, has cast doubt on this hypothesis. Redford believes that the Egyptian army under Ahmose and his successors was too weak to cause such ruin. He reminds us that the Egyptians were unable to take Avaris, the Hyksos capital, by storm; moreover, they needed all of three years to take control of Sharuhen, a relatively small city in the south of Canaan. Even 60 years later, Thutmose III, the 'Napoleon of Ancient Egypt', was forced to spend seven months capturing Megiddo – a medium-sized city in Palestine. Redford rightly notes that we have absolutely no proof that the destruction of the Canaanite cities was carried out by the Egyptian army. He suggests that either these devastations should be ascribed to a later period, that in which Thutmose III waged his campaigns, or responsibility for them should be placed on Mitanni. If it was indeed the Hurrians who invaded Canaan in the second half of the 16th century B.C.E., then it becomes understandable why the Hyksos were defeated: they were forced to wage war on two fronts and during the decisive phase of the battles with the Theban pharaohs they had to make do without help from their allies in Canaan. Whatever the case, we must admit one obvious fact: from the second half of the 16th until the beginning of the 15th century B.C.E., part of Canaan's ruling elite were Hurrian and Indo-Aryan in origin. These changes in the make-up of the population of Palestine occurred when the 'house of Jacob' and the 'house of Joseph' lived in Egypt, so the arrival of the Hurrians and the Indo-Aryans could not have affected the Hebrew epos.

The emergence of Israel

During the rule of the 19th Dynasty pharaohs (Seti I, Ramesses II, and Merneptah), Egypt was successful in regaining control over Canaan for almost the entire 13th century B.C.E. However, this was possible only at the cost of regular punitive expeditions. And yet the power of the pharaohs in Canaan held up as long as the Egyptian army was located there. When it left, Egyptian rule became purely nominal. One of the objectives of the Egyptian military raids was to pacify the northern Hebrew tribes, who became much more active in the second half of the 14th century B.C.E. Egyptian military pressure on the Habiru led to their retreat from many cities and to a substantial diminishment of their territory. Quite possibly, they were forced to give up all that they had conquered during the years of the weakening of Egyptian power. But this retreat also played a positive role, helping to consolidate the northern tribes, for on their own, these tribes were not strong enough to resist Egypt and its local vassals. We do not know exactly when the Israelite tribal league was formed, but we may suppose that it was in the second half of the 13th century B.C.E., while Ramesses II was still ruling. Strangely perhaps, the Israelite tribes formed their alliance not during the years when Egyptian rule in Canaan was weak, but when it was at its strongest. Such paradoxes are evidently typical of Jewish history. It is worth remembering that the United Monarchy was also established at the height of the Philistines' military aggression against the Hebrew tribes. It is probable that the Egyptian army's attacks on the Habiru in Canaan forced several northern tribes to unite.

Thanks to the Amarna letters, we know that in the second half of the 14th century B.C.E., Israel did not yet exist as a tribal confederation. Otherwise, it would have undoubtedly been mentioned in one of the numerous letters sent by the local rulers. The territory on which the 'house of Joseph' settled was under the control of Labayu, the ruler of Shechem. His rival from Jerusalem, Abdi-Heba, earnestly informed the Egyptian pharaoh of any contact between Labayu or his sons and the Habiru, but he made no mention of Israel. On the other hand, we have irrefutable proof of the fact that Israel already existed in Palestine by the end of the 13th century B.C.E., when Pharaoh Merneptah (1213-1204 B.C.E.), son of Ramesses II, ascended the throne. Merneptah is famous for his Israel Stele, which is his triumphant report on his military campaign in Canaan. Composed in poetic form, the text of the stele lists the cities and peoples of Canaan over which the Egyptians won victories. It mentions Ashkelon, Gezer, Yanoam, and, most importantly, Israel – the first mention of Israel in non-biblical history. "Israel is laid waste, his seed is no more," reads the text of the stele, which is dated approximately 1207 B.C.E. Although the line dealing with Israel is extremely laconic, it provides a basis for several conclusions. First of all, the very fact that Israel is mentioned proves that the Israelite tribal confederation already existed in Canaan at the end of the 13th century B.C.E. Next, the Egyptian hieroglyph symbolizing Israel was used to depict not countries, but peoples. This is evidence that the Israelite tribes had still not settled on the land or that this process was far from complete. Judging by the place given to Israel among the other peoples and cities of Canaan, we may say that at the end of the 13th century B.C.E., Israel did not dominate in Palestine and, consequently, the conquest of Canaan had only just begun. We cannot help remembering the words spoken by the biblical soothsayer and sorcerer Balaam with regard to Israel: "I see a people who live apart and do not consider themselves one of the nations" (Numbers 23:9). Thus Israel was already a separate people, but did not yet have its own land. Later, the 'house of Jacob' found itself in exactly the same position when it left Egypt at the beginning of the 12th century B.C.E. At that time, the region of the Israelite tribal league was probably limited to the regions of the city of Shechem and late-stage Samaria, i.e.

A Stele of the Egyptian Pharaoh Merneptah,
which mentions Israel. Thebes.

the tribal territory of the 'house of Joseph'. Finally, Pharaoh Merneptah's campaign in Palestine is even more proof that neither his father Ramesses II nor his grandfather Seti I succeeded in pacifying Canaan and subduing the local peoples.

There is no need to repeat that the Israel mentioned on the stele of Merneptah was an alliance of only several northern Hebrew tribes. The other northern tribes, not to mention the southern ones (the 'house of Jacob'), lived at the time in the Nile Delta in Egypt, and continued to suffer from having to provide forced labor for the Pharaoh. Israel came into existence as a tribal confederation of several northern tribes only in Canaan and not earlier than the second half of the 13ᵗʰ century B.C.E. Therefore, to search for traces of the Israelite alliance in Egypt, especially during the time of the Hyksos, would be completely pointless.

Merneptah's military raid into Canaan turned out to be the last campaign waged by the pharaohs of the 19ᵗʰ Dynasty. Merneptah's successors lost control not only of Canaan, but of part of their own country as well. At the beginning of the 12ᵗʰ century B.C.E., Egypt once again fell into the maelstrom of a 'time of troubles' – a time of battles for power, court intrigues, and pretenders to the throne. These years were decisive for both groups of Hebrew tribes. The 'house of Joseph' began conquering Canaan while the 'house of Jacob' began its famous exodus from Egypt, as described in detail in the Book of Exodus. Meanwhile, both Egypt and Canaan found themselves facing a new and serious ordeal – invasion by the 'Sea Peoples'. In Asia Minor, the mighty Hittite Empire collapsed beneath the blows of these peoples. In Amurru and Syria, coastal cities were destroyed. Suddenly the Egyptians and the Western Semites found themselves face to face with a new enemy – the Indo-European peoples who had arrived from the north.

CHAPTER FIVE

The second exodus of the Western Semites from Egypt

Ramesses II: the oppressor pharaoh

The defeat of the Hyksos pharaohs led to the beginning of the mass exodus of the West Semitic population out of Egypt. This process began immediately after the surrender of Avaris and the flight of the Hyksos army into southern Palestine. It reached its climax in the 15th century B.C.E. during the reign of Thutmose III, when the majority of the Amorites left the Nile Delta and moved into Canaan, the Lebanese coast, and Syria. This enormous migratory wave included several northern Israelite tribes and, most importantly, their core – the 'house of Joseph'. But it was by no means all the Western Semites who left Egypt after the expulsion of the Hyksos: some continued living in the Nile Delta. We do not know why they remained when the majority of their fellow tribesmen had left Egypt, but we may assume that there were two main causes. Firstly, the tribes that stayed had no relation to the Hyksos and had not participated in the latter's wars with the Theban pharaohs. Secondly, they lived in the most remote regions of the Nile Delta and thus posed no threat to the population centers in Lower Egypt. It is possible that economic considerations also played a role: the pharaohs of the New Kingdom did not want to leave the Nile Delta completely empty and were planning to use the remaining Amorites for forced labor in the service of the state. Whatever the case may be, the southern Hebrew tribes or 'house of Jacob' were among those who stayed behind. In the 15th-14th centuries B.C.E. they were probably in quite a good position; otherwise, they would have left Egypt together with their fellow tribesmen. Their situation changed markedly for the worse only when the pharaohs of the new 19th Dynasty came to power at the beginning of the 13th century B.C.E. In contrast to the preceding 17th and 18th Dynasties of Theban pharaohs, these new rulers originally came from the north, from the Nile Delta, the east of which – the land of Goshen – was at that time home to the Hebrew tribes. The founder of the 19th Dynasty, a former army officer who had subsequently become a minister, was a native of the region of Avaris, the former capital of the Hyksos. Upon accession to the throne, he took the name of Ramesses I, but reigned for only two years, during which he failed to properly make his mark. However, his son, Seti I, and especially his grandson, Ramesses II, both achieved incomparably more. In contrast to the southern pharaohs, who as a rule erected new cities and temples in Upper Egypt, the new dynasty concentrated its efforts on building in the north, in the Nile Delta region that was its original homeland.

This circumstance proved fateful for the 'house of Jacob' and those Amorites who remained in the Nile Delta. Ramesses

II is famous for his feverish building activity: none of the other Egyptian pharaohs built so many cities and temples. Needing a giant labor force, he placed a heavy burden of work duties on the Western Semites living in the direct vicinity of his main building projects. It was here, in their lands, that he built a majestic new city – Piramese (meaning the 'property of Ramesses') – and it was this that the southern Hebrew tribes were forced to build. The burdens of this period left such an impression on the memory of the 'house of Jacob' that they were even mentioned in the Bible: "So they put slave masters over them to oppress them with forced labor, and they built

A black granite statue of Ramesses II wearing the War Crown.
1279-1212 BCE. Turin Museum.

Pithom and Rameses as store cities for Pharaoh" (Exodus 1:11). It was Ramesses II who was the pharaoh oppressor to whom the Bible dedicated its scant lines on Egyptian slavery. It was under Ramesses II that "the Egyptians worked them ruthlessly. They made their lives bitter with hard labor in brick and mortar and with all kinds of work in the fields; in all their hard labor the Egyptians used them ruthlessly" (Exodus 1:13-14).

He was the pharaoh who commanded, "Every boy that is born you must throw into the Nile, but let every girl live" (Exodus 1:22). Unfortunately for the 'house of Jacob', Ramesses II

Brickmaking in Egypt. Thebes, tomb of Rekh-mi-Re. By this labor,
Egyptians fatigued the 'house of Jacob'.

reigned for a surprisingly long time – approximately 67 years.
It is difficult to say whether the terrible order to kill new-born
males was actually carried out. However, it was this order that
was the cause of Moses falling into the hands of one of the Pharaoh's daughters and being adopted as a son. Had this command
been carried out over any length of time, it would have led not
only to the complete disappearance of the Hebrew tribes in the
Nile Delta, but to a sharp deficit in the labor force, a result which
would have been highly undesirable for the Pharaoh. But the
Bible tells us of no such effects, so clearly this awful command
had no consequences for the people as a whole. In general, the
sense of this order was completely at odds with the true intentions of the Pharaoh. After all, the Bible tells us that the Pharaoh
had no wish to be rid of the Hebrews, but instead tried his hard-
est to keep them back in Egypt for use as slave labor. Why was it
necessary to destroy that which he had done his best to protect?
It is likely that the real point of the command was something
else. Fearing a mood of mutiny among the West Semitic tribes

who were in their power, the Egyptians at all times required the Hebrews to send at least some of their rulers' sons to the court of the Pharaoh. Thus they achieved two goals at one stroke: the rulers' children were in effect hostages for the loyal conduct of their fathers and, the longer they spent being educated at the Pharaoh's court, the more spiritually cut off they became from their own families and peoples and the more they became devoted servants of Egypt. Later, some of these sons were sent as Egyptian governors to rule their tribes and peoples, while others remained captives at the royal court until the end of their lives.

A similar system was used not only in Egypt, but over the entire ancient Near East. There is nothing surprising in the son of the ruler of the Hebrew tribe of Levi finding himself at the Pharaoh's court. We must not forget that all the names mentioned in the books of the Pentateuch belonged, as a rule, to the leaders of tribes and clans, as well as members of their families, not to ordinary tribesmen. Therefore, it is for good reason that the Bible lists the names of Moses' parents: this was the family of the ruler of a tribe or prominent clan. It may well have been the case that in order to compel recalcitrant rulers to obey, the Pharaoh threatened to kill their newborn sons if they refused to give them up willingly to the Egyptians. The miserable parents faced a difficult choice: they had to agree to either the spiritual or physical death of their sons. This horrible duty, however, concerned only the tribal elite and in no way affected the ordinary people. Something similar was probably the case with the Hebrew midwives Shiphrah and Puah, whom the Pharaoh commanded, "When you help the Hebrew women in childbirth and observe them on the delivery stool, if it is a boy, kill him; but if it is a girl, let her live" (Exodus 1:16). Not trusting the rulers of the Hebrew tribes and clans, the Egyptians were evidently trying with the aid of the midwives to kill the successors of their potential enemies in order to replace them with pupils of the royal court. All these stories about the Egyptians' machinations were preserved in the narrative of the 'house of Jacob' and were subsequently, three centuries later, set down in the initial version of the Book of Exodus in an incomplete and more importantly, inaccurate form.

The origin of the name 'Moses' has given rise to much debate. In Hebrew, 'Moses' is 'Moshe'. According to the Bible, the Pharaoh's daughter "named him Moses, saying, 'I drew him out of the water'" (Exodus 2:10). However, 'Moshe' is a Semitic name that comes from the root of the verb 'mshkh', 'to pull out'. An Egyptian woman from the Pharaoh's family is unlikely to have named her foster son by a foreign Semitic name. The Hebrew name 'Moshe' probably arose at a later date on the basis of the ancient Egyptian word 'mose' ('son'). It may well be that Moses's Egyptian name was composed, as was the custom at the time, of two parts ('Thutmose', for instance, was son of the god Thut; 'Ahmose', son of the Moon-god; and 'Ra-mose', son of the god Ra). But for his family and friends, Moses's name was just 'mose', i.e. 'son'. This is all the more likely to have been so, since in the ancient Egyptian judicial and economic documents of the 13th century B.C.E. the name 'Mose' is encountered in its pure form, without any addenda or prefixes. Probably, Moses's fellow Hebrew tribesmen could not be bothered to get their tongues around his Egyptian name, but instead quickly reshaped it into the Semitic word 'moshe', which was more comprehensible to them. Subsequently, in the national legend about Moses, the origin of his name was linked with the circumstances of his being saved and adopted. Still later, an additional shade of meaning was added to this name when it was interpreted not as 'pulled out', but as 'pulling out' his people from Egyptian slavery. In any case, this widely known Jewish name is ancient Egyptian in origin and recalls the stay in Egypt.

Fortune was kind to Moses. He escaped the common lot of those who were brought up at the court of the Pharaoh and, despite everything, did not remain indifferent to the sufferings of his people. But his first attempt to take their side led to conflict with the Egyptians. Still worse, there were also those among Moses's own tribesmen who were ready to betray him to their oppressors. Finding himself in mortal danger, he was forced to flee from Egypt to the east to take refuge with nomads in the desert. He was given shelter by distant relatives of the Hebrews, the Midianites, who traced their roots to Abraham. The Midianites' legendary forefather, Midian, considered himself the son of Abraham by the latter's second wife, Keturah. The Midianites lived nomadically at the time on a vast territory in Sinai and northwest Arabia. We do not know where Moses encountered them. Most likely, he did not take off just in any direction when he left Egypt, but knew in advance where and with whom he could find refuge; to roam in the desert at that time meant certain death. Jethro, the ruler and high priest of the Midianites, gave Moses his daughter Zipporah in marriage. This fact is further evidence that Moses came from a distinguished and well-known family – probably from the family of the rulers of the tribe of Levi, since the ruler of Midian, as the Bible terms his father-in-law, would not have given his daughter to an unknown fugitive of humble origin and, moreover, would not have concealed him from the Egyptians. The biblical text mentions in passing that "Moses himself was highly regarded in Egypt by Pharaoh's officials and by the people" (Exodus 11:3), but does not, unfortunately, reveal the exact nature of Moses' significance for the Egyptians.

We do not know how much time Moses spent with the Midianites. The Bible merely says that so much time had passed that the Pharaoh and all those striving to kill Moses had already died. During these years Moses had at least two sons. The biblical narrative does not tell us about any other children, but this does not mean that there were none. The fact that he knew about the changes in Egypt means that he had kept contact with relatives and with other people he trusted. Moses was undoubtedly in close touch with his own family from childhood onwards; after all, his own mother was his wet-nurse. The Egyptians did not object to this since they were planning to place him as their own ward at the head of the tribe of Levi in the future. While with the Midianites, Moses must have been in contact not only with Egypt, but also with neighboring Canaan. He must have known that a new tribal confederation was forming in central Canaan – the alliance of Israel, which comprised related Hebrew tribes who, just like his own tribe, had formerly lived in the Nile Delta. It may be assumed that Moses was in touch with the 'house of Joseph' and that he even had agreements of some kind with these tribes regarding a future alliance in the event of the southern tribes managing to leave Egypt. The main problem lay in the fact that action could be taken only when Egypt and its power over Canaan weakened substantially; it was therefore necessary to endure a long wait, right up until the beginning of the 12th century B.C.E.

When did the biblical Exodus happen?

Among biblical scholars the opinion prevails that the Hebrews' exodus from Egypt took place during the rule of Ramesses II, sometime in the middle or second half of the 13th century B.C.E. The main reason that forces us to date the exodus precisely to this period is the stele of Pharaoh Merneptah, which mentions Israel as a people that was already in Canaan at the end of the 13th century B.C.E. Taking into account the fact that, according to the Bible, the Hebrew tribes had spent 40 years in the desert before they could set about conquering Canaan, the date of the exodus must be moved back to the middle of the 13th century

B.C.E. However, this supposition does not take into account two important circumstances. First and foremost, the significance given to the Merneptah Stele in dating the exodus is fundamentally erroneous, since in reality there was not one exodus but two. The tribal league of Israel that is mentioned in the Merneptah Stele comprised only several northern Hebrew tribes, which left Egypt for Canaan in the middle of the 15th century B.C.E.; the remaining Hebrew tribes could not have left Egypt before the beginning of the 12th century. Secondly, during the rule of Ramesses II, Egypt's military and political power was at its height; there was almost no chance for an entire group of tribes to depart against the Pharaoh's will. The exodus of some of the northern tribes and of the rest of the Hebrews happened in completely different circumstances. The 'house of Joseph', just like the majority of the Amorites, was forcibly driven out from Egypt during the period when the latter's military power was growing. The 'house of Jacob', on the other hand, was forcibly kept back by Egypt for use as slave labor. To break free from Egypt, the 'house of Jacob' had to wait for a period of national crisis. For this reason, we must look for a date pertaining to the exodus of the southern Hebrew tribes, and of the Amorite tribes which had joined them, in the years of the decline of Egypt's military might and the abrupt weakening of its central power. On this basis, the period from the end of the 19th to the beginning of the 20th Dynasty, i.e. between the final years of the reign of Queen Tausret and the rule of Pharaoh Setnakht, is the most likely time for the biblical exodus. This was a period of troubles in Egypt. During the course of several years, the country was paralyzed by internal feuds, revolts, and court intrigues; and this was followed by the accession to the throne of the Syrian usurper, Irsu. We have evidence of the complete chaos enveloping Egypt at this time, and, even more importantly, there are mentions of an uprising of 'Asiatics' who challenged the authority of the Pharaoh. There is, unfortunately, no absolute agreement among

Egyptologists as to when Queen Tausret and Pharaoh Setnakht ruled. Nevertheless, most favor dates between 1192 and 1182 B.C.E. Hence, it is during this period that we need to look for the exact year of the exodus of the 'house of Jacob' from Egypt.

There can be no doubt that Moses was born during the rule of the pharaoh oppressor, Ramesses II. It is also clear that he was forced to flee from Egypt either at the end of Ramesses II's reign or at the beginning of the rule of his son, Merneptah. Much more difficult to determine is when Moses returned. This was a period of decline in Egypt. Having reached the zenith of its power under Ramesses II, it began to weaken under his successor, Merneptah. Having come to power at an old age, Merneptah realized perfectly well that he had little time to accomplish large-scale projects and so devoted all his strength to retaining already conquered territories. His death was followed by the rapid decline of the 19th Dynasty; Egypt began to slip into serious, internal political crisis. At the moment when Merneptah died, his son, the crown prince, was evidently absent from court and the throne was seized by his brother, Amenmessu. But the rule of this usurper proved very short. Merneptah's lawful successor, Seti II, ascended the throne in unclear circumstances. Guided by the desire to wreak vengeance on his brother, he not only attempted to erase all memory of the latter, but also punished everyone who had helped him. But Seti II was likewise not destined to reign for long. When he died, he was replaced, for want of a better candidate, by his sick young son, Siptah. The latter's mother was, however, one of the very youngest wives of the Pharaoh, so official power rested with Seti II's principal wife, Tausret, as queen regent. Upon the untimely death of Siptah, Tausret then became lawful ruler of Egypt. Real power in the country, however, belonged not so much to her, as to her all-powerful favorite – chancellor Bay, a Syrian by origin. When Queen Tausret died, the Syrian chancellor attempted to seize power and rule under the name of Irsu. The time of troubles came to an end when a new dynasty, the 20th, was founded by Setnakht, a person of unidentified origin. The rule of Setnakht, however, also lasted no longer than three years; the cause of his death is unknown. Such was the historical background to Moses' return and the exodus of the 'house of Jacob' from Egypt.

From the Book of Exodus, we know that upon returning to Egypt, Moses was unable to immediately obtain his people's freedom. In order to organize and prepare for the exodus of the Hebrew tribes, he needed several years. He certainly could not have returned to Egypt earlier than the death of Pharaoh Merneptah, but must have been in the country not later than the rule of the child Siptah and Queen Tausret. The famous exodus described in the Bible happened after the death of Queen Tausret, when power had been seized by chancellor Bay and the country was caught up in a civil war. The pharaoh with whom Moses negotiated was the Syrian chancellor who was later known by the name of Irsu. The ten Egyptian plagues were mixed together with natural catastrophes and the disasters caused by internal wars. The exact period of the exodus coincided with the time when the new pharaoh, Setnakht, had begun winning victories over his adversaries and was attempting to restore order in the country.

Moses's mission

We know nothing about the many years when Moses lived with the Midianites. The Bible only speaks of the most important episode in his life there, when God laid upon him a special mission to save his people from Egyptian slavery. This took place on Mount Horeb, which was regarded as a holy site not only by the Hebrews, but also by all the nomadic West Semitic peoples, including the Midianites. This episode is extremely important in several respects. First of all, it signified God's sanctification of the role of Moses as savior and leader of his people; henceforth, no one could challenge Moses from a position of distinction, wealth, or supremacy in the tribal hierarchy since Moses had been chosen by God himself. This circumstance was crucial for the time, since Moses's position in the tribal hierarchy of the 'house of Jacob' gave him no claim to supremacy. He was merely chief of the tribe of Levi, which in numerical terms was inferior to the other southern tribes of Reuben, Simeon, and especially Judah. Secondly, the episode was God's sign to the 'house of Jacob' that they needed to leave Egypt and conquer the land of Canaan. There could be no resisting this plan, for such was the will of God. It is entirely possible that among the chiefs of the Hebrew tribes and clans in Egypt, there was no consensus about what to do. There were evidently those who proposed accepting enslavement and remaining in the Nile Delta to hold out for better times. Others probably doubted the choice of destination (land of Canaan), realizing that conquering it would not be easy. In short, this divine injunction was needed to induce the Hebrew tribes to recognize not only Moses's claim to leadership over the 'house of Jacob', but also the necessity of leaving Egypt for Canaan. In addition, help was needed from an influential leader among the Hebrew tribes in Egypt itself, a leader who could confirm Moses's authority and the divine character of the directions given to him. Such an authority was Aaron, and it was for this reason that in referring to God's Will, the biblical text clearly defined the role and significance of Aaron as Moses's principal assistant, Number Two in the exodus of the people from Egyptian slavery.

The Bible calls Aaron the brother of Moses. However, here, just as in the case of the forefather Jacob-Israel, the first authors of the Pentateuch decided to combine two different families for political considerations. Moreover, it is possible that Moses and Aaron were even from two different tribes. Indeed, who was Aaron? There is reason to think that he was head of the priestly clan of the 'house of Jacob', i.e. he was the high priest of the southern Hebrew tribes and simultaneously closely linked with the most prominent such tribe, the tribe of Judah. According to the Bible, the brother of Aaron's wife was ruler of this tribe. Furthermore, it may have been that Aaron himself came from one of the most esteemed families in this tribe. The idea that Aaron and Moses were close relatives and had common origins in the tribe of Levi arose later, during the period of the United Monarchy, and was intended to bring together the northern Levites and the southern Aaronites.

The episode in which Moses was given his mission to save his people in Egypt had great significance from another point of view as well: it united the southern tribes' cult of Yahweh with the northern tribes' cult of El and thus paved the way for their merging. It reminded the Hebrews that the God of the 'house of Jacob' was the same as that of the 'house of Joseph' and that the Yahweh of the southern tribes was known to the forefathers Abraham, Isaac, and Jacob by the name of El or Elochim (the plural of the word El'), to whom they prayed and to whom the northern tribes in Canaan also prayed. It is not by chance that the Bible discloses the name of the Lord – Yahweh (the Eternal One) – for the first time in this episode. This name, designated by four Hebrew letters – the so-called tetragrammaton – was certainly known to the southern tribes even earlier. After all, even the name of Moses' mother, Yocheved, was derived from 'Yahweh'. But on this occasion, it was necessary to emphasize that no one should be disturbed by the fact that the southern and northern Hebrew tribes had different names for God, since in reality these names designated one and the same Lord of the 'house of Jacob' and the 'house of Joseph'. The merging of the two religious cults was the logical conclusion to the unification of the names of the Hebrew tribes' two forefathers, Jacob and Israel. Just as these initially distinct tribal leaders had become a common patriarch, so the two distinct religious cults of El and Yahweh merged into a single faith in a God with different names.

The growing crisis of authority and the country's general weakening not only made it possible for Moses to return to Egypt, but also allowed him to take the lead in fighting for his people's exodus. But until the beginning of the civil war in Egypt, Moses could put forward only the most 'harmless' and natural requests that would not call into question either the authority of the Egyptian rulers or the loyalty of the Hebrew tribes. Such were the requests for the restoration of the Western Semites' rights to conduct pilgrimages to the Mountain of God, where they had previously held ceremonial services. The Mountain of God was located in Sinai, a three-day journey from the eastern border of the Nile Delta; Moses' plan envisaged that, instead of returning to Egypt, the Hebrew tribes would flee into the mountainous regions of the Sinai or Midian, where with the help of the Midianites they could hide from the pursuing Egyptian army. It might have seemed that this was a request that the Egyptians would be unlikely to turn down, given that it concerned fulfillment of the religious duties of the 'house of Jacob' and that the Egyptians themselves worshipped both their own and other people's gods. But as long as Queen Tausret and her favorite, chancellor Bay, retained a firm hold on power, they spurned such petitions, seeing them as an attempt to restore the Western Semites' former rights and freedoms. Unsurprisingly, the incensed leaders of the Hebrews interpreted all the natural catastrophes that befell Egypt as God's retribution for Egypt's refusal to let His people go and serve Him. The situation changed when, after the death of Queen Tausret, chancellor Bay proclaimed himself the new pharaoh, taking the name Irsu upon his accession to the throne. Many at court and especially in the army refused to recognize the Syrian usurper. Then another pretender, Setnakht, appeared and, with the support of the Egyptian army, took up arms against the former chancellor. The ensuring fight for power called the authority of Pharaoh Irsu into question. Sensing that he was losing the support of his adherents, Irsu had no choice but to change tactics and, not wishing to aggravate his position through a new conflict with the West Semitic population, expressed his readiness to let them go to the Mountain of God. However, suspicious that they intended to leave Egypt forever, he forbade them to take their families with them. Later, as the situation in the country deteriorated, he agreed to let their families go as well, but without taking their cattle or property. This hindered Moses's plans; without cattle and stocks of food, life in the desert would be impossible. Negotiations were again interrupted and the Hebrew leaders entered into contact with Setnakht.

The final plague resulting in the death of the 'first born sons' was completely different in character from previous punishments. While the invasions of locusts, lice, and frogs, as well as the wholesale death of cattle, and the devastating hail, harmful dust, and reddening of the Nile's waters could all be explained as natural catastrophes that were real events in Egypt's history, the death of the firstborns could have only resulted from an intervention of supernatural powers or an act of human hands. What probably happened during the night known as the Passover was that the adversaries of the usurper pharaoh attempted a coup, trying to eliminate both the Pharaoh and all his supporters. It must be remembered that by 'firstborns' the Bible meant the heads of clans and families, i.e. those who usually had power and wealth and who ruled the country. It was against them that a kind of Bartholomew's Night was organized. We may assume that the conspirators counted on help from Setnakht's army, which was located on the approach to the Nile Delta. It may have been that Setnakht's messengers promised the enslaved Semites freedom or important indulgences if they helped during the storming of the capital. In any case, Pharaoh Irsu's adversaries regarded the Hebrew tribes, who were displeased with their position, as potential allies; and so it was that the 'angel of death' passed over their homes. It was not for nothing that Moses warned that there would be a "loud wailing throughout Egypt – worse than there has ever been or ever will be again. But among the Israelites not a dog will bark at any man or animal. Then you will know that the Lord makes a distinction between Egypt and Israel" (Exodus 11:6-7). Some of the Hebrews probably lived near and perhaps even among the Egyptians and in order to be able to tell the two peoples apart, the conspirators advised the leaders of the 'house of Jacob' to mark the dwellings of their fellow tribesmen. This explains Moses's command to smear the doorposts and lintels of the entrance doors with the blood of sacrificial animals and not to leave the house until morning. Most likely, the coup attempt was unsuccessful, but there were large numbers of victims. "Pharaoh and all his officials and all the Egyptians got up during the night, and there was loud wailing in Egypt, for there was not a house without someone dead" (Exodus 12:30). Frightened by the bloodbath, the Pharaoh's court made haste to prepare for battle with Setnakht's approaching army. It was for this reason that they hurried to eliminate all who could help Setnakht's army at this critical moment.

The Book of Exodus especially emphasizes the fact that the Hebrews did not simply leave or independently break out of Egypt, but were sent out by the Egyptians themselves in great haste. "During the night Pharaoh summoned Moses and Aaron and said, 'Up! Leave my people, you and the Israelites! Go, worship the Lord as you have requested. Take your flocks and herds, as you have said, and go.' [...] The Egyptians urged the people to hurry and leave the country [...] So the people took their dough before the yeast was added, and carried it on their shoulders in kneading troughs wrapped in clothing [...] With the dough they had brought from Egypt, they baked cakes of unleavened bread. The dough was without yeast because they had been driven out of Egypt and did not have time to prepare food for themselves" (Exodus 12:31-34, 39).

That this was not a voluntary departure but a forced expulsion was said on more than one occasion even before the night of the Passover: "Then the Lord said to Moses, "Now you will see what I will do to Pharaoh: Because of my mighty hand he will let them go; because of my mighty hand he will drive them out of his country" (Exodus 6:1).

There is a further interesting fact that deserves attention. The Bible repeatedly and insistently mentions things of gold and silver and expensive clothing that the 'house of Jacob' takes with it out of Egypt. The first oblique mention of this comes in the prophetic dream of Abraham, the patriarch: "Know for certain that your descendants will be strangers in a country not their own, and they will be enslaved and mistreated four hundred years. But I will punish the nation they serve as slaves, and afterward they will come out with great possessions" (Genesis 15: 13-14). Subsequently, Moses is told this many times over – first, in the episode when he is invested with the mission to save his people from captivity in Egypt: "And I will make the Egyptians favorably disposed toward this people, so that when you leave you will not go empty-handed. Every woman is to ask her neighbor and any woman living in her house for articles of silver and gold and for clothing, which you will put on your sons and daughters. And so you will plunder the Egyptians" (Exodus 3: 21-22); then on the day before the Passover; and finally following the Passover night: "The Israelites did as Moses instructed and asked the Egyptians for articles of silver and gold and for clothing. The Lord had made the Egyptians favorably disposed toward the people, and they gave them what they asked for; so they plundered the Egyptians" (Exodus 12: 35-36). On the face of it, this deed seems not only ethically unattractive on the 'house of Jacob's' part, but also illogical from the Egyptians' point of view: how could they give up their own precious possessions to a people whom they were driving out from their country? The fact that the Pentateuch's authors accentuated this event by mentioning it several times in the biblical text suggests that it actually did happen. So, although the taking of gold, silver, and other fine things out of Egypt constitutes a detail of secondary importance in the history of the exodus, it can help us establish the precise time and circumstances of the departure of Moses's tribes.

We currently have only two ancient Egyptian sources relating to the time of Pharaoh Setnakht's rule. The first of these, the Harris Papyrus, is the largest ancient Egyptian document written during the rule of Ramesses IV, Setnakht's grandson. Unfortunately, it gives very incomplete information on the founder of the 20th Dynasty and the three years of his rule. The second source for our knowledge of this period is the stele erected by Setnakht himself on the island of Elephantine in Upper Egypt. Both of these documents tell of Setnakht's fight against disturbances and rebellions that encompassed the entire country. More interestingly, they describe the uprising of the 'Asiatics' – as the West Semitic population was then called – in Egypt. But the most fascinating thing is that both inform us of something that is mentioned in the Bible many times – the gold, silver, and copper items that the Egyptians gave up, or were supposed to give up, to the 'Asiatics'. Setnakht calls 'mutineers' those Egyptians who, after plundering Egypt, tried to reach an agreement with the 'Asiatics' with the help of the treasures they had previously plundered. These non-biblical pieces of evidence to some extent shed light on the events of that period and on the reasons for the 'house of Jacob's hurried departure from Egypt. It is likely that during the period when chancellor Bay and Setnakht were contesting the throne, the Hebrew tribes became the decisive factor shaping the balance of forces in the region of the Nile Delta. Each of the parties involved in the struggle tried to draw the Hebrew tribes onto its side. Possibly, it was the followers of Setnakht who, after organizing the conspiracy on the night of the Passover, helped the 'house of Jacob' to arm itself. The Book of Exodus makes an unexpected admission: "The Israelites went up out of Egypt armed for battle" (Exodus 13:18). This in itself contradicts the idea that the kindness of the Pharaoh was instrumental in allowing the enslaved peoples to leave Egypt. In this way, the ruler of Egypt was forced to deal not with a crowd of unarmed slaves, but with armed and organized tribes whose stance could determine the outcome of the fight for the throne. After the events of the Passover night, no one believed any more in the loyalty of the Hebrew tribes, as in that of the Western Semites who remained. It was necessary to send them out of Egypt as quickly as possible – before the arrival of Setnakht's army. Having no wish to open a new front in the war, this time with the Semites, the Pharaoh's court decided to achieve its goal not through force but with the help of gold and silver. So the things of gold and silver and expensive clothes that are repeatedly mentioned by the Bible came into the possession of the Hebrew tribes as a reward for leaving Egypt without delay. This episode became part of the biblical texts only 200 years later, which explains why it underwent changes that made it illogical and ethically unattractive.

Also possible is a slightly different interpretation of how the events developed. Fed up with lengthy and fruitless negotiations with Pharaoh Irsu, Moses and Aaron were compelled to use force to put pressure on the Egyptians. On the night that became 'Passover', armed detachments of Hebrews massacred the Egyptian 'firstborns', after which Pharaoh Irsu considered it best to get rid of the West Semitic population with all possible haste. True, this time he had to buy them off – otherwise, they were threatening to join forces with his enemy, Setnakht.

Meanwhile, the civil war in Egypt finished earlier than the Egyptians and the Hebrews expected: to seize the Nile Delta and the capital turned out to be easier and, more importantly, quicker than Setnakht himself had calculated. Irsu was overthrown and declared a mutineer, and all agreements made in his name were declared invalid. With the power struggle now over, there was no longer any need for the Hebrew tribes as allies. However, the latter were once more required as an unpaid workforce. After concluding military operations in the Nile Delta, Setnakht's army threw itself into pursuit of the departing Semites. Foreseeing this, Moses led his tribes towards the desert, heading for places where the lay of the land would have made it difficult to employ the most dangerous weapon of that time, the war chariots. "When Pharaoh let the people go, God did not lead them on the road through the Philistine country, though that was shorter. For God said, 'If they face war, they might change their minds and return to Egypt.' So God led the people around by the desert road toward the [Sea of Reeds]" (Exodus 13: 17-18). Realizing that the Egyptians were catching up with them too quickly and that he had no time to go round the Bitter Lakes, Moses decided upon a dangerous and risky maneuver: he chose to use the extreme ebb of the tide caused by a strong east wind to cross to the lake's opposite shore over dry land or through shallow water. It is difficult to say whether this was a clever plan thought up in advance or inspiration from above at a moment of mortal danger. The crucial idea was that the muddy sea bottom would prove no obstacle to cattle and people on foot, but would be impassable for the wheels of the Egyptian war chariots. And this is indeed what happened. "He made the wheels of their chariots come off so that they had difficulty driving." (Exodus 14: 25). Stranded and broken, the chariots held up the progress of the Egyptian army at a dangerous moment and in a dangerous place. "At daybreak the sea went back to its place... The water flowed back and covered the chariots and horsemen—the entire army of Pharaoh that had followed the Israelites into the sea. Not one of them survived" (Exodus 14: 27-28). Stripped of their main advantage – the war chariots, – the Egyptians did not dare continue the pursuit of the armed tribes and, demoralized by their losses, turned back the way they had come. Thus ended the 430-year stay of the 'house of Jacob' in Egypt. The most likely date for the exodus is the first or second year of the rule of Pharaoh Setnakht.

It is impossible not to notice that the description of the crossing in the biblical text consists of two versions that have been imposed on one another. One version attributes the event to Moses having the original idea of taking advantage of natural phenomena. It, for instance, links the ebbing waters to the fact that a strong easterly wind had blown all night and ascribes the destruction of the chariots to the damage suffered by their wheels as a result of the viscous, muddy sea bottom. Bearing in mind that all this happened not in deep sea, but in a shallow lake that was overgrown with reeds, we get a plausible picture of a cunning military maneuver that exploits natural phenomena. The second version speaks of an unconditional miracle: "Then Moses stretched out his hand over the sea, and all that night the Lord drove the sea back with a strong east wind and turned it into dry land. The waters were divided, and the Israelites went through the sea on dry ground, with a wall of water on their right and on their left" (Exodus 14:21-22). This second version came into being much later, when memories of salvation had become overgrown with new details and the event began to be perceived as a real miracle. By the time this narrative was recorded, – i.e. approximately two centuries later – the two versions had become so intertwined that they complemented one another.

The very first version of the Book of Exodus, which was composed during the United Monarchy, contained an account in which both groups of Hebrew tribes left Egypt simultaneously. However, all the biblical texts that describe the preparations for the exodus and the exodus itself preserve absolute silence regarding the role of the northern tribes; they make no mention of either the 'house of Joseph' or the northern tribes. The first naming of the northern tribes' leader – Joshua, son of Nun – comes during the battle with the Amalekites. It is difficult to say whether his name was inserted into this episode later or whether the episode in fact took place at a later date, when the tribes of Moses had united with the 'house of Joseph'. On the other hand, not only are the southern tribes (Reuben, Simeon, and Levi) mentioned on the eve of the exodus, but all the 'heads of their father's houses' – the clans that make up these tribes – are listed in detail. It is true, however, that our attention is drawn to something else as well: the lack of detailed information on the largest southern tribe, the tribe of Judah. What sense can we make of this? Did this tribe really leave Egypt before its fellows from the 'house of Jacob'? Probably not. The problem was that following the exodus from Egypt, the tribe of Judah absorbed numerous Edomite and Midianite nomadic clans (Sutu), which quickly rose to leading positions within it. However, to list the tribe of Judah's clans' heads without the noblest Judahite families – for instance, of Kenazzite origin, who never lived in Egypt – would have been unthinkable, so the biblical writers preferred not to mention this tribe at all.

The Book of Exodus gives the total number of Hebrews who came out of Egypt as "about six hundred thousand men on foot, besides women and children" (Exodus 12:37). If we add to this figure a number of women and children proportional to the number of men, then we end up with a total considerably larger than two million. Of course, all the Hebrew tribes in Egypt and Canaan could not muster such numbers, even if counted together. The population of Egypt itself at that time is hardly likely to have exceeded this figure. And it would be reasonable to ask whether a large family of 70 persons could produce a nation of several millions in the space of four centuries. Theoretically, yes, this was possible. As an example, consider two groups of people from the same region – the Arabs of Israel and the Gaza Strip. From 1950 to 2000, i.e. over a period of a mere 50 years, these groups quintupled in size – as a result of natural growth. If natural growth had occurred at a similar rate among the Hebrews, then over the 400 years they spent in Egypt their population would have increased to 27,343,750 – in the light of which the biblical figures seem more than moderate. But the 'house of Jacob' at that time did not have access to the advantages of modern medicine, sanitary conditions, and hygiene enjoyed by the Israeli and the Gaza Arabs today, so we would be wrong to use the latter's model of demographic growth.

But where did the biblical writers get their figure of 600,000 adult men? Most scholars today agree that this figure derives from the census conducted for purposes of taxation during the rule of King Solomon. The census included not just the northern and southern Hebrew tribes, but also the entire non-Israelite population of Canaan. In this way, the authors of the Book of Exodus took figures relating to the middle of the 10th century B.C.E. and applied them to the beginning of the 12th century, equating the population of the Hebrew tribes who came out of Egypt with the entire male population of the United Monarchy. This kind of handling of numerical evidence must make us extremely wary of all numbers given in the early biblical texts. There can be no doubt that all these figures reflected genuine contemporary facts, but at the time of being written down the chronology and geography of these facts were arbitrarily altered. An idea of the overall number of those who came out of Egypt may possibly be gained from the advice given by Moses's father-in-law Jethro, leader of the Midianites. Seeing how difficult it was for his son-in-law to make all the decisions by himself, he suggested appointing commanders for every ten, fifty, hundred, and one thousand people. Which is to say that he did not suggest appointing commanders for every ten thousand or more people; one thousand was the largest unit he had in mind. Therefore, we may very tentatively suggest that in reality the total number was several tens of thousands. This is indirectly confirmed by another episode from the Bible:

"Whenever the ark set out, Moses said,
  "Rise up, Lord!
  May your enemies be scattered;
  may your foes flee before you."
Whenever it came to rest, he said,
  "Return, Lord,
  to the countless [in the Hebrew Bible "tens of"]
  thousands of Israel» (Numbers 10: 35-36).

Here Moses himself speaks not of hundreds of thousands, but of tens of thousands only. It is not for nothing that the biblical text contains an admission that the people of Moses were fewer in number than most of the peoples of Canaan, for which reason he had to stick closer to God and His commandments. It is likely that the northern Israelite tribes who were already in central Canaan were similar in number, so the union of the two Hebrew groups was vitally important for both.

The biblical description of the exodus contains a very short, but telling phrase: "Many other people went up with them, as well as large droves of livestock, both flocks and herds" (Exodus 12:38). Who were these "many other people" who left Egypt together with the 'house of Jacob'? This is an important question because they were numerous and subsequently became part of the alliance of Hebrew tribes. Undoubtedly, these "many other people" included Egyptians too – but only those who were bound by bonds of kinship with the Semites. Forsaking Egypt for the lifeless desert brought many difficulties and deprivations and could not in any way be considered an attractive option for the Egyptians even during times of bloody troubles and civil war. The same may be said with regard to the slaves in Egypt. Unlike the West Semitic tribes, the slaves belonged to various ethnic and racial groups, and were disunited and unarmed. No one could have driven them out of Egypt and it is unlikely that slaves from Nubia, Cush, and Libya would have left by their own free will for the waterless Sinai Desert in the company of the Semites, a people who were alien to them. It is no coincidence that even Moses's fellow tribesmen reproached him on more than one occasion: "They said to Moses, 'Was it because there were no graves in Egypt that you brought us to the desert to die? What have you done to us by bringing us out of Egypt? Didn't we say to you in Egypt, 'Leave us alone; let us serve the Egyptians?' It would have been better for us to serve the Egyptians than to die in the desert!" (Exodus 14: 11-12). Judging by the hurriedness of the departure – or, to be more exact, the expulsion – of these people together with the 'house of Jacob', most of them must have occupied the same place in Egyptian society as the southern tribes, i.e. they were Western Semites just like the Hebrews themselves. We have every reason to suppose that the 'house of Jacob' was not the only tribe to remain in Egypt following the departure of the main body of the Amorites for Canaan and Syria. The West Semitic tribes that remained shared the fate of the 'house of Jacob' in every respect in the Nile Delta. However, they never had their own Moses or their own keepers of the tradition like the Levites and Aaronites, who might have been able to tell of their history and lineage prior to their arrival in Egypt. Evidently, in terms of ethnic origin, they differed little from the Hebrews. We may tentatively suppose that the West Semitic population (of Amorite origin) who joined the 'house of Jacob' at the time of its departure from Egypt included tribes like Issachar and Zebulun. Significantly, their founders are named as the sons of patriarch Jacob by his first wife Leah, making them part of the family tree of the southern tribes of Reuben, Simeon, Levi, and Judah. The biblical texts preceding the departure for Egypt contain no mention of the tribes of Issachar and Zebulun. It is likely that the formal alliance with these tribes was formed on Mount Sinai as part of the general covenant with one God, when the 'house of Jacob' and its 'adoptive sons' took upon themselves identical obligations. But the union of the southern Hebrews with these tribes lasted only a short period of time – from the exodus from Egypt to the moment of unification with the tribal league of Israel. Subsequently, the southern and 'adopted' tribes went their separate ways, the latter joining the northern Hebrews and, following the break-up of the United Monarchy, remaining in the kingdom of the northern tribes, i.e. Israel. This was probably no coincidence since from the point of view of geography and tribal genealogy they felt much closer to the northern than the southern Hebrew tribes. The same goes for two other northern tribes, Gad and Asher, whose founders were held to be the sons of Jacob by Zilpah, the slave girl of his wife Leah. The fact that the primogenitors of these tribes were born to a woman of low social status is a sign of their subordinate and secondary position in the tribal hierarchy of the 'house of Jacob'. Gad and Asher also became 'adoptive sons' of Jacob during the period between the exodus from Egypt and the arrival in Canaan. But the lower social status of the tribe's founders is evidence that they joined the alliance as junior partners. Nevertheless, the departure of the 'house of Jacob' and its 'adoptive sons' was the final stage in the long process by which the Amorites migrated from the Nile Delta to Canaan and Syria. Unfortunately, we know only of the last stage in this process, and then only because its participants included the keepers of the biblical tradition, the Levites and Aaronites.

CHAPTER SIX

On the path to
the old homeland

FOLLOWING THE EXODUS FROM Egypt, Moses's position
became even more difficult. His authority as a leader was constantly in question and he was periodically required to carry out
supernatural feats in order to prove his right to be leader. The
first year of wandering through the desert consisted of unceas-
ing attempts at mutiny against Moses's rule and his monotheistic concept of faith. This is something that comes as a surprise
to anyone who knows anything about relations within Bedouin
tribes in the Middle East. Usually, members of nomadic tribes
are bound fast by an iron discipline and disobedience to the
leader is an extraordinarily rare phenomenon. That Moses's and
Aaron's positions were so unsteady is explained, above all, by the
fact that there were other Amorite tribes that had likewise been
expelled from Egypt in the same way as the 'house of Jacob'. It
was they who cast doubt on Moses's leadership because he represented the smallest Hebrew tribe. On the other hand, during
the four centuries that they had remained in Egypt, the Hebrew

tribes had time to become settled. Some of them had lived amongst the Egyptians and the severe discipline of their previous nomadic life had long since softened. Furthermore, since the rule of Ramesses II, when the enslavement of the Amorite tribes in the Nile Delta had begun, the Egyptians had done everything to weaken the authority of the tribal leaders and replace it with the rule of their own civil servants. It was thus that two new types of 'bosses' had emerged. They are described in the Bible as 'oppressors', i.e. Egyptian civil servants who directed compulsory construction work, and 'supervisors', who monitored the performance of such work. The 'supervisors' were chosen by the Egyptians from among the Western Semites themselves, and in such a way as to create a counterbalance to the authority of the traditional leaders. Once they found themselves in the desert, the Hebrew tribes experienced an unfamiliar vacuum of power: the tyranny of the Egyptian rulers no longer existed; the former supervisors had lost all legitimacy; and the authority of their own leaders had been badly undermined by the long years of enslavement in Egypt. It should not be forgotten that many of Moses's fellow-tribesmen had no intention of leaving Egypt and still less of conquering Canaan. The biblical texts contain eloquent admissions that the Hebrews "did not listen to [Moses] because of their discouragement and cruel bondage" (Exodus 6:9). Moreover, seeing that initially Moses's mission only exacerbated their position, they unthinkingly started bitterly reproaching him and Aaron: "and they said, 'May the Lord look upon you and judge you! You have made us a stench to Pharaoh and his officials and have put a sword in their hand to kill us'" (Exodus 5:21). If the Egyptians had not themselves expelled the Hebrew tribes and not paid to hasten their departure, a substantial part of Moses's fellow-tribesmen would undoubtedly have stayed on in Egypt. For, in spite of enslavement and oppressive forced labor, the West Semitic population did not go hungry in the Nile Delta. For this reason, every time when they were tormented by thirst and hunger in the desert, they set about reproaching Moses and Aaron: "The Israelites said to them, 'If only we had died by the Lord's hand in Egypt! There we sat around pots of meat and ate all the food we wanted, but you have brought us out into this desert to starve this entire assembly to death'" (Exodus 16:3). It was not for nothing that in Rephidim, "Moses cried out to the Lord, 'What am I to do with these people? They are almost ready to stone me'" (Exodus 17:4).

The precise route taken by Moses is almost impossible to establish today, since the texts dealing with the wanderings through the desert are arranged not in strict chronological order, but by degree of importance for the first authors of the Pentateuch. Furthermore, we cannot identify all the places mentioned in the texts. Modern archaeology is unable to help us here since it is very difficult to discover nomadic camps, and these camps provide insufficient material for any conclusions. It is likely that, to begin with, Moses chose his route taking into account the possibility of pursuit by the Egyptians and so as to minimize their main advantage – the war chariots. Afterward, he focused more on sources of water and food for the people and cattle. Here he was helped by the experience of nomadic life and the knowledge of places in Sinai and northwest Arabia that he had acquired while living with the Midianites. However, the oases and springs in the desert were never vacant and Moses had to use them in a way that would avoid conflict with the local nomadic tribes. Inevitably, with some of them – the Amalekites, for instance – he ended up quarrelling, but others, the Midianites, with whom he had earlier joined in marriage, gave him a great deal of help and support. Moses did not intend to remain long in the desert. His goal was Canaan, where his plan was to unite with the 'house of Joseph', which had arrived there from Egypt in the 15th century B.C.E. It was only in alliance with the 'house of Joseph' that it would be possible to conquer Canaan. However, on the way to the Promised Land he had to once again organize both his own, southern tribes and those Amorite tribes that had joined him during the departure from Egypt. He strove to create a military, political, and religious alliance capable of conquering Canaan. But the main criteria of unity at the time were considered to be tribal origin and faith. The first condition was already obtained: Moses's tribes belonged to the Western Semites of Amorite origin. The second – a shared faith in the one God and the covenant with him – had yet to be created. So the next task following the exodus was the religious and spiritual consolidation of the 'house of Jacob' and those who had joined it.

The birth of monotheism

The Book of Exodus mentions several times the Mountain of God ('har elohim'), which was situated in the desert, three days' travel from the region where the Hebrew tribes lived in the Nile Delta. It was this mountain that Moses had in mind when he asked that his people be let go so that they could worship God. It was on this mountain that Aaron met Moses when the latter was returning to Egypt from the Midianites. And it was on this mountain that the Hebrews were supposed to make a sacrifice when they were released, or rather expelled with haste, from Egypt. Possibly, the Mountain of God had been well known from way back and was used as a place of worship by the Amorites who had settled in the Nile Delta. Before the rule of Ramesses II, the Western Semites had no problems accessing the Mountain of God. But when Ramesses II came to the throne, he started to enslave them and the mountain could no longer be used for regular sacrifices. Moses, however, did not lead his people straight to the former holy place, but headed for another mountain – Sinai or Horeb, – where he was invested with the mission of saving the 'house of Jacob'. It is likely that the Mountain of God was very close to the Nile Delta and the Hebrew tribes would have been overly vulnerable to unexpected attack by the

Egyptian army. The distance, which was three days' journey for the entire people (burdened, of course, by herds of cattle), could have been covered in less than two days by the Egyptian infantry and even more quickly by their war chariots. Today it is difficult to identify where the Mountain of God was located, but, judging by the fact that three days' journey was needed to reach it, the mountain was situated in an easily accessible place with a landscape that allowed the Egyptians to use their most powerful weapon, their chariots. However, there was a further reason why Moses avoided this mountain. It was associated with the old pagan gods and their rituals, and this made a very poor fit with the monotheistic spirit of Moses's faith. Essentially, he wanted to breathe new content into his people's old tribal religion and this required a different setting and a different holy place. The mountain he chose was relatively far from the Nile Delta and the lay of the land there not only ruled out unexpected attack by the enemy, but also deprived the latter of all ability to maneuver. The biblical texts have different names for this mountain, where the Ten Commandments were handed down to Moses. In one case it is named as Horeb; in another, as Sinai. Do both names refer to the same mountain? Possibly, this is something that was unknown even to the redactors of the Pentateuch. But they did not dare make amendments to the ancient texts and restricted themselves only to arranging them. If different mountains are in fact meant, then it is possible that during their wandering in the desert Moses brought his people to both and conducted an act of worship on each. Mount Sinai is well known; it is situated at the southern end of the Sinai Peninsula. As for Horeb, it might have been somewhere in northwest Arabia, near Midian, and could have been an extinguished volcano. Although the biblical texts that give an account of Moses's receipt of the Torah derive from different sources, they all draw the same picture – which is very similar to the awakening of a previously extinguished volcano: "Mount Sinai was covered with smoke, because the Lord descended on it in fire. The smoke billowed up from it like smoke from a furnace, the whole mountain trembled violently" (Exodus 19:18); "To the Israelites the glory of the Lord looked like a consuming fire on top of the mountain" (Exodus 24: 17). On the other hand, if the city of Hebron in south Palestine underwent three name changes in ancient times alone, why could Mount Sinai not have had a second name, Horeb. Mount Hermon, for example, had a second name, Sirion; and Mount Nebo was also known as Avarim. Given that the first books of the Pentateuch were composed 200 years after the exodus from Egypt, biblical writers were already confused on which of the sacred mountains was meant by the 'Mountain of God'. This is an example of how the biblical texts describing the exodus and the wanderings in the desert reflect real historical events of the time, but cannot give a precise idea of these events' chronology or geography.

The cult of Yahweh was probably the primordial faith of the southern Hebrew tribes ('house of Jacob'). They brought it with them from their original motherland in northwest Mesopotamia. At the same time, they also accepted the national gods of those countries they had lived in for a long time. In Sumer, they prayed to the local pagan gods, and in Canaan they gave up the latter for a new cult – that of El, which was common in Palestine and Syria. Abraham's new faith was likewise pagan; it was either adopted from the Canaanites or took shape under their influence. Abraham's 'El Elyon' – the 'Almighty' – was probably the same god to whom the Hebrews' neighbors, the Jebusites from the city of Urushalem (Jerusalem), also prayed. Abraham merely exchanged the Mesopotamian gods for Canaanite ones, as is indirectly confirmed by the words spoken by Joshua at the end of his life to his fellow tribesmen: "Throw away the gods your forefathers worshiped beyond the River [Euphrates] and in Egypt, and serve the Lord. But if serving the Lord seems undesirable to you, then choose for yourselves this day whom you will serve, whether the gods your forefathers served beyond the River, or the gods of the Amorites, in whose land you are living. But as for me and my household, we will serve the Lord" (Joshua 24: 14-15). Here, Joshua effectively admits that the Hebrews worshipped pagan gods not only in Sumer and Haran, but in Egypt as well – i.e. during the period when they were supposed to be following the new, 'monotheistic' faith of Abraham. At the same time, the Aaronites and Levites, who were the keepers of the tradition and the authors of the Old Testament, preferred to trace the tradition of monotheism back to Abraham, though in reality the real credit for creating a monotheistic faith belonged not to him, but to Moses. It is no coincidence that in the episode where Moses is invested with the mission of taking his people safely out of Egypt so much breath is spent on explaining that the God of the forefathers – Abraham, Isaac, and Jacob – is identical to Moses's Yahweh. This helped solve two problems at once: first, it created a bridge between the Southerners' cult of Yahweh and the Northerners' cult of El and, secondly, it linked Moses's monotheistic faith with the worship of El, which the forefathers adopted following their arrival in Canaan. In the Nile Delta, the Western Semites lived for a long time by themselves, prevailing numerically over the Egyptians, which is why the Egyptian cults took almost no hold among them. During the 430 years of life in Egypt, the cult of El that had been brought from Canaan weakened considerably among the southern tribes, giving way to the old tribal worship of Yahweh. However, before Moses the cult of Yahweh was pagan. It was Moses who breathed into it new, monotheistic content. We do not know whence Moses took this concept of God that was so revolutionary for the time. The ancient world knew nothing like it, so this religious and philosophical idea could not have been borrowed from anyone in that distant age. Certain historians have tried to draw an analogy with the religious reform of the Egyptian Pharaoh Akhenaten (Amenhotep IV). But they fail to take into account the fact that the cult of Aton, the Egyptian sun god, was essentially pagan.

What the reformer pharaoh proposed was not monotheism, but an improved form of paganism amounting to the worship not of multiple gods and idols, but of a single pagan god. At best, his reforms may be regarded as a step towards monotheism, but no more than that. There is another and no less important aspect: almost one and a half centuries separate the time of Akhenaten from that of Moses. How could have the ideas of Akhenaten influenced Moses if they were condemned and utterly forgotten a mere few years after the death of the reformer pharaoh?

Evidently, Moses's monotheism could not have been the result of a development of religious and philosophical thought from even the most developed and civilized parts of the ancient world of that time, e.g. areas such as Egypt and Babylonia. So there is nothing surprising in the fact that Moses's fellows and successors could not sustain the elevated nature of his concept of God and descended to a considerably lower level in their understanding of monotheism. Only much later, under the Juda-hite kings Hezekiah and especially Josiah, do we see a return to Moses's concept, but again only for a short time. It was, in fact, only in the 6th and 5th centuries B.C.E., following the Babylonian exile that the Judeans began to truly understand the monotheistic nature of Moses's teachings (this underlines the extent he was in advance of his own time). Many elements of his unique concept – the law regarding the Sabbath, for example – were understood by the surrounding world only a thousand years later. For the first time in history, many hundreds of years before the apogee of the Hellenistic and Roman civilizations, a law was made to create a special day of the week, and not just for rest from hard physical labor, but for worshipping God and for the spiritual and intellectual development of all people, including the most oppressed and dispossessed – the slaves.

The adoption of the Sinai commandments simultaneously became a ceremony of swearing an oath of loyalty to the new alliance of tribes that had come out of Egypt. On Sinai, not only was a covenant with the one God created, but there came about an alliance of southern Hebrew tribes, both with one another and with those Amorite tribes who had taken part in the exodus from Egypt. It was on Mount Sinai that they all committed to conquering Canaan. Now, Moses led not a motley crowd, but a unified people bound together by a shared faith, laws, and purpose.

Religious and tribal conflicts

The new tribal union did not escape the occurrence of internal conflicts. The most serious such conflict happened as a result of the 'golden calf'. For a reason that was not clear to his people, Moses was absent for considerably longer than expected. Believing their leader to be dead, the tribes chose as their new head Aaron, Moses's fellow and the high priest. Now that he had supreme authority, Aaron went back to the old pagan concept of the cult of Yahweh, a concept that was clearer and more comprehensible to the people than the invisible and impalpable God of Moses, a God who also rejected any form of coexistence with other gods: "They have been quick to turn away from what I commanded them and have made themselves an idol cast in the shape of a calf. They have bowed down to it and sacrificed to it and have said, 'These are your gods, O Israel, who brought you up out of Egypt'" (Exodus 32:8). The unexpected appearance of Moses during the pagan celebrations caught everyone off their guard. But Aaron and his supporters were in no hurry to give power back to Moses. There was a period of dual rule – which, as might have been expected, led to fratricidal clashes between the Hebrew tribes. The conflict concerned not just which concept of the cult of Yahweh – pagan or monotheistic – would win out, but also who would have authority over the newly created tribal alliance. The tribes and clans took sides with some supporting Moses and others Aaron. The tribe of Levi was entirely on the side of Moses: "So he stood at the entrance to the camp and said,

'Whoever is for the Lord, come to me.' And all the Levites rallied to him" (Exodus 32:26). This episode is further confirmation of the fact that Moses was not only a member of the tribe of Levi, but also its leader and high priest. But the tribe of Levi was one of the smallest and without the support of other tribes would have been bound to be defeated. Unfortunately, the biblical text does not say who else supported Moses. We may suppose that the tribes of Simeon and Reuben took his side. Among the southern tribes a latent fight for supremacy had been going on for a long time. Following the exodus from Egypt, this fight began to take more open forms. The main and longest-running contender (in the 'house of Jacob') was the largest tribe, Judah, although in the tribal hierarchy it occupied only fourth place after Reuben, Simeon, and Levi. The Aaronites, who were closely linked with, and possibly derived from, the tribe of Judah, supported this tribe's claim of primacy. For their part, the three other southern tribes feared the strengthening of Judah and considered its claims to rule over them unlawful from the point of view of traditional tribal law. It is difficult to say what position was taken by the Amorites who had joined the 'house of Jacob'. Possibly, they remained neutral, not wishing to take part in internal disputes between the Hebrew tribes.

The biblical text maintains an eloquent silence concerning the position taken by Aaron during the fratricidal conflict within the 'house of Jacob'. This in itself tells us that it was he who led Moses's opponents. The internal struggle left no clear winner. The balance of forces between Judah and the three small tribes (Reuben, Simeon, and Levi) was approximately equal, although possibly it even favored the former. At any rate, Moses and the Levites were unable to restore the previous state of affairs. The Bible indirectly admits that not Aaron, but Moses was obliged to leave the common camp. "Now Moses used to take a tent and pitch it outside the camp some distance away, calling it the "tent of meeting." Anyone inquiring of the Lord would go to the tent of meeting outside the camp" (Exodus 33:7). As far as we can tell, Aaron's tent was in the camp itself and he was visited there by members of the tribe of Judah. We do not know how long this stalemate lasted, but among the hardships of the desert any internal conflict was against the interests of all the tribes, and this is why a reconciliation took place. Probably, it was then, following the incident with the golden calf, that the his-

Bronze statuette of Baal covered with gold. Megiddo. 12th century BCE.

toric agreement was reached by which supreme authority over the tribes returned to Moses and primacy in performing sacred rites was established as belonging to the kin of Aaron. The Levites were forced to accept second place after the Aaronites in the worship of Yahweh. At the same time, Moses managed to secure important guarantees for members of his tribe in the future. After taking Canaan, all the tribes had to accept the Levites as priests of the cult of Yahweh and regularly give them a part of their income. The latter gave the Levites disproportionately large privileges in the tribal alliance and provided them with a steady material sufficiency, regardless of possible redistribution of the tribal lands in Canaan. But supreme authority was given back to Moses only for the duration of his life – on the condition that after his death it would not pass to his sons or the tribe of Levi. This agreement must have had the effect of reconciling the

Hebrew tribes and likewise of rationalizing relations between the Levites and the Aaronites. But the compromise satisfied by no means everyone: some of the Levites remained unhappy with the fact that supremacy in matters of religion had been surrendered to the Aaronites, while the tribe of Reuben, which was the first in the tribal hierarchy of southern tribes, felt badly done by in the 'house of Jacob'.

The episode with the golden calf contains serious accusations against Aaron: "He [Moses] said to Aaron, 'What did these people do to you, that you led them into such great sin?'" (Exodus 32: 21); "Moses saw that the people were running wild and that Aaron had let them get out of control and so become a laughingstock to their enemies" (Exodus 32: 25). There can be no doubt that these words were written by Levites, descendants of Moses, who were in competition with the Aaronites. On the other hand, it was the Aaronites who introduced into the biblical text an unusually brusque condemnation of the forefathers of the tribes of Simeon and Levi: "Let me not enter their council, let me not join their assembly, for they have killed men in their anger and hamstrung oxen as they pleased. Cursed be their anger, so fierce, and their fury, so cruel! I will scatter them in Jacob and disperse them in Israel" (Genesis 49: 6-7). It is difficult to get rid of the thought that this very sharp condemnation does not only concern the massacre in Shechem following the rape of Dinah, the daughter of forefather Jacob. The angry tirade against Simeon and Levi probably was a reaction not so much to their cruelty to the Hivites from Shechem, as to their treatment of their own brothers from the tribe of Judah in the incident with the 'golden calf' – especially given that these accusations were set down during the period of the United Monarchy when the country was ruled by the dynasty of David, which derived from the tribe of Judah, and worship in the Temple was supervised by the Aaronites, who were closely bound up with the same tribe. It was then too that the Aaronites attributed the creation of the golden calf not to any initiative of Aaron, but to the bad conscience of the people itself. "Do not be angry, my lord," Aaron answered. "You know how prone these people are to evil. They said to me, 'Make us gods who will go before us. As for this fellow Moses who brought us up out of Egypt, we don't know what has happened to him'" (Exodus 32: 22-23). Over the course of centuries, right up to the destruction of the First Temple, the two priestly clans, the Aaronites and the Levites, competed with one another in sometimes overt, sometimes concealed rivalry for the main role in celebrating the cult of Yahweh. This rivalry was a reflection of the old battle for power within the 'house of Jacob'.

The historical literature contains speculation about whether Moses could have been an Egyptian by origin and, moreover, an Egyptian priest (a supporter of the religious reform of Akhenaten) who joined the Semites on their exodus from Egypt. However, the path taken by Moses during his entire life and his readiness to sacrifice himself and to share all the sufferings of his people are evidence of the contrary. It is difficult to find more convincing proof of love for the 'house of Jacob' than the following: "So Moses went back to the Lord and said, 'Oh, what a great sin these people have committed! They have made themselves gods of gold. But now, please forgive their sin—but if not, then blot me out of the book you have written'" (Exodus 32: 31-32) It is unlikely that an Egyptian official or priest would have been ready to show so much love for the Semites, an alien people, that he would have been prepared to lay down his life for them without the slightest hesitation.

Alliance with the Midianites and confrontation with the Amalekites

During the difficult period in its history, the 'house of Jacob' had an important ally in the Midianites. The Midianites had saved Moses and concealed him from the Egyptians and, after the southern Hebrew tribes had left Egypt, helped them cope with the difficulties of living in the desert. The Book of Exodus records several important episodes taken from meetings with the Midianites. One such episode deals with the arrival of Moses's father-in-law, Jethro, ruler of Midian, at Moses's camp. Jethro came together with his own daughter, Moses's wife Zipporah, and two of their sons. His visit was a goodwill gesture and constituted support of the 'house of Jacob', which now found itself in unfamiliar conditions in the barren desert. As a man experienced in nomadic life, Jethro helped Moses organize his tribes in the desert and get a judicial system up and running. This interesting fact is evidence that the leaders of the Hebrew tribes lacked management experience given that in Egypt they had been allowed to perform only priestly functions. It is likely this that explains the importance attributed to supervising celebration of religious rites, for the priest automatically became a leader for his fellow tribesmen, who had been accustomed to obey only Egyptian civil servants and their supervisors. The fact that Jethro took part in a joint religious service and made sacrifices to Moses's one God is evidently a sign that some sort of alliance had been joined between part of the Midian tribes and the 'house of Jacob' – and this alliance reinforced the relationship of kinship between Jethro and Moses. Another episode has to do with the request made by Moses to his brother-in-law, Hobab, the Midianite: "But Moses said, 'Please do not leave us. You know where we should camp in the desert, and you can be our eyes. If you come with us, we will share with you whatever good things the Lord gives us'" (Numbers 10: 31-32). During the years of wandering through the desert, the tents of the Midianites stood next to the tents of the Hebrews. This West Semitic nomadic people of Amorite origin became the 'house of Jacob's' strategic ally. The Midianites were guides, advisors, and helpers in the vast and lifeless desert. Moses would have liked to see some of the tribes of Midian – the Kenites, for instance – join his new tribal alliance. Bonds of kinship with the Midianites reinforced the position of the tribe of Levi and helped Moses both during periods of conflict with the priestly clan of Aaron and during moments of disquiet among the Amorite tribes who had left Egypt together with the 'house of Jacob'. Two other southern tribes – those of Judah and Simeon – were also keen to ally themselves with their kin among the tribes of the desert. It was at this time that Judah and Simeon were joined by a large number of Midianite and Edomite nomadic clans who wanted to go with Moses to conquer southern Canaan. The alliances with the nomadic clans and tribes were reinforced by marriages their leaders entered into. Zimri, the leader of the tribe of Simeon, followed the example of Moses in taking one of the daughters of the ruler of Midian as his wife. The southern tribes of Levi, Simeon, and Judah saw alliance with the Midianites as a counterbalance to the growing influence of the Amorite tribes who had left Egypt at the same time as they did. The new allies strengthened Moses's position and weakened the influence of the priestly clan of Aaron, which was linked to the old tribal aristocracy of the 'house of Jacob'. This could not but arouse the dissatisfaction of the Aaronites. But while the 'house of Jacob' was in the desert, union with the Midianites remained a vital necessity and the Aaronites were compelled to put up with it.

Of a completely different character were relations with another desert people, the Amalekites. Amalek, the forefather of this nomadic people, was considered to be the grandson of Esau, Jacob's brother – which made him, from the point of view of blood kinship, closer to the Hebrews than the Midianites. However, Amalek's mother, Timnah, was merely the concubine of Esau's son Eliphaz, and for this reason Amalek's status in the tribal hierarchy of Edom was relatively low. Moreover,

Timnah came not from the Western Semites, but from the so-called 'Horites' – cave-dwellers who inhabited Mount Seir in southern Transjordan. The Horites were most likely descendants of the ancient pre-Semitic population of Canaan and, in spite of the closeness of their ethnonym to the Hurrians, are unlikely to have been related to them, since the latter arrived in Palestine no earlier than the 16th century B.C.E. It should be noted that the name 'Amalek' itself is clearly not of Semitic origin. This reinforces the supposition that the Amalekites were a mix of Amorites with the Neolithic population of southern Canaan. Their tribal lands were in the Negev Desert and northeastern Sinai. The Amalekites almost certainly regarded the 'house of Jacob' as their potential enemy, correctly assuming that following the return from Egypt, the 'house of Jacob' would try to occupy its old tribal lands in southern Canaan – lands which they (the Amalekites), of course, included in their own territories in central Negev. Furthermore, the Amalekites regarded many wells and oases in Sinai as their monopoly and were extremely suspicious of newcomers appearing in these places. Evidently, the leaders of the Amalekites had decided to attack first without waiting for the Hebrew tribes to arrive, so as to catch them unawares. Confrontation with the Amalekites constituted a great danger for the fugitives from Egypt, given that the latter were not ready for war. In the first half of the 12th century B.C.E., the Amalekites were at the zenith of their short-lived power and were a serious military force in southern Canaan and Sinai. It is no coincidence that the biblical text cites Balaam, a wizard and soothsayer of the time: "Amalek was first among the nations, but he will come to ruin at last" (Numbers 24:20). The first battle between the two peoples took place in Rephidim, in Sinai, but produced no winner. The Amalekites' attacks were successfully beaten off, but their main forces were able to escape in an eastward direction. The Bible talks only of "a weakening of the Amalekites through the force of the sword."

This attack was perceived by the Hebrews as a flouting of all standards of West Semitic tribal morality. Firstly, they were blood relations – and, unlike the Midianites, quite close ones at that: Amalek was a grand-nephew of forefather Jacob. It is hardly surprising that the southern Hebrew tribes for a long time did not allow themselves to fight with either Moab or Ammon, and still less with Edom, given that they were relatives of one another. They expected the Amalekites to behave likewise, but were disappointed. Secondly, Amalek's attack was completely unprovoked: the 'house of Jacob' had not violated the borders of the former's tribal territory. Memory of the treachery of the Amalekites in falling upon the 'house of Jacob' at an extremely difficult moment in its history persisted for a long time, which is why the Bible contains an unprecedentedly sharp condemnation of this: "Then the Lord said to Moses, 'Write this on a scroll as something to be remembered and make sure that Joshua hears it, because I will completely blot out the memory of Amalek from under heaven.' [...] He [Moses] said, 'For hands were lifted up to the throne of the Lord. The Lord will be at war against the Amalekites from generation to generation'" (Exodus 17: 14, 16). The second battle with the Amalekites mentioned by the Bible occurred on the border of the Negev. This time, the Amalekites were in alliance with the Canaanites and forced the 'house of Jacob' to retreat back into the Sinai Desert. Subsequently, relations between the two peoples were marked by especial hostility and enmity. For many centuries, the nomadic tribes of the Amalekites carried out attacks on the southern Hebrew tribes until at the end of the 8th century B.C.E., Hezekiah, King of Judah, crushed them completely. But the memory of their hatred for the 'house of Jacob' remained: the name of Amalek became a synonym for Israel's cursed enemy.

When he brought his people out of Egypt, Moses did not intend to spend many years in the desert. Moreover, his fellow-tribesmen would never have left the Nile Delta had they known how long they would have to wander through the waterless desert. Was it really fear of the inhabitants of Canaan, as the Bible explains in the incident with the spies, that forced Moses's people to retreat? And could a single unsuccessful battle with the Amalekites and Canaanites have led to rejection of the idea of conquering Canaan for almost 40 years? It is likely that both these biblical episodes are really merely the tip of the iceberg projecting above true events that are hidden in the depths of history. They cannot be understood independently of the development of the political situation in Egypt and Canaan.

The strengthening of Egypt and split of Moses's tribes

The civil war in Egypt, which allowed Moses to bring the Hebrew tribes out of the Nile Delta, finished a lot earlier than might have been expected. In only the second year of his rule, Pharaoh Setnakht was able to deal with his opponents and strengthen his position on the throne. And although he ruled for only one year after this, he was replaced by a worthy successor, his son, Ramesses III, who was to become Egypt's last great pharaoh. Ramesses III quickly established order in the country and, even more importantly, prepared it for the serious military trials approaching from the west and north. In the fifth year of his reign, a mutiny of Libyan tribes flared up in the western part of the Nile Delta. The Libyans supposed that after several years of civil war and troubles Egypt would be rather different from the country they had known under Ramesses II and Merneptah. But, as it turned out, they were mistaken. Ramesses III delivered a crushing defeat to those who tried to put him to the test. However, this was only his first military examination. His main test came in the eighth year of his reign, when the Sea Peoples – a considerably more serious opponent than the Libyans – attacked Egypt from the north. The Sea Peoples consisted of various peoples of Indo-European origin whom many years of drought and famine had forced to look for a new motherland. In about 1200 B.C.E., they devastated the powerful Hittite Empire and set fire to the largest cities of northern Syria, including Alalakh and Ugarit. Their next goal was to seize the Nile Delta and Canaan. As far as we can tell, Ramesses III was very well informed about the danger that threatened Egypt. He sent part of his army in good time to Gaza in the southwest of Canaan to reinforce the Egyptian garrison there and met the naval attack against the Nile Delta in full strength. His crushing of the previously unconquerable foreigners on sea and land was his greatest success and placed him on equal footing with great pharaohs such as Ramesses II and Thutmose III.

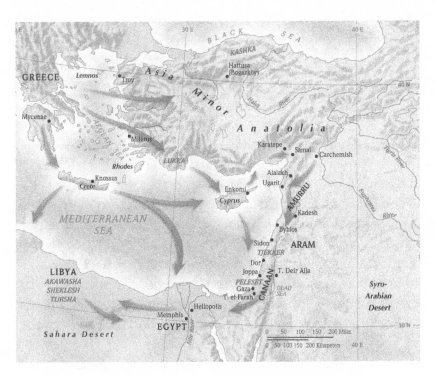

Invasion of the Sea Peoples. Beginning 12th century B.C.E.

By the same token, Egypt demonstrated its ability not only to defend itself, but also to hold onto southern Canaan, which was under its rule. In the 11ᵗʰ year of his reign, Ramesses III once more shattered the Libyans when they attempted to challenge Egypt.

The naval battle between Egyptians and Sea Peoples.
Relief from the Medinet Habu.

Naturally, all these dramatic events did not escape the attention of Moses and the leaders of the 'house of Jacob'. They understood well that, while Egyptian power was strengthening, to conquer Canaan would be a difficult task and that they would meet opposition not only from local peoples, but also from the Egyptian army, which had shown itself to be no less effective than before. In short, for as long as Egypt was ruled by a pharaoh such as Ramesses III, there was no hope of success. What thought could there be of an attack on southern Canaan if Egypt was moving reinforcements to Gaza and the Sea Peoples were advancing to Palestine like a roller, destroying whatever cities in Syria and on the Lebanese coast they met on their way? Clearly, this bad news was discussed by the leaders and elders of the houses of Jacob and Joseph. Judging by the biblical texts, the result was serious disagreement between the leaders of the Hebrew tribes, the majority of whom considered the conquest of Canaan under such conditions unthinkable and blamed Moses and Aaron for coming up with an idea – the exodus from Egypt and return to Canaan – that had been doomed to failure from the very start. "All the Israelites grumbled against Moses and Aaron, and the whole assembly said to them, 'If only we had died in Egypt! Or in this desert! Why is the Lord bringing us to this land only to let us fall by the sword? Our wives and children will be taken as plunder. Wouldn't it be better for us to go back to Egypt?' And they said to each other, 'We should choose a leader and go back to Egypt'" (Numbers 14: 2-4). For Moses and Aaron, the situation must have been critical; they were forced to escape the wrath of the people in the Tent of Meeting, by the Ark of the Covenant (the Tabernacle), a sacred religious object: "But the whole assembly talked about stoning them. Then the glory of the Lord appeared at the Tent of Meeting to all the Israelites" (Numbers: 14:10). Salvation came in the form of support from their own southern tribes and their allies, the Midianites. Support for Moses and Aaron also came from the head of the 'house of Joseph', Joshua, son of Nun, who was also a member of the tribal council. For the few northern Hebrew tribes who were in central Canaan at the time, the only possibility of seizing the entire country was to be in alliance with the 'house of Jacob'. They had no intention of abandoning this hope and decided merely to postpone its fulfillment to a more fitting time. Some of the Hebrew tribes tried to break through into central Canaan on their own, but without support from the others suffered the defeat described in the Bible. 'The house of Jacob' returned to the desert to wait for better times and its ally, the 'house of Joseph', remained in its positions in central Canaan.

Another serious trial for the authority of Moses and Aaron and their union was the mutiny raised by Korah from the tribe

of Levi, supported by Dathan, Abiram, and On, leaders of the
tribe of Reuben. Here, everything came together – terrible
fatigue due to living in the unfamiliar desert conditions; disappointment with Moses's unfulfilled promises (to lead his people
into Canaan); and, finally, dissatisfaction with the fact that the
tribal hierarchy had been violated and junior partners in the
alliance were giving orders to their seniors. To cap it all, a dangerous plague – evidently, an epidemic of some kind of serious
disease – was raging in the camp of the Hebrew tribes. Initially,
the mutiny of Korah, one of the leaders of the tribe of Levi and
a relative of Moses, was directed against the excessive power
wielded by Aaron and the primary role played by the latter's
kin in performing religious services. The Levites felt hard done
by and insufficiently involved in the celebration of the tribes'
shared religion. Dissatisfaction with the Aaronites probably
affected not only the top people in the tribe of Levi, but also the
leaders and elders of other tribes and clans. Moses's attempt to
calm them and protect Aaron merely fueled the fire: "and [they]
rose up against Moses. With them were 250 Israelite men, well-
known community leaders who had been appointed members of
the council. They came as a group to oppose Moses and Aaron
and said to them, 'You have gone too far! The whole community
is holy, every one of them, and the Lord is with them. Why then
do you set yourselves above the Lord's assembly?'" (Numbers
16: 2-3). Seeing that the mutiny was growing, Moses tried to use
force and "summoned Dathan and Abiram, the sons of Eliab",
who, together with other members of the 'house of Jacob', were
obliged to give support to their leader. However, Dathan and
Abiram openly joined the mutineers. "But they said, 'We will not
come! Isn't it enough that you have brought us up out of a land
flowing with milk and honey to kill us in the desert? And now
you also want to lord it over us? Moreover, you haven't brought
us into a land flowing with milk and honey or given us an inheritance of fields and vineyards. Will you gouge out the eyes of

these men? No, we will not come!"' (Numbers 16: 12-14). At the most difficult moment for Moses and Aaron, help probably came from the tribe of Judah, which was always ready to support the Aaronites, and likewise from the Midianites, Moses's allies. The principal mutineers were punished with a terrible death: they were chased into the notorious quicksand of Sinai, where "the earth opened its mouth and swallowed them." This episode is a further reminder of the tribe of Reuben's claim to primacy in the 'house of Jacob' and of the contrived nature of the pretext that had deprived it of primacy. Reuben's 'offence' was 'dug up' by the Aaronites from the epic lore of the southern tribes and inserted into the biblical text at a later date to justify the primacy of the tribe of Judah. As time went on, the most junior partners of the southern tribal alliance in the 'house of Jacob', Judah and Levi, began dominating the elder ones, Reuben and Simeon, and this led to conflicts between them – at least, initially. Evidently, Moses's inability to quickly carry out his promises and the excessive influence of the Aaronites were responsible for their partners in the alliance deciding to redistribute the balance of power between the tribes. This was the background to Korah's mutiny. At the same time, the mutiny was further proof of how deep and long-lasting the rivalry was between the Aaronites and Levites, a sign of the fact that originally they had belonged not only to different families and kin, but to different tribes as well. The mutiny was so serious that the biblical text reproaches Aaron and his sons for excluding "their brothers, the Levites," from performing religious services.

The unexpected strengthening of Egypt's military might during the rule of Ramesses III caused considerable complications for Moses's plans. The conquest of southern Canaan was now an impossible feat given that the Egyptians viewed these lands as their eastern border. A degree of freedom of action remained in central and northern Canaan, where the 'house of Joseph' was. But to break through the lands of Egypt's vassals without triggering the intervention of the army of Ramesses III did not seem possible. Part of the 'house of Jacob' – the tribes of Judah and Simeon, – having drawn closer to their Midianite and Edomite allies, preferred to wait in the oases of the desert until the Egyptians left southern Canaan. However, the majority of the tribes were impatient to head north to unite with the 'house of Joseph' and together win back the lands that had once been their tribal territory. Desiring to preserve unity, Moses tried to reconcile the interests of the two groups and to hold on for as long as possible on the border with southern Canaan, but in vain. The mutiny by Korah had shown that people no longer wanted or were no longer able to wander in the desert and that delay of any kind could lead to an uprising among the tribes and to death at their hands. It became inevitable that the 'house of Jacob' would split up. This happened not just because most of the tribes that had accompanied the 'house of Jacob' in the exodus from Egypt belonged to the northern, Israelite, tribes and were closer to the 'house of Joseph'. This circumstance did not, for instance, prevent the southern tribe of Reuben and part of the Levites subsequently joining the Northerners. The main reason for the split was, in fact, that the southern tribes of Judah and Simeon were under the influence of their more numerous allies, the Midianites and Edomites. The kinship and alliance between Moses and the Midianites, and the help given by the latter in the waterless wilderness, had negative as well as positive consequences. The new allies began to prevail numerically over the old members of the tribe of Judah, and it is probable that the same threat faced the tribe of Simeon. Eventually, leadership of the tribe of Judah passed from the old tribal aristocracy into the hands of desert chieftains who had no part in the exodus from Egypt. Interestingly, during the departure from Egypt and the first months of stay in the desert, the Bible mentions Nahshon, son of Aminadav, as leader of the tribe of Judah. Nahshon was brother-in-law of the high priest Aaron. However, beginning with the episode relating to the spies sent into Canaan, Caleb, son of Jephuneh and head of the Kenazzites (Edomites), is constantly named as the new leader of the tribe of Judah. And yet the episode with the spies occurred at the very beginning of the forty-year stay in the desert. But that is not all. While the Book of Exodus lists in detail the genealogy of the southern tribes of Reuben, Simeon, and Levi - tribes that had been in Egypt, - it refrains from doing the same in relation to the fourth southern tribe, that of Judah. And this is no coincidence, because the new nomadic clans and their leaders who displaced the old tribal aristocracy had never been in Egypt. Caleb and the other desert leaders imposed their own decision on the two southern tribes of Judah and Simeon – to remain in the desert they knew so well until the Egyptians left southern Canaan. This turn of events was especially unpopular with the priestly clan of the Aaronites: the transfer of power to the desert leaders deprived them of their traditional support from the old tribal aristocracy among the tribes of Judah and Simeon. The situation changed when, after the death of the extremely aged Aaron, the position of high priest was occupied by his energetic and decisive son Eleazar. The new high priest began to openly resist any form of closer relations with the Midianites, seeing any convergence as a threat both to the privileged position of his own family and to the 'house of Jacob'. Taking advantage of the fact that Moses had considerably aged and weakened, he began imposing on him his own strategy aimed at breaking off the alliance with the Midianites. In order to provoke a conflict with the latter and put Moses in an impossible position, Phinehas, son of Eleazar, killed the leader of the tribe of Simeon and his Midianite wife. It was probably at this moment that the Aaronites seized power from the dying Moses. Eleazar, under the cover of Moses's name, embarked on a bitter war against one of the groups of Midianite tribes, showing no mercy to either its women or children. Much later, the keepers of the biblical tradition from this family tried to justify the split with the Midianites, arguing that the latter had tempted the Israelites with the pagan cult of Baal of Peor, as a result of which God had sent a pernicious plague to punish His people. From this moment onwards, relations between the Hebrews and the Midianites soured, but the memory of their touching friendship during the time of Moses remained forever.

The split with the Midianites accelerated the break-up of the 'house of Jacob' too. The southern tribes of Judah and Simeon, who had intermarried with the numerous Midianite and Edomite clans, refused to join the 'house of Joseph' in order to conquer central and northern Canaan. Under the influence of their new relatives and allies, they preferred to stay within the borders of southern Canaan, in the oases that they knew so well, where they could wait for the Egyptians to leave. They were joined by those Levites and Aaronites who had led the worship of Yahweh in those tribes. The remaining tribes, including the southern one of Reuben and most of the Levites, left together with Moses and Eleazar to seize central and northern Canaan. In this way, the original 'house of Jacob', which had consisted of the four southern tribes, was split: the tribes of Judah and Simeon remained for forty more years in the desert while the tribe of Reuben and the majority of the Levites joined the Northerners and the 'house of Joseph'. However, the split affected not just the 'house of Jacob', but the Levites and Aaronites too. They divided between the Northerners and Southerners, but very unevenly: most of Levites joined, together with Moses, the Israelite tribal confederation, while the majority of Aaronites stayed with the Judahites and their new allies in southern Canaan. Despite the fact that high priest Eliazar and his family went with Moses and the Levites to the north, most of the Aaronites preferred to remain with the Judahites, with whom they were connected closely.

Meanwhile, the strengthening of Egypt turned out to be short-lived, lasting only as long as Ramesses III himself, who ruled for 31 years. He was replaced by his son, Ramesses IV, who in spite of desperate prayers to the gods to extend his life, ruled for a mere six years. In his lifetime, the military might of the Egyptians weakened considerably and the 20th Dynasty began to wane. Ramesses IV did not undertake any military campaigns, but continued to use the quarries on Sinai and the copper mines in Timnah. His successor, Ramesses V, ruled for an even shorter length of time – four years – and by the end of his reign, Egypt had lost all its possessions in Asia, including southern Canaan. Moreover, at this time the country experienced serious internal political difficulties and perhaps even a civil war. When the next Ramesses, the sixth, took over, Egypt's greatness and might vanished forever and the country's eastern border moved to the eastern edge of the Nile Delta. Even the quarries on Sinai were abandoned. In this way, forty years after the 'house of Jacob' left the Nile Delta, Egypt lost entirely and for far into the future all control over Canaan. And it was at this point that the painful wanderings of the two southern Hebrew tribes in the desert likewise came to an end. Following the example of the northern Israelite tribes but only forty years later, they began conquering southern Canaan.

CHAPTER SEVEN

The Peoples of pre-Israelite Canaan

ON THE EVE OF its conquest by the Hebrew tribes, Canaan was ethnically a hotchpotch. All the peoples of this country can be divided into four main categories: 1) Western Semites; 2) the primordial pre-Semitic population of Canaan; 3) peoples of an Indo-European origin; and, finally, 4) Hurrians. Of the biblical sources, the Book of Genesis provides the most complete list of the peoples of Canaan. It names ten of them: "the Kenites, Kenazzites, Kadmonites, Hittites, Perizzites, Rephaites, Amorites, Canaanites, Girgashites and Jebusites" (Genesis 15: 19-21). Later books of the Bible – Deuteronomy, for instance – mention only seven peoples: "the Hittites, Girgashites, Amorites, Canaanites, Perizzites, Hivites and Jebusites" (Deuteronomy 7:1). And, finally, the biblical texts make separate mention of the Philistines and Maachatites.

The West Semitic population

The absolute majority of people living in Canaan were Western Semites. All were very close to one another and spoke in different dialects of one and the same language. The first of these groups to arrive in Palestine, in the second half of the 4th millennium B.C.E., was the Canaanites; for this reason they occupied the districts that were most convenient and favorable for agriculture – the strip along the Mediterranean shore, the valley of the Jordan River, the fertile Jezreel Valley, and Shephelah, the foothills in the southwest of the country. It was the Canaanites who gave their name to this country – Canaan. However, they occupied not just Palestine, but the entire coast of Lebanon and Syria. The people whom the Greeks later called Phoenicians also considered themselves to be Canaanites. The Bible gives the Canaanites another name too, calling them Sidonians after Sidon, a port in Canaan (today called Saida). This was not just a settled farming people; it was also the most developed ethnos in Palestine in terms of social, economic, and cultural activity.

The second, even larger, part of West Semitic peoples consisted of the Amorites. Unlike the Canaanites, they divided into nomadic and settled groups. The majority of the Amorite nomads were driven by prolonged droughts to move gradually into the Nile Delta, into Egypt. The sedentarized Amorites established themselves in the interior and mountain districts of Palestine and in northern Transjordan. It was to these settled Amorite peoples that the 'Amorites, Perizzites, Hivites, and Jebusites' mentioned in the Bible belonged. Evidently, these Amorite peoples appeared in Canaan at the same time as the northern Hebrew tribes – at any rate, before the arrival of Abraham and his tribal alliance. The Amorites lived in northern and central Transjordan, where the kingdoms of Sihon and Og were situated, and also in certain districts of inner Palestine. The Perizzites inhabited part of southwestern and central Canaan, and the Jebusites held Jerusalem, or Jebus, as it was then called. The Hivites lived both in the center of the country, in Shechem, and in more southern parts, in Gibeon, Kephirah, Beeroth, and Kiriath Jearim. There were also nomadic and semi-nomadic Amorite peoples who had failed to settle by the 12th century B.C.E. These included relatives of the 'house of Jacob' – the Moabites, Ammonites, and Edomites, who were led into Canaan by the biblical patriarch Abraham. The first two groups of tribes settled in the central part of Transjordan, while the Edomites, who were the people closest to the 'house of Jacob', inhabited the region of Mount Seir in southern Canaan. In central Negev, there were camps used by another Amorite people, the Amalekites, with whom the Hebrews had extremely hostile relations. The Bible also mentions the Kenazzites as a people living in Canaan. The Kenazzites were an Edomite nomadic tribe that had joined the tribe of Judah before the conquest of Canaan. It cannot be ruled out that it was they who were the tribe of Shasu which, according to the ancient Egyptian sources, worshipped Yahweh. According to the Bible, as reward for loyalty to the common cause, their leader Caleb, son of Jephuneh, was distinguished first by Moses and then by Joshua, son of Nun, who gave him Hebron, the best part of southeastern Palestine. In addition to peoples who were settled or led a nomadic life in Canaan on a permanent basis, there were also tribes of Amorite nomads who occasionally ventured into this country from Sinai, northwest Arabia, and the Syrian Desert. Such were the Midianites and the Ishmaelites – peoples of the desert. Another people that periodically visited Canaan was the Kenites – those same Midianite tribes with whom Moses had intermarried when he was hiding from the Egyptians. Certain scholars have, on the basis of the Kenites' name, thought them to be clans of nomadic blacksmiths.

Among the West Semitic peoples living in Canaan there were also Habiru – Amorite tribes who had returned from Egypt following the defeat of the Hyksos pharaohs. During the centuries that they had lived in the Nile Delta, their tribal lands in Canaan had been occupied by other peoples, meaning that these fugitives from Egypt found themselves without a home. Many Habiru in Canaan belonged to several northern, Hebrew, tribes who had returned to Palestine in the 15th century B.C.E. However, for as long as Egypt ruled Canaan, there could be no thought of regaining this lost land; early Israelites were forced to make themselves comfortable in the inconvenient and little used lands of central and northern Palestine.

Judging by the biblical texts, the Hebrews never regarded themselves as Amorites. They looked upon the latter sometimes as their allies – for instance, during the time of Abraham – and sometimes, as during the conquest of Canaan, as their enemies. They identified themselves using the name 'Ivri / Ibri', which initially sounded like 'Habiru' or 'Apiru'. Ethnically, however, all Habiru, including the Hebrews, belonged to the West Semitic tribes of Amorite origin. We should not be put off by the fact that the Israelites, being Amorites by origin, denied their connection with this ethnos and never used this name to identify themselves. This kind of thing happens often. Many peoples reject the ethnonym of the largest and most well-known tribes with which they have at some time been closely linked and prefer to use other names to identify themselves. However, this should not stand in the way of an understanding of the blood ties between such ethnic groups. The Book of Genesis gives a list of descendants of Canaan, the legendary forefather of the Canaanite peoples. Among them are the Amorites, the Jebusites, and the Hivites – i.e. peoples of Amorite origin. In this way, the Hebrew epic tradition preserves memories of the blood ties between the Canaanites and the Amorites; moreover, the Amorites are mentioned as descendants of the Canaanites. This ancient narrative reflects the true picture: the Canaanites and the Amorites were initially one ethnos when they lived in their ancestral motherland in northwest Mesopotamia. Those who subsequently came to be called Canaanites were the first to leave; they went in a southwesterly direction – into Syria, Lebanon, and Palestine. Approximately 1000 years later, another part of the same ethnos, which was given the ethnonym 'Amorites', followed along the same path. It is possible that the ethnonym 'Amorites' came mainly to signify the settled part of this ethnos, while the name 'Habiru' initially applied only to nomadic Amorites. And although the Habiru did not consider themselves to be Amorites, they were undoubtedly an integral part of that people. Here we could adduce an analogy with the fellahin (peasants) and Bedouin (nomads) in Arabic countries. Among the Bedouin, you still find the view that only the fellahin and not they – the Bedouin – are Arabs. It is likely that something similar existed among the settled Amorites and the semi-nomadic Habiru.

In spite of the periodic conflicts and collisions between the various Canaanite and Amorite peoples in Palestine, the only difference between them was in their level of social and economic development and lifestyle. Ethnically and linguistically, they were almost identical. Moreover, in most cases the Amorites were very quick to assimilate the Canaanite culture and religious rites.

In the 12th century B.C.E., groups belonging to one more West Semitic people – the Arameans – began penetrating into northeast Canaan. Among them were the Girgashites and Maachatites mentioned in the Bible, who established themselves in the north of Gilead and on the Golan Heights. However, at the time of the conquest of Canaan by the Hebrew tribes, the Aramean population in Canaan was still of inconsiderable size.

The primordial pre-Semitic peoples

Probably, the most numerous people after the Western Semites were the indigenous inhabitants of Canaan, who had lived there from at least Neolithic times. Unfortunately, we know nothing of either their ethnic origins or their language. The Old Testament is the only literary source that mentions them. According to the biblical description, these ancient inhabitants of Canaan were in no way related to the Semites. They were distinguished by being far taller than the average for Semite peoples. It was their great height that made the strongest impression on the 'spies' of the 'house of Jacob' sent by Moses to 'spy out' the promised land. The latter reported that "We can't attack those people; they are stronger than we are [...] All the people we saw there are of great size. We saw the Nephilim there (the descendants of Anak come from the Nephilim). We seemed like grasshoppers in our own eyes, and we looked the same to them" (Numbers 13: 32-34). This ancient people lived in all parts of Palestine and Transjordan. The Semites who came to Canaan had different names for their tall neighbors. The Israelites called them 'Anaks' and 'Rephaim'; the Moabites, 'Eimim'; and the Ammonites, 'Zamzumim'. In southwest Palestine, in the region of Gaza, they were known as 'Avim'. Of these many names, only one – Rephaim (Rephaites) – was in any way connected with how this people called itself; they believed their mythical forefather to be Rapha. According to the books of Judges and Joshua, the entire district of modern Hebron in the south of Palestine once belonged to the leaders of the gigantic Rephaim – Sheshai, Ahiman, and Talmai, sons of the legendary Anak; and the city of Hebron itself was founded by the same people and was previously called after the 'greatest of the Anaks', Kiriath-Arba (Judges 1:10; Joshua 14:15, 15: 13-14). The same people produced the king of the Bashan region of Transjordan, Og. Another descendant of this people was the giant Goliath, who was chosen by the Philistines to fight David in single combat. However, this ancient autochthonous people very soon dissolved among the West Semitic peoples who arrived in Canaan. By the time the Israelites conquered Canaan, the Neolithic giants had become Semites in terms of language and culture. This fact confused the authors of the biblical books, which accounts for why in some cases they called this people by their old name of 'Rephaim' while in others they called them 'Amorites' or 'Canaanites'. The best example of this is the region of Hebron, whose population is described in turns as Rephaim, Amorites, and Hittites. The last mentions of the Rephaim are connected with the Philistines. In southwest Canaan, which was later known as Philistia, there lived a large number of Rephaim who had, even before the arrival of the Sea Peoples, assimilated the language and culture of the Canaanites. The Bible specifically emphasizes that the Philistines did not touch the Rephaim and, judging by much later reports, actively exploited their outstanding physical qualities in their own army. Many of the best warriors in the Philistine army were of Rephaim origin. The Book of Kings mentions among them not only the celebrated Goliath from the city of Gath, but also the then famous warriors Yishbi and Sapha, who were also 'descendants of Rapha', this people's legendary forefather. It is difficult to say why these tall and physically strong people retreated so quickly before the Semite newcomers, but it is likely that they were considerably inferior in terms of social organization; they were also less numerous. By the time the Hebrew tribes returned from Egypt, the larger part of this autochthonous people had merged with the Western Semites who were all around them. The remnants of the Rephaim mixed with the Israelites so quickly that in the biblical Hebrew their name became a synonym for what was long past. The Book of Joshua noted: "No Anakites were left in Israelite territory; only in Gaza, Gath and Ashdod did any survive" (11:22). Today the only reminder of this legendary people is the unusually tall Jews who have inherited their genes.

When describing the war of the southern Canaanite kings against the Amorite rulers of Syria, the Book of Genesis provides an interesting ethnographic account of Canaan in the 20th-19th centuries B.C.E. It turns out that in eastern Canaan, in Transjordan, before the Ammonites and Moabites arrived there, the dominant presence consisted of non-Semitic peoples. These included the tall Rephaim, the Zamzumim, the Eimim and, in the very south, the Horites, who were subsequently assimilated by the Edomites. However, to the west and the south of the Jordan River, Amorite peoples were the more numerous. The Amorites controlled the Ein-Gedi oasis on the west bank of what is now the Dead Sea. Possibly, Abraham's Amorite allies – Aner, Eshkol, and Mamre – were the very same Hittites that the Bible several times mentioned when giving an account of the times of the patriarchs. The same episode, which deals with the invasion of outsiders from Syria, talks of the Amalekites as if they were the injured party, although Amalek, their forefather and a great-grandson of Abraham, should have appeared much later (Genesis 14: 1-7). Either this is an historical anachronism deriving from the fact that the events of this war were recorded only 1000 years later, or it is evidence that initially the Amalekites had no relation to Abraham's tribal group. If the latter is true, then it may explain the extreme hostility between the descendants of Jacob and Amalek.

Indo-Europeans

The history of the Indo-European peoples in Canaan is no less intriguing. The Bible makes frequent mention of the Hittites – initially as neighbors of the patriarch Abraham, then as a people who lived in Canaan immediately before it was conquered. But in the 20th-19th centuries B.C.E., when Abraham was a nomad in southern Canaan, there could not have been any Indo-European Hittites living there – given that they had not yet left the borders of far-away Anatolia. On the other hand, present there were the Amorite or Canaanite 'Hittites' who, according to the biblical narrative, were descended from the mythical Canaan. The Indo-European Hittites came to Canaan much later, after the collapse of the Hittite Empire around 1200 B.C.E. The Hittites served the local rulers as mercenary colonists, and most were not so much Hittites as Luwians – Indo-Europeans from north Syria. The biblical writers regrettably made no distinction between the West Semitic Hittites of the age of Abraham and the Indo-European Hittites who were their own contemporaries, so subsequently the different ethnic groups began to be perceived as one and the same people.

An incomparably more important role in the life of Canaan belonged to another people of Indo-European origin – the Philistines. The Philistines appeared in the southwest of Canaan at the beginning of the 12th century B.C.E., i.e. shortly before the second wave of Hebrew tribes returned from Egypt. Moreover, to begin with, the Philistines came as raiders and enemies of Egypt and then as the latter's mercenaries and colonists, having been given the region of Gaza as a place in which to settle. The Philistines belonged to the so-called 'Sea Peoples' – a group of peoples of Indo-European origin who came from over the sea, from the northwest. We do not know the reasons why there was a mass migration of various Indo-European tribes from north to south at the end of the 13th century B.C.E., but we may conjecture that this was a result of natural phenomena that brought droughts and famine to the places where they had lived up to this point. It cannot be ruled out that they were forced to move south by other Indo-European peoples coming from the north. And it is notable that Asia Minor at this time suffered a drought so severe and prolonged that the Hittite rulers were forced to ask Egypt to send them as much grain as possible. The few literary monuments that were found on the site of the Philistine cities – for instance, inscriptions on the stamps from Ashdod – belong to the so-called Minoan Linear A script. Unfortunately, this ancient system of writing, which made its first appearance on Crete, has yet to be deciphered. However, limited information on the Philistines may be gleaned from objects that are products of their material culture – their ceramic ware, for instance, which bears the distinctive marks of the Mycenaean style. This points to the Philistines' Aegean and, moreover, Achaean, origin. The Bible gives different names for the country from which the people came. In one case, it calls it Cyprus; in another, Crete. However, it is likely that Cyprus or Crete was only an intermediate stopping place for the Philistines' ancestors. Their most probable birthplace was Mycenae, in the south of Greece, the native city of legendary King Agamemnon. In the second half of the 13ᵗʰ century B.C.E., Doric tribes invaded the Peloponnese from the north. During the course of the next century, they destroyed not just Mycenae, but also the entire Achaean civilization as well. Part of the population was enslaved; the remainder emigrated to islands in the Aegean Sea, Crete, and Cyprus. In their search for a new motherland, the Achaean Greeks – and, together with them, other displaced tribes, possibly from Asia Minor – chose the Nile Delta and Canaan, which was then ruled by Egypt. Bas reliefs and frescoes from the temple of Ramesses III at Medinet Habu on the site of ancient Egyptian Thebes depict warriors from these peoples together with carts in which their families are sitting. What we see here is not plundering raids but a forced migration of entire peoples. However, in the decisive battle with the army of Ramesses III, the coalition of Sea Peoples was defeated and the Philistines came to the southwest of Canaan not as conquerors but as mercenary colonists in the service of the Pharaoh. But several years later, following the death of Ramesses III, Egypt's rule in southern Canaan came to an end and the Philistines became masters of this country's southern shore. Until the Philistines arrived, the local population in these parts consisted of Canaanites and, intermarried with the latter, Avim (Rephaites), descendants of the ancient inhabitants of Canaan. The newcomers were numerically inferior, but superior in terms of military organization and quality of weaponry. It was the Philistines who brought the Iron Age to Canaan. They knew the secret of how to produce iron and used this metal to make weaponry. They seized the Canaanite cities and created their own communities there under the command of their own leaders, called 'seranim' ('tyrants'). The Philistines' country was known as the Pentapolis, i.e. the union of the five cities of Gaza, Ashkelon, Ashdod, Ekron, and Gath. The Philistines quickly assimilated with the West Semitic people they had conquered. They began using the Canaanite language and their gods now had Semitic names. It is significant that thoroughly Mycenean pottery is to be found only in Ashdod and Ekron – the Philistines' original settlements. Subsequently, their pottery was made in a mixed style, with the adoption of Canaanite and Egyptian motifs. It cannot be ruled out that the people who came from Mycenae constituted only a part of the Philistines, even if the dominant one. Possibly, among them were representatives of other tribes from the Aegean and Asia Minor. In any case, the Philistines were not the only Sea People to settle in Canaan. Another Indo-European people of Aegean provenance, the Tjeker, settled on the northern coast of Palestine, in the region of the city of Dor. And finally a third Sea People, the Sherden, managed to find itself a home in the northern valleys of Canaan. Historians have at their disposal an important ancient Egyptian document dating to approximately 1100 B.C.E., 'The Journey of Wen-Amon', which deals with the journey of an Egyptian dignitary through Canaan to Byblos to buy cedar wood. For a time, Wen-Amon stayed in Dor and was witness to the fact that the city belonged to one of the Sea Peoples, the Tjeker. From his tale, it follows that the rulers of other cities on the coast of Canaan were also from Indo-European peoples from the Aegean or Asia Minor who, together with Western Semites (the Phoenicians), monopolized maritime trade in the eastern part of the Mediterranean. It has to be supposed that Wen-Amon's information on the Sea People who settled in northern Canaan was relatively reliable. The Egyptians were by this time familiar with people from these tribes, given that many of the latter had served as mercenaries in the Egyptian army from the 14th century B.C.E. The Amarna archive contains letters mentioning the Sherden. The latter served the Egyptian Pharaoh and, under Ramesses II, took part in the battle against the Hittites at Kadesh. Later, during the rule of Pharaoh Merneptah, some of the Sea Peoples – the Sherden, Shekelesh, Lukka, Tursha, and Avakasha – joined the Libyans to initiate a series of attacks on Egypt. Yet the Egyptians learned most about the Sea Peoples during the time of Ramesses III, when these peoples began to migrate en masse to the eastern Mediterranean, into Asia Minor, Syria, Canaan, and the Nile Delta. If the Lebanese and Syrian coast suffered badly from the attacks of the Sea Peoples and if some of these peoples settled in the southwest of Canaan, then there is nothing surprising in their being present in north Canaan also. It cannot be ruled out that the name 'Hittites' actually indicated large numbers of immigrants from the Sea Peoples immediately prior to the conquest of Canaan.

Hurrians

Yet another ethnic group in pre-Israelite Palestine was the Hurrians – a people who were unrelated to the Semites, the Indo-Europeans, or the primordial inhabitants of Canaan. Incontrovertible evidence of their presence in the country is provided by letters in the Amarna archive mentioning rulers of Canaan with names that are of clearly Hurrian provenance. Furthermore, a large number of stamps of the kind that are characteristic of the Hurrians of Mitanni, but which were made after the latter state's destruction, have been found in Palestine. It is highly likely that the Hurrians first came to Canaan in the second half of the 16th and at the beginning of the 15th centuries B.C.E., during a period when the state of Mitanni was expanding more rapidly than at any other time on the one hand, and there was a vacuum of power in

Canaan on the other. This was a time when the Hyksos, the main power in Canaan, were trying unsuccessfully to fend off attacks by the pharaohs of Thebes and the Egyptians were still too weak to subjugate neighboring Palestine. It was at this moment that both the Indo-Aryan (Maryannu) and Hurrian groups entered Canaan from Mitanni, seizing power in a number of Canaanite cities. In the Bible we sometimes find names – for instance, the Jebusite Aravenna (Arauna) – that indicate an Indo-Aryan or Hurrian origin for their bearers. But both these ethnic groups were small in number, since we have no evidence of the presence of any large Hurrian or Indo-Aryan population in Canaan. Judging by the letters from the Amarna archive, both the former and the latter formed the ruling elite in certain Canaanite city states – which tells us that they entered Canaan by no means peacefully, but as the result of conquering certain of its cities. Later, in the 14th and 13th centuries B.C.E., the defeats suffered by Mitanni in the war with the Hittites and then with the Assyrians led to the appearance in Canaan of a new wave of Hurrians – this time, not conquerors but fugitives. Some scholars have linked the Hurrians with the biblical Horites, based on the evident closeness of their ethnonyms. However, they are unable to propose a satisfactory explanation for how the Hurrians, who in the 20th to 18th centuries B.C.E. lived in northern Mesopotamia with its plentiful natural resources and water, came to be found in the drought-ridden region of Seir, 1000 miles from the place of habitation of their own people. Moreover, unlike the biblical Horites, who were in the position of subordinates in the semi-desert of Edom, the historical Hurrians, who made their appearance in Canaan much later, belonged to the ruling class – and were, moreover, rulers not among the nomads on the outskirts of this country, but in the prosperous cities. The Bible tells us that Esau, the forefather of the Edomites, drove the Horites ('the cave dwellers') out from the region around Mount

Seir and settled there himself in their place. But Esau lived in the 18th-17th centuries B.C.E. Moreover, it follows from the biblical text that the Horites lived in Seir long before the arrival of Esau – which rules out any link between them and the Hurrians, who at the time were living in northeastern Mesopotamia. It is likely that the Horites were part of the primordial population of Canaan, but their ethnic origins are unknown – just as it is unclear whether they were in any way related to the Rephaim. Evidently, the Horites assimilated with the descendants of Esau and became an integral part of Edom. At least, the genealogy of the Amalekites given in the Book of Genesis is clear confirmation of the Horites mixing with the Edomites. Subsequently, the Bible mentions the Horites again, telling us that the tribe of Simeon drove them out from the area of southern Palestine where they had settled after the conquest of Canaan. Since this implies the second half of the 12th century B.C.E., authentic Hurrians could also here have gone by the name of Horites. Of course, for the biblical authors who were writing down the texts several centuries after the event, the Horites, of the age of Esau, and the Hurrians, of the time of the conquest of Canaan, had turned into one and the same people – all the more so since by that time both peoples had ceased to exist, having merged with the Western Semites who surrounded them. It is likely that this was a repeat of the confusion that had happened with the Indo-European and West Semitic Hittites.

It is possible that the Hurrians were also called Hittites in the Bible. In general, the ethnonym 'Hittites', which is many times mentioned in the biblical texts, is evidently a collective name which covers not so much the Hittites themselves as various Indo-European and Hurrian groups among the population in Canaan. An interesting fact is that in spite of the frequent mentions of Hittites, no book in the Bible tells us of a Hittite ruler or city in Canaan. At the same time, we possess a large number of mentions of Amorite, Canaanite, Hivite, and Jebusite cities and rulers. There is even mention of a Rephaite ruler Og, but not a single Hittite. This is a sign that the Hittite and Hurrian presence in Canaan was well-dispersed; it consisted of colonists, mercenaries, merchants, and fugitives who were scattered all over Palestine and went by the general name of 'Hittites'. There is nothing surprising in the fact that, unlike the majority of local peoples who lived in dense groups, the Indo-European and Hurrian elements very quickly assimilated with the Western Semites who formed the majority of the country's population.

CHAPTER EIGHT

The re-conquest of Canaan

Moses's people join the Israelite tribal league

The second wave of Hebrew tribes, which came out of Egypt under the leadership of Moses, tried to join up with several Israelite tribes that had been in central Canaan since the middle of the 15th century B.C.E. Both tribal groups made an effort to merge with one another; however, they were separated by territories belonging to the Canaanite and Amorite city states, which for their part tried to impede the unification of their potential opponents. We do not know what actions were taken by the Israelite tribes, but the Bible tells us the approximate route taken by their brothers, who left Egypt in the beginning of the 12th century B.C.E. Initially, they tried to break through into central Canaan by the shortest route, through the Negev, but in the region of Arad they encountered serious resistance from local rulers. They lost the first battle, but the second was more successful. However, Moses refused to head directly north. He turned to the southeast and went by the longest route, through

Transjordan, bypassing the western part of Canaan. His decision was not accidental. In southern and central Canaan, he would have encountered an entire coalition of Canaanite and Amorite rulers, war with whom, as the battles near Arad had shown, he was ill-prepared for, without additional support. Furthermore, there was a fear that an open invasion of southern Canaan might provoke a response from Egypt, which considered southern Palestine to be its eastern boundary. It is probable that the leaders of the Hebrew tribes had no clear idea of the extent to which Egypt had lost its power over Canaan; nor did they anticipate that Egypt would make no attempt to defend its position there.

War with King Sihon's semi-nomadic Amorite kingdom in Transjordan was the first joint campaign by the Israelites and Moses's tribes – who had recently arrived from Egypt. The 'house of Joseph' attacked from the west, from the direction of the Jordan River, and the tribes led by Moses from the east, from the desert. It cannot be ruled out that the Moabites, who had been at war with Sihon at an earlier time and had to give up part of their territory to him, also took part, attacking Sihon from the south. Facing attack from three directions simultaneously, Sihon suffered complete defeat. This was a very important victory, since it involved a territorial unification of several Israelite tribes who had returned to Canaan in the 15th century B.C.E. and the tribes that Moses had brought out of Egypt at the beginning of the 12th century B.C.E. For the first time since the exodus from Egypt, the Hebrews received a piece of land of their own in Transjordan from where they could launch a joint campaign to conquer Canaan. The considerable expansion of the Israelite tribal league, in the absence of any kind of reaction from Egypt, made it possible to crush another Amorite ruler as well – King Og of Bashan. The Bible notably describes the Hebrew tribes as 'a multitudinous host', although it is unlikely that the people of Moses could have increased in number during the period that they had wandered in the desert. This is undoubtedly indirect evidence of the already existing tribal alliance of Israel having been joined by tribes newly arrived from Egypt. If prior to the unification of the Hebrew tribes the Bible had usually referred to them by a single name (either Jacob or Israel), following their union the biblical texts began to use the two names simultaneously. After the passing of many centuries, the redactors of the Old Testament managed to ensure that both these names – Jacob and Israel – were taken as representing a single people, and regarded as stemming from a single forefather. However, the most ancient texts contain traces of the fact that these names had originally represented two different groups of tribes. For instance, "There is no sorcery against Jacob, no divination against Israel. It will now be said of Jacob and of Israel, 'See what God has done!'" (Numbers 23:23). At least until the emergence of the United Monarchy, the simultaneous use of both these names was not a poetic technique, but recognition of the objective reality of two different tribal groups in a shared union. Only subsequently did the redactors of the Old Testament take pains to erase all memory of the two related peoples having different ancestors. Simultaneous mention of their names began to be perceived as synonyms referring to one and the same people. For example, "How beautiful are your tents, O Jacob, your dwelling places, O Israel!" (Numbers 24:5). Confirmation of the fact that Jacob and Israel indeed united and that they together seized Transjordanian territories belonging to kings Sihon and Og is to be found in the fact that these lands were divided between them. The southern part went to the tribe of Reuben, which claimed to be eldest in the 'house of Jacob', and the northern one to the tribe of Manasseh, which represented the 'house of Joseph', i,e. the eldest of the Israelite tribes. Moreover, a chunk of the conquered Transjordan was given to the Amorite tribe of Gad, which had left Egypt together with the 'house of Jacob'. In this way each group that was part of the union – Israel, Jacob, and those Amorites who had joined Israel and Jacob – received a share of the spoils from the first joint conquests in Canaan.

Regarding the fate of the Transjordanian Amorite population, the Bible gives contradictory information. In Deuteronomy, we find the following unambiguous assertion: "At that time we took all his [Sihon's] towns and completely destroyed them—men, women and children. We left no survivors. But the livestock and the plunder from the towns we had captured we carried off for ourselves" (Deuteronomy 2:34-35). But the earlier Book of Numbers mentions the intention of the tribes of Reuben, Gad, and Manasseh, prior to departing to conquer Canaan, to build city walls to defend their families from the local inhabitants: "Meanwhile our women and children will live in fortified cities, for protection from the inhabitants of the land" (Numbers 32:17). Thus, if it was necessary to think about protection from the local population, that means there were indeed local people still living there. Which of the books of the Bible gives a more credible picture? Probably, the earlier book of Numbers; its initial version was written down during the age of the United Monarchy, while Deuteronomy was created much later, in the 7th-6th centuries B.C.E.

The arrival of the new Hebrew tribes in Transjordan and their joining up with the Israelite tribal alliance was extremely troubling for their closest relatives, the Moabites. "And Moab was terrified because there were so many people. Indeed, Moab was filled with dread because of the Israelites. The Moabites said to the elders of Midian, 'This horde is going to lick up everything around us, as an ox licks up the grass of the field'" (Numbers 22: 3-4). The Moabites, frightened by the unification of the Hebrew tribes, tried to form an alliance against them with the Midianites, but without success: the Hebrews beat them to it by dealing the Midianites a crushing defeat. The change in the balance of forces in favor of the Israelite tribal league forced their kinsmen – the

Edomites, Moabites, and Ammonites – to stay neutral and to not enter into any coalition that would be hostile to the Hebrews. On the other hand, we cannot help but notice the strict prohibition in the Pentateuch against going to war against Edom, Moab, and Ammon – even if subsequently this prohibition was violated. The reason for the prohibition was not just kinship with these peoples, but also the strategy pursued by Moses and Joshua, which aimed at securing a friendly rear and, if possible, at winning potential allies during the conquest of Canaan. This strategy proved successful. In spite of the anxiety felt by these peoples in the face of the expansion of the Israelite tribal alliance, they nevertheless refrained from supporting the Israelites' opponents even during the most difficult years of re-conquest.

Judging by the archaeological facts at our disposal, all the Transjordanian peoples, including both the Amorites from the kingdoms of Sihon and Og and the relatives of the 'house of Jacob' – the Edomites, Moabites, and Ammonites – were, in the 12th century B.C.E., not yet settled peoples with a developed urban culture, but, like the Hebrew tribes, were still only at the initial stage of settling on the land.

According to the Bible, a 'count' of the Israelite tribes was held immediately prior to the conquest of Canaan. And although the numbers given probably refer to a later time – the period of the United Monarchy, – they are nevertheless of great interest, since they may be assumed to reflect the proportionate numerical 'weights' of the various tribes. They tell us that Judah and the 'house of Joseph' (Manasseh and Ephraim) were the largest tribes among the Southerners and Northerners respectively; and, conversely, the tribe of Levi was so small that it should really be called a large clan. If in all other tribes the men were counted from the age of 20 upwards, in the tribe of Levi they were counted from one month old and, in spite of this trick, the tribe was still nearly the smallest. For this reason, Moses requested for his tribe not an allotment of land in Canaan, but an allotment in service to God – something that could give a great deal more than all that this tribe would have been able to count on as its share of the parceling out of Canaan.

The Book of Joshua gives another interesting number: there were 40,000 'advance troops' who moved through the steppe of Jericho to conquer Canaan. Given that the 'house of Joseph' was already in central Canaan, this number must refer to those tribes that had left together with Moses. Quite possibly, it was much closer to the real number of Moses's fellow-tribesmen than the figure of '600,000 men on foot' mentioned immediately after the departure from Egypt.

Moses's death on the eve of the crossing of the Jordan forced the Hebrew tribes to choose a new leader. Prior to unification, each tribal group had its own leader. The newly arrived tribes were led by Moses and the Israelite tribes by Joshua. Both these leaders had long since wanted an alliance of the two groups and were convinced that without it conquest of Canaan would be impossible. From the very start, Moses led the 'house of Jacob' into Canaan to join with Israel and only the unforeseen strengthening of Egypt under Ramesses III threw his plans into disarray, resulting in the split of the 'house of Jacob' and forcing the two southern tribes to spend 40 years wandering the desert. The first territorial unification of the tribes of Moses and Joshua occurred in central Transjordan as a result of the crushing defeat of the kingdom of Sihon. Thus the majority of the Hebrew tribes (10 out of 12) were together again after two and a half centuries of divided history (from the middle of the 15th to the beginning of the 12th centuries B.C.E.). One may suppose that in recognition of his advanced age, experience, and record of achievements, Moses was recognized as nominal head of the union. But Moses was already too old and ill to rule, so real power over the Hebrew tribes was in the hands of Joshua, leader of the 'house of Joseph', and Eleazar, head of the priestly clan of the 'house of Jacob'. To begin with, the creation of the alliance of Hebrew tribes changed little in their lives, at least until the crossing of the Jordan. Each group was managed by its leader and had its own army and religion. Relations between the two groups resembled a temporary coalition against a common enemy and were unlikely to have differed greatly from the ordinary alliances entered into by city states in Canaan at the time. However, the death of such a universally acknowledged leader as Moses and the difficulties arising from the forthcoming conquest of Canaan forced the leaders of the Hebrew tribes to organize their alliance in a new way. The principal factor in the redistribution of power was the 'relative weight' of each tribal group, i.e. its numerical size and military strength. Two factors considerably weakened the 'house of Jacob'. First, the split between the Southerners, as a result of which two tribes – those of Judah and Simon – together with their Midianite and Edomite allies, had remained in the deserts of southern Canaan. Secondly, the fact that following Moses's death the 'fellow travelers' – the Amorites who had left Egypt together with the southern Hebrew tribes – preferred to stay close to the 'house of Joseph' rather than the 'house of Jacob'. Evidently, from the point of view of history and tribal genealogy, they were closer to the Northerners than the Southerners. Given the balance of forces between the tribal groups, leadership was transferred to Israel – or, to be more exact, to the 'house of Joseph', which was head of the northern tribes. The leading role taken by the 'house of Joseph', like the clash with the Midianite allies, was yet another cause of the split within the 'house of Jacob'. The southern tribes of Judah and Simeon did not recognize Joshua's right to be Moses's successor and preferred their own leader, Caleb. For this reason it was important not to underestimate the relevance of the part of the 'house of Jacob' that did join Israel – the Levites and the tribe of Reuben – and thus strengthened it. Significant concessions had to be made for such a significant ally. Today, biblical history gives us an understanding of the distribution of power within the Israelite tribal alliance. Military and political leadership was given to Joshua, the head of the Northerners. All the tribal troops were merged to form a single army and placed under the command of Joshua. Priestly functions, on the other hand, were given to Eleazar, the leader and high priest of the 'house of Jacob'. However, in order to lead religious services on behalf of the entire alliance, there needed to be a common religious cult, and this did not yet exist: the southern tribes worshipped their own God, Yahweh, while the northern tribes had long since adopted El and Baal, the principal gods of the Canaanite pantheon. But a genuine alliance required sacrifices and concessions from each party and so the leaders of the Northerners adopted the God of the 'house of Jacob' as the main religion of the new union and Eleazar as the high priest of the entire alliance. The position of the northern tribes was made easier by the fact that Yahwism of that time was quite content to be the principal worship among a number of cults. Once it had received this status, it co-existed peacefully with the pagan gods. The few Aaronites who joined the Northerners were accepted as supreme priests in perpetuity. Nor were the Levites forgotten: their function was to hold religious services among all tribes in the new alliance; they received adequate maintenance from each tribe and, moreover, retained a secondary role in the central religious services. In short, the old agreement between Aaron and Moses regarding the distribution of powers between Aaronites and Levites was part of the agreement regarding the alliance with the northern tribes. It is difficult to say whether this was an achievement to be credited to Moses himself, the result of the care he showed for his own tribe before his death, or whether it was a condition laid down by Eleazar, who had a strong interest in the Levites strengthening the cult of Yahweh among the northern tribes.

Return to the rite of circumcision

For the Amorites who had come out of Egypt together with the 'house of Jacob', the adoption of the latter's religious cult meant that they had to go through the rite of circumcision. And indeed, in the Book of Joshua, we find the execution of this rite confirmed by a very important episode: "At that time the Lord said to Joshua, 'Make flint knives and circumcise the Israelites again.' So Joshua made flint knives and circumcised the Israelites at Gibeath Haaraloth. Now this is why he did so: All those who came out of Egypt—all the men of military age—died in the desert on the way after leaving Egypt. All the people that came out had been circumcised, but all the people born in the desert during the journey from Egypt had not. [...] and these were the ones Joshua circumcised. They were still uncircumcised because they had not been circumcised on the way" (Joshua 5:2-5, 7). This explanation seems extremely strange and illogical if we take into account that upon leaving Egypt, the people were liberated from all compulsions and constraints of the Egyptians and, even more significantly, were led at this time by Moses, the lawgiver himself, who kept a very close eye to ensure that all commandments and rites were properly carried out. If this rite was observed even during the time of slavery in Egypt under the oppressor pharaohs, why did the southern Hebrew tribes stop observing it under the lawgiver and liberator? All arguments based on the special conditions that obtained in the desert fail to convince: if in those same desert conditions failure to observe other laws (for instance, the law of the Sabbath) could be punished by death, what reason could there have been for not enforcing the rite of circumcision? Probably, the true reason was something else altogether: the Amorite tribes had not undergone circumcision at all prior to their joining the Israelite alliance. That said, the rite of circumcision was in itself initially in no way associated with either the cult of Yahweh or the monotheism of Moses.

It should not be forgotten that the ancestors of the Hebrews did not conduct circumcision either in Sumer or in Haran, from where they had come. It is likely that the West Semitic people of Amorite origin to whom the Hebrew tribes belonged did not initially practice circumcision. The best examples of this are the Hivites of Shechem and the Midianite tribes of the Kenites: being Amorite in origin, they knew of the existence of this rite, but did not practice it themselves. The rite was likely adopted from the Jebusites, Abraham's neighbors and allies, who had themselves taken it from the Canaanites. However, the Canaanites, like the Amorites, did not initially practice circumcision. They also adopted the rite from their own precursors – people of the Ghassulian culture. We possess incontrovertible proof that the inhabitants of southern Palestine practiced circumcision from as far back as the end of the 4th millennium B.C.E., i.e. 1000 years before the Amorites arrived and, quite possibly, before the arrival of the Canaanites. The evidence in question is the Battlefield (Vultures) Palette, an ancient Egyptian palette dating to approximately 3200 B.C.E., on which the Egyptians depicted naked prisoners from southern Palestine, all of them circumcised. The same is seen on another ancient Egyptian slate, the so-called Narmer Palette, which dates to a slightly later period, 3000 B.C.E., when Egypt was ruled by one of its very first pharaohs, Narmer. Another piece of evidence that confirms this rite belongs to profound antiquity is the use of flint knives, even though in Joshua's time bronze was universally available and iron was gradually coming into general use. The mention of flint knives for this rite places its origins in the Neolithic Age. Thus the custom of circumcision is a very ancient and undoubtedly pagan ritual that was practiced by the pre-Canaanite population of southern Palestine. When they arrived in this region, the Canaanites adopted this religious ritual, and were followed by the Amorites when the latter arrived in their turn. Exactly the same happened with the southern Hebrew tribes who settled in these parts. Evidently, the cult of God the Almighty (El Elyon) and the custom of circumcision, which prevailed in the Jebusite city of Urushalem (Jerusalem), merged with the old tribal beliefs of the 'house of Jacob'. In addition to the southern Hebrew tribes, many other nomadic Amorite peoples who traced their family history back to patriarch Abraham, including the Ishmaelites, adopted the circumcision rite. Very likely, this rite was also practiced by the Transjordanian relatives of the Hebrews – the Edomites, Moabites, and Ammonites. At any rate, reason to think so is furnished by certain sayings of the prophet Jeremiah. It may be supposed that most West Semitic peoples who derived from Abraham were practitioners of the rite of circumcision. But this custom was practiced less and less the greater the distance from southern Canaan. Evidently, in central and northern Palestine not all peoples practiced circumcision. The Hivites of Shechem, for instance, as we see from the Book of Genesis, likewise did not practice this rite. Clearly, the custom of circumcision made its appearance initially in southern Palestine, where it came to be most widely practiced. However, there is evidence to suggest that circumcision was practiced in the northern regions of Canaan as well. An ivory slate found in Megiddo and dating to 1350-1150 B.C.E. depicts the procession of a local ruler in which there are two prisoners without clothing and both are circumcised. Ancient Megiddo was situated in the fertile Jezreel Valley, which, even after it had been conquered by Israelite tribes, had a population exclusively of Canaanites. The latter – or some of them – also inherited the ancient Palestine custom of circumcision. In general, one may here discern a distinct pattern: the longer this or that people inhabited Canaan or the closer it lived to the south of that country, the greater was the likelihood that it practiced circumcision. The 'house of Joseph', although it mainly practiced the pagan cults of El and Baal, was also circumcised, given that by the time the tribes of Moses came out of Egypt, it had already been in Canaan for at least two and a half centuries.

Moses's attitude to circumcision is very interesting. There can be no doubt that this rite was practiced by the southern tribes in Egypt and Moses himself was circumcised. But, as the Bible tells us, he for some reason did not circumcise his sons by his Midianite wife Zipporah. The Book of Exodus contains an episode of great significance in this regard: "At a lodging place on the way, the Lord met Moses and was about to kill him. But Zipporah took a flint knife, cut off her son's foreskin and touched Moses' feet with it. 'Surely you are a bridegroom of blood to me,' she said. So the Lord let him alone. (At that time she said "bridegroom of blood," referring to circumcision)" (Exodus 4:24-26). In saving her seriously ill husband, Zipporah made a sacrifice to the Lord, symbolically giving him back his son. Clearly, then, this is a rite that was resorted to in extreme circumstances even by those Amorite peoples who did not practice it in daily life. However, even among the Ten Commandments that Moses handed down to his people there is none that mentions or, still less, requires circumcision. One has the impression that Moses did not regard this rite as part of his monotheistic faith but, quite possibly, considered it to be one of the pagan rituals that he personally fought against. For this reason, we cannot rule out that the Bible in this case is literally correct: Moses's people did not practice circumcision under his leadership. Only after his death, when the Aaronite Eleazar became the high priest of the entire alliance, did Eleazar require a return to the old ritual that Moses had ignored. Later, the editors of the Old Testament arranged the texts in such a way that the rite of circumcision was legitimized by the lawgiver. However, they were afraid to discard the two blatant instances of this rite being violated by Moses himself: he did not have his own sons circumcised and did not require his people to practice circumcision – and not just during the period of wandering in the desert, but also upon their arrival in Canaan. Judging by the character of his teachings, Moses evidently believed that genuine proof of his alliance with God was not the cutting off of a foreskin, as practiced by the pagans at the time, but the fulfillment of God's commandments, and that it was not a person's foreskin that needed to be circumcised, but his spirit. There is another fact that is of interest here. Many Arab tribes of the pre-Islamic period practiced circumcision although they were utter pagans. In short, the circumcision rite had nothing at all to do with belief in the one God, or with monotheism in general; rather, it was a sign of the alliance – or, to be more precise, of the covenant regarding the alliance both with the patron divinity and with Moses's own people. The rite had a political as well as religious significance. The circumcision of the patriarch Abraham in Canaan signified not just rejection of the old Sumerian gods and adoption of the cult of the Almighty God, but also a military and political alliance with his new neighbors – the Jebusites of Urushalem (Jerusalem). Exactly the same was implied by the Hivites of Shechem when they agreed to patriarch Jacob's requirement that they conduct the rite of circumcision. At this time, the rite signified an agreement regarding a permanent alliance. Circumcision among the Amorites who returned from Egypt constituted not only acceptance of the religion of the southern Hebrews, but also the conclusion of an alliance with both them and the northern Israelite tribes.

As Yahwism started to become a monotheistic religion, the rite of circumcision began to lose its former pagan character and gradually transformed into a symbol of union with the one God. At the same time, circumcision presents itself essentially as the cultural and historical connection between the Jewish people and their ancient homeland Canaan, where this rite was first born.

The re-conquest of Canaan in the light of biblical and archaeological data

The history of the conquest of Canaan by the Hebrew tribes is mainly given in the Book of Joshua, where it is depicted as a simultaneous military campaign. Unfortunately, at present archaeology is unable to confirm or refute the version set out in the Bible. The problem is that many of the Canaanite cities mentioned have yet to be identified or excavated. Archaeologists continue to argue about the precise location of cities such as Horma, Libnah, Makkedah, Lasharon, Madon, Shimron-Meron, and Goiim. But even those cities that have been identified – such as Geder, Adullam, Tapuah, Hepher, and Achshaph – have for various reasons not been excavated in the proper way. It is, of course, impossible to conduct archaeological excavations in cities such as Jerusalem or Gaza in the event that modern buildings have been erected directly on the site of ancient ruins. Other cities have been identified and excavated only for it to turn out that they have been destroyed at different times and by different conquerors. The coastal cities of Ashdod, Ashkelon, Ekron, Aphek, and Dor, for instance, were destroyed by the Sea Peoples in the 12th century B.C.E., while Hazor and Bethel fell to Israelite tribes in the 13th century B.C.E. Still other cities were burned and abandoned by their inhabitants long before Joshua's conquest. The best examples of this category of cities are Ai and Arad, which flourished during the early Bronze Age but were destroyed at the end of the 3rd millennium B.C.E., their lands remaining uninhabited right up to the arrival of the Israelite tribes. On the other hand, cities such as Yokneam, Kedesh, Taanach, and Lachish were indeed destroyed by the Israelites – and, moreover, precisely during Joshua's military campaign, in the 12th century B.C.E. There is other evidence too that confirms the information found in the Bible. For instance, Shechem, a city in central Canaan that is of great importance for Israelite history, is never mentioned among those seized or destroyed, and there is a good reason for this: archaeological data tells us that it already belonged to the Israelite tribes or was their ally. The same goes for cities such as Jerusalem, Debir, Yarmuth, Gezer, Beth-shean, and Akko, which are mentioned as unconquered cities. As archaeologists have established, these cities contain no traces of Israelite culture. In short, the archaeological facts partially confirm the biblical version and partially contradict it.

Currently, archaeology furnishes us with only two unconditional conclusions. First, the Hebrew tribes' conquest of Canaan was not a simultaneous military campaign, but one that stretched over several centuries. Second, the Israelites were not aliens in Canaan, but rather had been closely connected with, and were an integral part of it. Their material and spiritual culture speaks of a continuity between them and the Canaanites – and all the more so because biblical Hebrew was merely a dialect of the Canaanites' language. These facts have allowed the American archaeologist William Dever to assert that the early Israelites were actually Canaanites who were displaced within their own country.

Interpretation of the archaeological data is made more complicated by the fact that by no means all sackings of Canaanite cities in the 15th-12th centuries B.C.E. can be attributed to the Hebrew tribes. At the end of the 16th and beginning of the 15th centuries B.C.E., the northeastern part of Canaan was attacked by Hurrian and Indo-Aryan groups associated with the state of Mitanni. At the same time, southern Canaan was subject to military expeditions organized by the pharaohs of the 18th Dynasty from Thebes, who were trying to finish once and for all with the Hyksos and their local allies. In the middle of the 15th century B.C.E., the Egyptian pharaoh Tutmos III conducted regular depredatory marches into Palestine, resulting in the latter's subjection to Egypt. During the course of the 13th century B.C.E., the pharaohs of the 19th Dynasty – first Seti I, then Ramesses II, and finally Merneptah – repeatedly organized punitive expeditions into Canaan in an attempt to break the resistance of the local peoples. Each expedition of this kind was accompanied by the destruction of numerous Canaanite cities. Then, at the beginning of the 12th century B.C.E., the Philistines invaded southwestern

Canaan and seized the southern coastal cities. Other Sea Peoples – the Tjeker and Sherden – settled further north, in the region of Dor. At the same time, the cities of northeastern Canaan suffered pressure and perhaps invasion at the hands of the Arameans, a West Semitic people related to the Amorites. The Arameans are known to have settled in the region of Damascus, where they set up their own kingdom and gradually became the main opponent of the Israelite tribes in the north of the country. However, apart from invasions by foreigners, Canaan also suffered substantially because of internal conflicts between its competitive city-states. Evidence of these cities' frequent military conflicts is to be found in letters from the Amarna archive. It is not surprising, then, that archaeologists are frequently unable to determine with any unanimity the parties responsible for the destruction of a particular city.

The struggle for Canaan: three time periods

And yet, the discrepancies between the results of the archaeological digs and the biblical version of the conquest of Canaan are not accidental. The Book of Joshua, which tells of the seizing of Canaan, was most likely compiled and set down in the 7th to 6th centuries B.C.E., i.e. approximately 500 years after the events it describes. As a result of the enormous gap in time between the events themselves and their being recorded in writing, unrelated episodes from different centuries were compressed into a single, simultaneous military campaign led by a single leader. In such cases, confusion and mistakes with regard to the names of individuals, peoples, and cities are inevitable. But the main problem is something else: in the Book of Joshua, fragments taken from three different periods when the Hebrew tribes were fighting for Canaan have been lumped together. The first period begins in the 23rd century B.C.E., when the nomadic Amorite tribes arrived in Palestine; among them were northern Hebrew tribes (Israel). From this time onwards, the epic tradition of the Northerners contained narratives of the conquest of Canaanite cities. Possibly, the detailed story of the seizing of the city of Ai was taken from these legends. Later, in approximately the 20th century B.C.E., the biblical patriarch Abraham led another group of nomadic Amorite tribes out of northwestern Mesopotamia; among them were the southern Hebrew tribes (Jacob). The latter's arrival in southern Palestine was more peaceful, although they too were unable to escape conflicts with the Canaanite peoples. It is likely that the wars waged by the Southerners against the ruler of Arad belong to this, the earliest period of the fight for Canaan. The first stage of conquering the country ended with the departure of the northern and then the southern Hebrew tribes into the Nile Delta in Egypt, as a result of which the tribal lands they had conquered were gradually taken over by other Amorite and Canaanite peoples.

Upon the return of several northern (Israelite) tribes to Canaan in the 15th century B.C.E., the second stage of the fight for the country began. This time, what was involved was not so much conquest as re-conquest, the winning back of land that had previously belonged to the Hebrew tribes. But when Egyptian power was established in Canaan, this ruled out the return of the lost land and the northern tribes became Habiru – homeless, 'displaced persons' in their own country. They occupied regions that were vacant and ill-suited to agricultural use in central and northern Palestine, where they kept cattle and fought as mercenaries for local rulers. The situation changed for the better only in the second half of the 14th and at the beginning of the 13th century B.C.E., when the weakening of Egypt made its rule over Canaan purely nominal. It was during this period that the Habiru started attacking, and won back, part of their former territories. Yet when Egypt regained its strength in the 13th century B.C.E., Egyptian control over Canaan was revived and most of the land that had been won back was lost again. Possibly, it was the military campaigns of Seti I and Ramesses II during the zenith of Egyptian might that forced several northern tribes to join together to form the tribal alliance of Israel.

The third and most important period in the fight for Canaan began at the beginning of the 12th century B.C.E., when internal political conflicts in Egypt deprived it of control over Canaan, on the one hand, and, on the other, allowed the tribes of Moses to leave the Nile Delta. It was at this time that the extended Israelite tribal alliance embarked on the decisive phase in the conquest of Canaan, and it was this that became the basis for the Book of Joshua in the Bible. The final strengthening of Egypt under Ramesses III probably had no great impact on central and northern Canaan, where the Israelites continued to reinforce their positions. After the death of Ramesses III, the Egyptians finally left Canaan, making it possible for the two southern tribes – Judah and Simeon – to return from their 40 years of wandering through the desert and begin in their turn conquering part of the south of the country.

Here, in Canaan, the 'house of Jacob' united with Israel. Henceforth, Jacob was Israel and Israel, Jacob. The two groups of tribes became a single people with two parallel names. Five to six centuries later, the keepers of the tradition – the Levites and the Aaronites – linked to this third stage in the fight for Canaan a large number of narratives relating to the first and second periods, creating the impression that there had been a single, simultaneous military campaign, although there had been no such thing (and nothing of the sort, naturally, can be confirmed by the archaeological data). For the sake of fairness, it should be noted that the fight for possession of all of Canaan was completed only during the rule of King David, i.e. in the first half of the 10th century B.C.E. Despite this, the authors of the Book of Joshua included in it all the episodes known to them relating to the conquest of the country by the Hebrew tribes from the 23rd to the 10th centuries B.C.E. Of course, archaeology will never be able to confirm that all these episodes took place during a single short military campaign under the leadership of Joshua. Thus, the official biblical version is a result of a compilation of narratives belonging to the Southerners and Northerners taken from three different periods.

Why did the 'house of Jacob' – the group of southern Hebrew tribes – join forces with Israel and not with Edom, Moab, or Ammon, who were in fact closer to it? The main factor in this case was probably not tribal genealogy, but the fact that Israel and Jacob had historical fates and political interests in common. They were the only Habiru in Canaan, which is to say that only they had no tribal lands of their own. Jacob's relatives Edom, Moab, and Ammon had not left to go to Egypt, had not lived during the course of hundreds of years in the Nile Delta, and had not experienced either the prosperity that came during the rule of the Hyksos pharaohs or the persecutions that followed under the pharaohs of the New Kingdom. On the other hand, this was something that the Hebrew tribes had experienced in full. The Edomites, Moabites, and Ammonites possessed old tribal lands in Transjordan which were, with rare exceptions (for instance, Sihon's seizure of part of the territory of Moab) not subject to attack by their neighbors, the Amorites and Canaanites. The Hebrew tribes were in an entirely different position. During the long time that they had spent in Egypt, their lands had been taken over by the Amorite and Canaanite peoples. During four centuries of life in Egypt, the blood ties between the 'house of Jacob', on the one hand, and Edom, Moab, and Ammon, on the other, had grown so weak that the latter had no wish not just to help their kin but even to allow them to pass through their territory. Moreover, as we are told by the Bible, Balak, the ruler of the Moabites, looked upon the 'house of Jacob' as his potential enemy. It is hardly surprising, then, that in these conditions the only possible true ally of the southern tribes was Israel, which was headed by the 'house of Joseph' that had been patron to the 'house of Jacob' in Hyksos Egypt. This is the underlying reason of the political and military alliance between two different West Semitic groups of Amorite origin – 'Jacob' and 'Israel', who found themselves in position of 'Habiru' after return from Egypt to their motherland – Canaan. This alliance was later reinforced when the Northerners adopted the religious cult of Southerners - Yahweh. From this time onwards, the name Habiru or Ibri/Ivri became the common ethnonym for both parties in the new union of Israel and Jacob. The emergence of this alliance is an interesting example of how under the influence of historical circumstances different tribal groups (admittedly within the same West Semitic ethnos) can discover that they have incomparably more in common than with peoples that are more closely related to them and with whom they have a shared genealogy. However, this short-coming – the lack of a shared tribal genealogy – was successfully compensated for during the United Monarchy, when the biblical writers connected two forefathers – Jacob and Israel – into a single shared patriarch whom they invested with two names.

Israelites and Canaanites: peaceful co-existence and intermarriage

The re-conquest of Canaan during the time of Joshua had two important features. First, it was by no means a complete capture of the country. The lands that were most fertile and most suitable for agriculture – such as the valley of the Jordan River and the Jezreel and coastal valleys – remained, as before, in the hands of the Canaanites. The most important interior regions in terms of economic and strategic significance and the cities in these areas – such as Jerusalem – were, as before, under the rule of the Amorites. A peace agreement with the Hivites – an Amorite people from central Canaan – left their cities (Gibeon, Kephirah, Beeroth, and Kiriath-Jearim) intact. Almost the entire Mediterranean coast was outside the control of the Israelites.

Being semi-nomadic, the latter possessed neither wall-breaking instruments nor experience of storming heavily fortified cities, nor chariots for fighting in the valleys. For this reason, when talking of large cities, the authors of the Book of Joshua are frank in saying: "Yet Israel did not burn any of the cities built on their mounds—except Hazor, which Joshua burned" (Joshua 11: 13). The same went for the valleys: "all the Canaanites who live in the plain have iron chariots" (Joshua 17: 16). At that time the Israelites had no chariots, and this for a long time prevented them from taking control of those regions that were most suitable for farming. The incomplete and partial character of the Israelite re-conquest of Canaan is acknowledged by the Bible itself: "When Joshua was old and well advanced in years, the Lord said to him, "You are very old, and there are still very large areas of land to be taken over" (Joshua 13:1).

Secondly, in spite of appeals from the keepers of the tradition, the local peoples not only were not destroyed, but were not even driven off their lands. In general, the biblical texts contain overt contradictions regarding the fate of the population in cities that were conquered. On the one hand, their authors maintain that "Joshua subdued the whole region, including the hill country, the Negev, the western foothills and the mountain slopes, together with all their kings. He left no survivors" (Joshua 10:40). On the other, the Bible supplies a great deal of evidence to show that the Hebrew tribes in all regions of Canaan settled alongside the local peoples and without causing the latter any harm:

"Judah could not dislodge the Jebusites, who were living in Jerusalem; to this day the Jebusites live there with the people of Judah" (Joshua 15:63);

"They did not dislodge the Canaanites living in Gezer; to this day the Canaanites live among the people of Ephraim but are required to do forced labor" (Joshua 16:10);

"Within Issachar and Asher, Manasseh also had Beth Shan, Ibleam and the people of Dor, Endor, Taanach and Megiddo,

together with their surrounding settlements (the third in the list
is Naphoth). Yet the Manassites were not able to occupy these
towns, for the Canaanites were determined to live in that region.
However, when the Israelites grew stronger, they subjected
the Canaanites to forced labor but did not drive them out completely" (Joshua 17: 11-13);

"Neither did Zebulun drive out the Canaanites living in Kitron
or Nahalol, who remained among them; but they did subject
them to forced labor" (Judges 1:30);

"Nor did Asher drive out those living in Acco or Sidon or
Ahlab or Aczib or Helbah or Aphek or Rehob, and because of
this the people of Asher lived among the Canaanite inhabitants
of the land" (Judges 1: 31-32);

"Neither did Naphtali drive out those living in Beth Shemesh
or Beth Anath; but the Naphtalites too lived among the Canaanite inhabitants of the land, and those living in Beth Shemesh and
Beth Anath became forced laborers for them" (Judges 1:33);

"But the Israelites did not drive out the people of Geshur and
Maacah, so they continue to live among the Israelites to this day"
(Joshua 13:13).

It is likely that instances of devastation and expulsion of
the inhabitants of seized cities were an exception to the rule.
From the economic point of view, there was greater profit to be
had from leaving the inhabitants where they were and making
tributaries of them – which is what tended to happen, in fact.
When the authors of the Book of Joshua assert that the populations of many Canaanite cities were put to their deaths in their
entirety, this is an absolutization of a number of extraordinary
instances; it has a purely didactic purpose – to demonstrate how
one should treat pagans. What actually happened, as the Book
of Judges shows, tended to be the exact opposite: "The Israelites lived among the Canaanites, Hittites, Amorites, Perizzites,
Hivites and Jebusites. They took their daughters in marriage and
gave their own daughters to their sons, and served their gods"

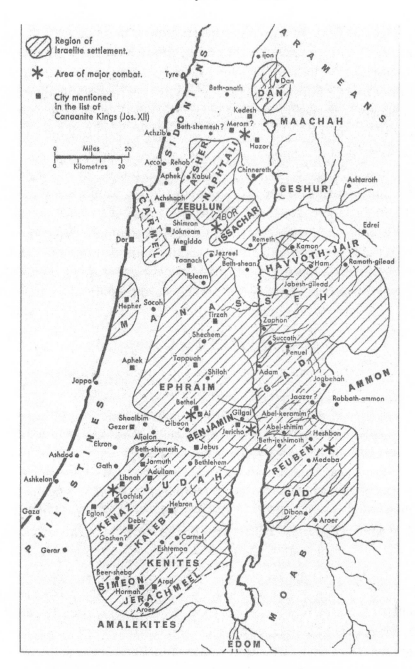

The Hebrew tribes and their neighbors in Canaan. 12-11 centuries
B.C.E. Y. Aharoni, The Land of the Bible.

(Judges 3: 5-6). In this way, the Hebrew tribes not only lived in peace with the peoples they had conquered, but also quickly assimilated with them. This led to what the keepers of the tradition, the Aaronites and Levites, were most afraid of: "They forsook the Lord, the God of their fathers, who had brought them out of Egypt. They followed and worshipped various gods of the peoples around them" (Judges 2:12). That the Hebrew tribes were adopting the religions of the Canaanite peoples was the principal danger for the position held by the Aaronites and Levites in the Israelite alliance. The problem was not so much that all these cults were pagan as the fact that conversion to them would result in loss of economic resources and political influence. The more the Hebrews were sucked into worshipping alien gods, the less they sacrificed to the Levites and Aaronites and the weaker was the latter's influence on them. In those days, the crux was not confrontation between monotheism and paganism, as it was subsequently depicted in the biblical texts, but a competitive struggle for material resources and for spiritual and political influence over the Israelite tribes. What was at stake was who would be the pastors of the people – the acolytes of Yahweh or the Canaanite priests who served Baal and Asherah. This was the reason for the extremely uncompromising attitude taken by the keepers of the tradition to the peoples of Canaan. It was not for nothing that when recording the biblical texts they repeatedly demanded the expulsion of the Canaanites, Amorites, Hivites, Jebusites, Perizzites, Hittites, Rephaim, and Girgashites, who had been conquered by the Israelites, with whom they lived and with whom they subsequently became completely intermixed in the cultural and physical senses. It was these peoples' religious cults that threatened the vital interests of the Aaronites and Levites. It is noteworthy that although the Israelites' most dangerous enemies in Canaan were the Philistines in the south and the Arameans in the north, the keepers of the tradition did not ask for their destruction or expulsion. And yet the damage and suffering caused by the Philistines, for instance, was something of a completely different order from the slight inconveniences that were created for them by the Hivites or Jebusites. The Israelites, however, did not lay claim to the Philistines' lands, did not live among them, and, most importantly of all, did not worship their principal divinity Dagan – which explains why the biblical writers did not call for their expulsion or destruction. Ironically though, the Israelites completely assimilated with precisely those peoples whose destruction or expulsion was called for by the Aaronites and Levites.

In trying to monopolize the performance of religious service, the Aaronites and Levites objectively played a centralizing role in the Israelite tribal confederation. They tried to suppress not just alien pagan cults, but also any attempts to create autonomous religious centers – even when the latter were related to the worship of Yahweh, – seeing such centers as a direct threat to their authority and economic position. By the same token, they were, even before the United Monarchy was established, the main opponents of all forms of separatism and division. The best example of this was the incident involving the construction of an altar of oblation on the land of the Transjordanian tribes of Reuben and Gad, and half of the tribe of Manasseh. On behalf of the entire Israelite alliance, the priests of the cult of Yahweh threatened these tribes with war in the event that the latter should tolerate autonomous worship or ignore the common tribal religious center. Pinhas, son of Eleazar, the high priest, was sent to negotiate with the Transjordanian tribes. Faced with such powerful resistance from the Aaronites, the leaders of the Transjordanian tribes retreated and unity was preserved.

Another incident that threatened the unity of the Israelite alliance was a result of the peace concluded with the Hivites of Gibeon. The Book of Joshua speaks of this as a fraudulent trick by the Hivites, who portrayed themselves as emissaries from a distant city that wished to become an ally of the Israelites. For their part, the leaders of the Israelites are depicted as simple-tons who were ignorant that Gibeon was situated a mere 20 or so miles from them and so took an oath of peace with the Hivites. When the deception was revealed, it was too late to change anything since seizing Gibeon would have meant breaking their oath. In actual fact, though, the purpose of this naïve story was to cover up serious disagreements between the leaders of the Israelite alliance. The Hivites were a relatively numerous Amorite people that had mainly settled in central Canaan, including in the region's largest city, Shechem. Correspondence from the Amarna archive gives us reason to suppose that the 'house of Joseph' had, since the middle of the 14th century B.C.E., been in alliance with the Hivites of Shechem. At the same time, the rulers of Shechem – Labayu and his sons – were planning with support from the Habiru to rid themselves of Egyptian rule over Canaan. But their plan failed and killers sent by the Egyptians dealt with the insubordinate ruler. Yet relations between the Hivites of Shechem and the 'house of Joseph' remained friendly. It is for good reason that Shechem is nowhere mentioned as a conquered city, even though it would have been impossible to not take it to secure a firm position in central Canaan. But the Hivites possessed not only Shechem, but other southern cities as well, including Gibeon, Kephirah, Beeroth, and Kiriath-Jearim. Joshua, the leader of the 'house of Joseph', was interested in prolonging the peace and alliance with the Hivites, but the tribe of Benjamin laid claim to the entire territory of the southern Hivites, including their principal city of Gibeon. Before the departure for Egypt, part of this region had possibly belonged to the tribe of Benjamin. In the end, the conflict was smoothed over, but its occurrence was in itself a reminder of the fact that, having returned to Canaan two and a half centuries earlier than the other Hebrew tribes, the 'house of Joseph' had time to create a system of relations with neighboring peoples in Canaan, and it strove to preserve this system even as the country was being conquered. The alliance with the Hivites of Gibeon was yet more proof that, in spite of what was asserted by the biblical writers, the Israelite conquest of Canaan did not lead to the expulsion or destruction of local peoples, but to intermarrying and merging with them. This is something that could not but be acknowledged by biblical authors themselves – although they viewed it as a violation of the covenant with Yahweh and laid all the responsibility for this on their own people: "and you shall not make a covenant with the people of this land, but you shall break down their altars. Yet you have disobeyed me. Why have you done this? Now therefore I tell you that I will not drive them out before you; they will be thorns in your sides and their gods will be a snare to you" (Judges 2: 2-3).

The Northerners and the Southerners - their separate conquests in Canaan

Analysis of the books of Joshua and Judges leaves the impression that the wars waged by Joshua in fact took place only in northern and central Palestine, while the two tribes of Judah and Simeon conquered the southern part of the country at a different, later time. It may very well be that the third and final stage in the conquest of Canaan under the leadership of Joshua divided in its turn into two distinct periods that differed from one another in both time and geography. In order to determine when the conquest of Canaan could have taken place, we must try to reconstruct the historical conditions in which the Hebrew tribes found themselves upon their return from Egypt. This is much easier to do in relation to the southern tribes (the 'house of Jacob'), since the biblical writers – the Aaronites and Levites – were from this same group. The tribes of Moses could not have left Egypt earlier than the beginning of the 12th century B.C.E., i.e. earlier than the internal political crisis resulting from the transfer of power, from the 19th to 20th Dynasty. It was only the disintegration of the Egyptian state and the paralysis – even if only short-lived – of its army and organs of power that could have allowed tens of thousands of bonded Semites to leave Egypt without hindrance. The biblical version of the compelled 40-year stay in the desert is entirely credible given that this was the period of Ramesses III's rule, when Egypt not only strengthened considerably, but also paid particular attention to southern Canaan, which was the target for incursions by the Sea Peoples. Admittedly, this did not concern all the Hebrew tribes – rather, only two of them. The biblical episode with the spies, an episode that led to the rejection of the idea of conquering Canaan immediately after the exodus from Egypt, was a reaction not to the strength of the resistance put up by the Canaanite rulers, but to a purely external factor – the arrival of Ramesses III's army in the southwest of the country. And, finally, the reason for the two southern tribes entering Canaan was not their sudden increase in strength or the fact that their Canaanite opponents had weakened, but the disappearance of the Egyptian military presence in the country. In this way, the two southern tribes – Judah and Simeon – could not have returned to Canaan earlier than the middle of the 12th century B.C.E., and consequently their conquest of southern Canaan could not have occurred earlier than the second half of the 12th century B.C.E.

It is much more difficult to trace the history of the northern tribes, especially given that prior to their unification with the 'house of Jacob' they had no Aaronites or Levites of their own who could have left us their Bible. We have reason to believe that some of the northern tribes – or, at any rate, the 'house of Joseph' – left Egypt after the expulsion of the Hyksos. Unlike the relatively precise dating we have for the exodus of the tribes of Moses, the time of the departure of their northern counterparts can only be conjectured. In any case, the northern tribes could not have left earlier than the end of the 16th century B.C.E., when the Hyksos were driven out, or later than the end of the 15th century B.C.E., when the Habiru had already flooded Canaan, Syria, and the coast of Lebanon. Most likely, their departure took place in the middle of the 15th century B.C.E., during the reign of Tutmos III. At that time, the Western Semites were not being kept by force in Egypt but, on the contrary, were being driven out as potential enemies and as heirs of the Hyksos pharaohs. The Bible points to the same time, telling us that the Temple of Solomon was built 480 years after the arrival of the sons of Israel from Egypt. The Temple of Solomon was erected around 960 B.C.E., so the approximate date we end up with for the departure of some of the northern tribes from Egypt is 1440 B.C.E. From this time forwards, West Semitic fugitives from the Nile Delta are mentioned as Habiru. But what might be the date for Joshua's conquests? We know that in the 15th century and the first half of the 14th B.C.E., Egypt kept a tight grip on Canaan, suppressing any attempts at insubordination. It was only in the second half of the 14th century B.C.E. that Egyptian control abruptly weakened – but if Israel had emerged at that time as a tribal league, it would certainly have been mentioned in the letters of the Amarna archive. Admittedly, it might be that the many wars waged by the Habiru in Canaan at the time passed through the epic tradition of the northern tribes to become part of the biblical version of Joshua's conquests. Most of the 13th century B.C.E., including the reigns of Seti I and Ramesses II, was extremely unfavorable for military endeavors of any kind, since Egypt was at the zenith of its might. The situation began to change for the better after the death of Ramesses II, the oppressor of the Hebrew tribes. His son, Pharaoh Merneptah, mentioned Israel on his stele as one of Egypt's opponents. Evidently, when several northern tribes ('house of Joseph') formed an alliance at the end of the 13th century B.C.E., they started to attack Canaanite cities, which the Egyptians considered as belonging to them. It was this surge of military activity of the northern tribes that brought them up against the Egyptians, causing Israel to be mentioned for the first time in non-biblical sources. It is well known that following the death of Merneptah, the 19th Dynasty quickly faded out and Egypt weakened considerably. It was probably at this time – the end of the 13th and beginning of the 12th centuries B.C.E. – that the northern (Israelite) tribes renewed their campaign to conquer Canaan. If northern and central Canaan were conquered even partially at the moment, then Joshua was not so much Moses's successor, as his ally and comrade-in-arms. When Moses was fighting to get the southern Hebrew tribes out of Egypt, Joshua was preparing several northern (Israelite) tribes for the conquest of Canaan. If this is so, then Moses could certainly have – and should have – had contact with Joshua or even plans for establishing a shared alliance with the aim of reconquering Canaan. But the two leaders could have joined forces properly only in the 1190s and 1180s B.C.E., at the time when the Israelite tribal confederation expanded and the biblical conquest of Canaan began. However, it should not be forgotten that due to the strengthening of Egypt during the rule of Ramesses III, the tribes of Judah and Simeon were unable to set about winning back their lands in southern Canaan and were forced to remain in the desert for four decades. If the situation developed in accordance with this scenario, then the conqueror of southern Canaan was not Joshua at all, but Caleb, the head of the tribe of Judah, a descendant of the Kenazzites. Incidentally, according to the Book of Judges, there were only two tribes fighting together for the south of Canaan – those of Judah and Simeon – and no mention is made of help given by the northern tribes: "Then the men of Judah said to the Simeonites their brothers, "Come up with us into the territory allotted to us, to fight against the Canaanites. We in turn will go with you into yours." So the Simeonites went with them" (Judges 1:3). The only true ally of the Southerners was one of the Midianite tribes, the Kenites, with whom Moses had intermarried following the flight from Egypt and which had repeatedly come to his aid during his stay in the desert: "The descendants of Moses' father-in-law, the Kenite, went up from the City of Palms with the men of Judah to live among the people of the Desert of Judah in the Negev near Arad" (Judges 1:16). The Kenites, like the Kenazzites, very quickly became part of the tribe of Judah. Such additions explain the fact that the tribe of Judah came to be so numerous – a kind of mega-tribe. Thus, if the central and northern regions of Canaan could have been conquered by Joshua in the first half of the 12th century B.C.E., then the south could not have been until, at the very earliest, the second half of the 12th century B.C.E. And consequently, the biblical stage of the conquest of Canaan, which is associated with Joshua, may have continued for almost a century. Support for this version is to be found in archaeological evidence that shows that the south of Palestine (historical Judea) was settled by Hebrew tribes at the end of the 12th and in the 11th centuries B.C.E., i.e. almost 100 years later than Samaria. Further proof is the Song of Deborah, possibly the earliest surviving piece of Hebrew literature, which dates to the 12th century B.C.E. The Song of Deborah lists all the Hebrew tribes with the exception of the two southern tribes of Judah and Simeon. What probably happened was that at a much later time the biblical writers combined two leaders – Moses the lawgiver and leader of the southern tribes, and Joshua, head of the northern tribes and conqueror of Canaan, – making the latter the successor of the former.

The fate of the tribe of Reuben

The fact that the two southern tribes of Judah and Simeon were absent from Canaan at least until the middle of the 12th century B.C.E., while the southern tribe of Reuben was present compels us to look again at Korah's mutiny in the desert following the exodus of the 'house of Jacob' from Egypt. Possibly, this had more serious consequences than the Book of Exodus tells us.

As we know, the dissatisfaction of some of the Levites headed by Korah was directed initially against the concentration of religious service in the hands of the Aaronites. However, due to the oppressive conditions involved in living in the desert and Moses's rejection of his former plans for conquering Canaan, this feeling very quickly transmuted into a broad and general opposition to the rule of Moses and Aaron. The malcontents were headed by the leaders of the tribe of Reuben – Dathan, Aviram, and On. Although the Bible asserts that the earth 'swallowed' the conspirators and that the latter 'disappeared without trace', it cannot be ruled out that this mutiny led to a split between the southern Hebrew tribe of Reuben and the 'house of Jacob' and to the former leaving for Transjordan of its own accord. It is possible that the Amorites who had joined the 'house of Jacob' when it was leaving Egypt, departed together with the tribe of Reuben. There, in Transjordan, fighting for a 'place under the sun', the tribe of Reuben and its Amorite 'fellow-travelers' became members of the Israelite tribal confederation and subsequently committed themselves to sharing the fate of the northern tribes. If events did indeed develop in this way, then it becomes clear why, according to the Song of Deborah, the southern tribe of Reuben was in Canaan earlier than its brothers and why the Book of Judges talks about the conquest of historical Judea by the two southern tribes (Judah and Simeon) only. In general, if you look through all the biblical narratives on Reuben, you find that he always had a special relationship with Joseph. It was Reuben who found the mandrakes for his mother, Leah – which allowed Jacob's second but beloved wife, Rachel, to become pregnant and give birth to Joseph. Reuben was the only brother who saved Joseph's life when his brothers had the idea of killing him. And again it was only Reuben who returned to the empty well to release Joseph, only to find that Joseph had already been sold by his brothers to the Ishmaelite merchants. Unlike his southern brothers Simeon and Levi, Reuben took no part in massacring the Hivites of Shechem, the traditional allies of the 'house of Joseph'. It is extremely probable that these stories, which passed into the Bible from the Hebrew epic tradition, reflect the historically close and amicable links between this southern tribe and the 'house of Joseph' – links that subsequently led Reuben to join the union of northern tribes. On the other hand, within its own 'house of Jacob' the tribe of Reuben was unjustly insulted when it was deprived of the supremacy in spite of its birthright. Moreover, Reuben lost his leadership to Judah, the very person who had proposed selling Joseph to the Ishmaelites. As subsequent events showed, the tribe of Reuben preferred the northern tribes to the 'house of Jacob', remained with them in the Kingdom of Israel, and shared their fate in everything. Admittedly, its southern origins were still felt to begin with and it acted like an outsider among the alliance of northern tribes. As the Song of Deborah tells us, the tribe of Reuben did not come to the help of the tribes of Zebulun and Naphtali when the latter fought with the Kingdom of Hazor. Evidently, Reuben was guided not so much by his relations with the northern tribes as by his own special ties with the 'house of Joseph'. It is interesting that in the same Song of Deborah, the tribe of Reuben is specifically identified among all the Israelite tribes as not offering support to its brothers. For some reason, it was Reuben that stirred up the most disappointment in the authors of this ancient work of poetry. While censuring in passing all who shied from offering help, the poem criticizes Reuben's position more than that of anyone else:

"In the districts of Reuben
    there was much searching of heart.
Why did you stay among the campfires
    to hear the whistling for the flocks?
In the districts of Reuben
    there was much searching of heart" (Judges 5: 15-16).

We may suppose that the closer attention given to this tribe was a consequence of the fact that it had been the first of the 'house of Jacob' to join the Israelite tribal alliance. In order to settle properly in Transjordan, it probably relied upon a great deal of help from its northern fellows; however, when its own turn to help came, it failed the test of loyalty.

Settlement on the land

Although modern archaeology is unable yet to give an answer to the questions of when the Israelites arrived and where from, it can determine, with a reasonable degree of accuracy, when they settled on the land in Canaan. This has been a considerable breakthrough in biblical archaeology over recent decades. Hundreds of new settlements belonging – judging by their material culture – to the Israelites have been found. According to statistics produced by the American archaeologist Laurence Stager, during the 12th and 11th centuries B.C.E. 633 completely new settlements with features of material culture characteristic of the Israelites appeared in Canaan. In the absolute majority of cases, these were small towns that did not even have fortified walls. They were made up of four-room, two-story pillared houses, of the kind that were typical for the Israelites. Their inhabitants engaged in both arable and cattle farming. Admittedly, unlike their Canaanite neighbors, they did not keep pigs. All these settlements were on hills or eminences in Samaria, Judea, and Galilee, while the Canaanite cities continued to exist in the valleys. The new settlements began appearing at the beginning of the 12th century B.C.E. – first in Samaria, then in Galilee, and, later still, in Judea and the Negev in the south. At approximately the same time, new settlements sprang up in Transjordan, where a similar process was likewise underway with the semi-nomadic population settling on the land. The American archaeologist William Dever notes a further feature that is typical of the Israelites alone – the collar-rim storage jar. This kind of ceramic ware, emphasizes Dever, is completely absent from Canaanite cities. He also points out that, judging by the archaeological finds, the inhabitants of the new settlements, unlike ordinary nomads, already had experience of crop-growing. Dever calls the Israelites 'pioneers of terrace arable farming' and is of the opinion that it was they who first invented this way of cultivating the land in Canaan.

At the same time, their studies of objects of material culture in the new settlements have led many archaeologists (including W. Dever, I. Finkelshtein, and A. Mazar) to conclude that, for all the differences between the Israelite and Canaanite settlements, there is no evidence that the Israelites were of an 'alien' origin, i.e. their material culture reveals no important difference from that of the local Canaanite population. The archaeological data provide unanimous support for the supposition that before settling on the land, the Israelites had already been a substantial length of time in Canaan and had managed to pick up a great deal of the Canaanite culture.

Regardless of when the majority of the Israelite conquests in Canaan were carried out, the alliance of all the northern and southern tribes, at least in the form in which it is described in the Bible, could have been created no earlier than the second half of the 12th century B.C.E. Moreover, the alliance continued to be dominated by the northern tribes and retained their name, Israel, as before. Only from this moment onwards, and not – it has to be stressed – from the age of the biblical patriarchs, was its second name (Israel) applied to the southern tribal group of Jacob. The Northerners – or rather, the 'house of Joseph', continued to play the main role in the alliance right up to the accession of David during the United Monarchy. The center of the alliance was the principal city of the northern tribes, Shechem, which was situated in the territory of the tribe of Ephraim. It was in Shechem that Joseph's bones, brought from Egypt, were buried, and it was there, in the hills of Ephraim, that Joshua himself was buried likewise. Moreover, it was on the tribal territory of the 'house of Joseph', in the hills of Ephraim, that high priest Eleazar of the 'house of Jacob' found his final resting place. However, in spite of sharing a center and a religious cult, the Israelite tribal league remained, as before, an extremely decentralized confederation, in which each tribe resolved its own problems independently and conducted its own policies. This tribal alliance was born out of the necessity to take back the Hebrews' former lands in Canaan, and it was for this purpose that they merged with one another. But as soon as the Hebrew tribes settled on the conquered land, their alliance in effect disintegrated. External conquerors were the only force capable of cementing together, even if for a short time, the separate elements in this amorphous union.

CHAPTER NINE

In the days when there was no king in Israel

The judges and their gods

The period following the conquest of Canaan and before the creation of the United Monarchy is usually called the period of the judges. However, 'judges' is an imprecise term for those who led the Hebrew tribes at that time – for they were not so much judges as leaders and military commanders. The Hebrew tribes who had settled in the land of Canaan acted independently of one another and tackled all problems each on their own. In characterizing this time, the Bible emphatically says that "in those days, when there was no king in Israel, each did as he pleased" (Judges 17:6). The biblical writers assess this period exclusively from the point of view of theosophy, i.e. from the point of view of loyalty to the cult of Yahweh: "[...] they [Israelites] forsook him [Lord] and served Baal and the Ashtoreths. In his anger against Israel the Lord handed them over to raiders who plundered them. He sold them to their enemies all around, whom they were no longer able to resist. Whenever Israel went out to fight, the hand of the Lord was against them to defeat them, just as he had sworn to them. They were in great distress. Then the Lord raised up judges, who saved them out of the hands of these raiders. Yet they would not listen to their judges but prostituted themselves to other gods and worshiped them. Unlike their fathers, they quickly turned from the way in which their fathers had walked, the way of obedience to the Lord's commands. Whenever the Lord raised up a judge for them, he was with the judge and saved them out of the hands of their enemies as long as the judge lived; for the Lord had compassion on them as they groaned under those who oppressed and afflicted them. But when the judge died, the people returned to ways even more corrupt than those of their fathers, following other gods and serving and worshiping them. They refused to give up their evil practices and stubborn ways" (Judges 2: 13-19). The authors of the Old Testament emphasized, above all, the opposition between the cult of Yahweh and all other religious cults in Canaan, implying a conflict between monotheism and paganism. In actual fact, not just during the period of the judges but during later times too, there was no such conflict. Firstly, worship of Yahweh was not at this time a monotheistic religion of the kind that it became many centuries later. Secondly, not just during the time of the judges but during the entire period of the First Temple, the cult of Yahweh co-existed reasonably peacefully with many pagan cults. The confrontation between the cult of Yahweh and the Canaanite cults was not a fight between monotheism and paganism, but a contest for political influence and material resources. The Aaronites and Levites were competing not for the triumph of faith in the one God over the pagan idols, but in order to preserve their own positions in the face of competition from priests belonging to other cults. This was the true reason for the bloody calls made by certain high priests for the total destruction of the already defeated enemies of Israel. That monotheism existed in this age is a myth that dates to later times. Most likely, the cult of Yahweh was during this period just as pagan as the Canaanite cults that it opposed. Moses's followers were unable to live up to the exalted nature of his religious and philosophical concept, quickly abandoning it for an old, pagan, perception of their tribal faith. Moses's death brought a revival of the pagan concept of the cult of Yahweh represented by high priest Aaron, at the time of the conflict arising from worship of the golden calf in the desert. However, this was natural and predictable given that the state of spiritual development of society at the time was not conducive to anything more elevated than paganism. It was Moses's consistent monotheism – a development for which there was no rational explanation and which had no chance of reaching fruition given society's lack of intellectual maturity – that was an unusual and striking phenomenon.

The books of Judges and Samuel abound with examples both of pagan rituals and beliefs contained in the cult of Yahweh itself, and of the cult's peaceful co-existence with other pagan cults. For instance, the story of judge Ehud, who liberated his people from the sway of the Moabite King Eglon, mentions idols – the 'graven images' that stood in Gilgal. But Gilgal was not some kind of Canaanite pagan place of worship. It was the first center of the alliance of the Hebrew tribes, a site where collective circumcisions were carried out (these circumcisions were a symbol of the alliance with Yahweh) – in short, a religious center run by the Levites and Aaronites.

Still more striking is the behavior of the judges themselves. These were the political and military leaders of the people. Gideon, who had defended the Israelite tribes from the plundering attacks of the Midianites, might have seemed to be rising up against the cult of Baal, who was worshipped not just by Gideon's family, but by his entire city. It was not for nothing that he was nicknamed 'Jerub-Baal' ('Let Baal contend with him'). Gideon had originally been the bright hope of the followers of Yahweh among the northern tribes. But to the disappointment of the latter, he began attributing his victories over his enemies not to Yahweh, but to another, pagan god. He made the pieces of golden jewelry that he had seized as plunder into "an ephod, which he placed in Ophrah, his town. All Israel prostituted themselves by worshiping it there, and it became a snare to Gideon and his family" (Judges 8:27). According to the text of the Bible, after all his victories over his enemies, "The Israelites said to Gideon, 'Rule over us—you, your son and your grandson—because you have saved us out of the hand of Midian.' But Gideon told them, 'I will not rule over you, nor will my son rule over you. The Lord will rule over you'"(Judges 8: 22-23). Evidently, Gideon realized that it was much more convenient to rule in the name of God than in his own name. (The advantages of theocracy were properly appreciated only during the time of the Second Temple.) But Gideon's Lord turned out to be nothing more than a pagan idol and not the Almighty One God of Moses.

While Gideon turned down the tempting proposal to become King of Israel, even if in favor of a Canaanite divinity, his son Abimelech was prepared to do anything – and with the help of any pagan idols – in pursuit of this goal. An interesting detail in the short history of his rule is that the people of Shechem, the principal city of the northern tribes, worshipped Baal-Berith – and it was from the latter's shrine that Abimelech obtained the money he needed to create his army of mercenaries. It was in the temple of Baal-Berith that the inhabitants of Shechem concealed themselves from Abimelech's army when the latter was storming their city, given that it was, evidently, the largest and best-fortified building in the city.

Still worse in this sense was the behavior of another judge, Jephthah. Jephthah 'gave the Lord his word' that he would make a burnt offering of the first person to emerge from the door of his home if he returned victorious from battle with the Ammonites. But the first to come out to congratulate him was his only daughter. "When he saw her, he tore his clothes and cried, "Oh!

My daughter! You have made me miserable and wretched, because I have made a vow to the Lord that I cannot break." "My father," she replied, "you have given your word to the Lord. Do to me just as you promised, now that the Lord has avenged you of your enemies, the Ammonites'" (Judges 11:35-36). But the God of Moses could not demand human sacrifice; he could not even tolerate such a thing. It was the pagan divinities that needed such sacrifices – for instance, the notorious Moloch, who was also worshipped by the Canaanites and to whom the latter sacrificed their children. In this way, neither Gideon's 'god' nor Jephthah's 'lord' had anything in common with Moses's Yahweh and the commandments handed down to Moses on Mount Sinai. From this it follows that the words 'God' and 'Lord' – like the tetragrammaton YHWH, used in

Bronze statuette of Baal covered with gold. Megiddo. 12th century B.C.E.

the biblical texts from the period of the judges to designate Yahweh – should not automatically be associated with the Almighty God of Moses. The 'Lord' of the majority of the judges, even if designated by the tetragrammaton YHWH, was merely one of the Canaanite divinities – probably, Baal. In the ancient oral narratives, these pagan divinities were called by their proper names, but the authors of the Old Testament replaced these names with 'Yahweh' or, more abstractly, 'God' or 'the Lord'. They dressed up the indubitable paganism of the period of the judges in a semblance of periodical enlightenment and a return to the cult of Yahweh – or, to be more exact, to the monotheistic concept of Yahweh, for which Moses had laid the foundation. It should not be forgotten that the biblical writers attributed all misfortunes and vicissitudes to befall their people to the fact that the Israelites had started worshipping new, pagan gods. Typical in this respect is the traditional leitmotif, "When they chose new gods, war came to the city gates" (Judges 5:8).

How the pagan cults flourished among the Israelites is clear from the story of Micah, who headed one of the clans of the Ephraim tribe. Setting up 'an idol and graven image' in his home, Micah turned his house into a pagan shrine and, furthermore, instructed his son to serve as a priest there. Subsequently, he appointed a Levite to command the priests in this shrine, and the Levite, without feeling the least bit embarrassed, served the pagan idol conscientiously. But the most interesting thing is this: at the moment when the tribe of Dan moved from the south to the north, this Levite took the idol from the house of Micah and set it up in the temple of the city of Dan (Laish) – and at the same time founded a dynasty of local high priests: "They continued to use the idols Micah had made, all the time the house of God was in Shiloh" (Judges 18:31). It should be remembered that the temple in Dan, like the similar temple in Bethel, subsequently became an alternative to the Temple in Jerusalem in the Northern kingdom (Israel). However, we need not dwell on ordinary Levites; a stronger example is provided by Samuel, the high priest himself, who built sacrificial altars and took part in sacrifices on the heights of numerous cities. And yet high priest Eleazar had responded to the creation of just such an autonomous sacrificial altar by threatening the Israelite tribes who had settled in Transjordan with war. The story of the conflict with the tribe of Benjamin likewise confirms the existence of several religious centers simultaneously. According to the Bible, representatives of all the tribes gathered to meet the Lord in Mizpah and at the same time came to the Lord at Bethel. The very fact that there were a large number of religious and political centers in the lands occupied by the Hebrew tribes – Gilgal, Shechem, Shiloh, Bethel, Kiriath-Jearim, and Ramah – is clear proof that they had no unified religious cult and that the alliance had disintegrated. Much depended on which of the tribes was dominant at what particular time, to which of the tribes the current leader belonged, and, possibly, which of the cults was then in the ascendance. Possibly the most precise characterization of the religious beliefs of the Hebrew tribes at the time is the following quotation from the Book of Judges: "[...] They served the Baals and the Ashtoreths, and the gods of Aram, the gods of Sidon, the gods of Moab, the gods of the Ammonites and the gods of the Philistines. And [because] the Israelites forsook the Lord and no longer served him" (Judges 10:6). Moses's consistent monotheism could hardly have been attractive to Hebrew society at that point in its spiritual development. An invisible, intangible, incorporeal God who was one God for everyone and everything in the world was something incomprehensible and alien to the primitive religious perceptions of people who were used to the objects of their worship being clearly visible and tangible. Intuitively, they were drawn to the pagan gods of the peoples who surrounded them, gods that were easily comprehensible and accessible to their minds and feelings. Moreover, the priests of Yahweh – the Aaronites and Levites, – like the priests of pagan divinities, tended to regard worship as, above all, a source of income rather than a duty arising from faith. The following words eloquently reveal the money-making emphasis in the functions of the priest: "Appoint me to some priestly office so I can have food to eat" (1 Samuel 2:36). The unsavory and sacrilegious behavior, debauchery, and corruption of the priests – and especially of the sons of the high priests Eli and Samuel – made it difficult for the people to see any difference between orgies in the pagan temples and sacrifices to the Lord.

The cult of Yahweh remained the principal religion of the southern tribes only, although even in the latter case Yahweh had to coexist with other, pagan, divinities. As for the northern tribes, although they recognized the Lord of their southern brothers as the main official God of the Israelite alliance, in daily life they nevertheless continued to favor Baal and Ashtoreth.

The disintegration of the Israelite tribal confederation

In contrast to what we are told in the Bible, the Hebrew tribes returned to Canaan not simultaneously, but in three stages and during the course of approximately 300 years – from the middle of the 15th century to the second half of the 12th century B.C.E. This determined the history of the formation of the tribal alliance. First taking shape in Canaan in the second half of the 13th century B.C.E., this alliance initially consisted only of the four northern tribes. Later, in the 1190s and 1180s B.C.E., these four tribes were joined by another seven who had just come out of Egypt. And, finally, 40 years later, the two southern tribes returned from the desert. Given this sequence of events, only ten tribes (not including the Levites) – and not 12 – could have taken part in Joshua's conquests. On the other hand, although Moses brought nine tribes, including the Levites, out of Egypt, only two of them – those of Judah and Simeon – wandered for 40 years in the desert.

The fact that the Hebrews returned to Canaan in three stages, coupled with analysis of their genealogy as given in the Bible, allows us to suppose that initially they consisted not of two but of three separate tribal groups – a northern group (Israel), a southern one (Jacob), and the Amorite tribes that had joined them at the time of their exodus from Egypt. There can be no doubt that the core of the northern tribes was the 'house of Joseph', which consisted of the tribes of Manasseh and Ephraim. The latter were joined by the tribe of Benjamin, which, like the latter two tribes, traced its roots to the same founder, Israel. As for the northern tribe of Naphtali, it is no coincidence that the Bible traces its origins not to Rachel, the favorite wife of Jacob/Israel, but merely to her slave girl, Bilhah. This is a sign not just of the tribe's inferior status in the tribal hierarchy, but also, evidently, of the fact that it was more distantly related. We do not know at what stage the tribe of Naphtali joined up with the 'house of Joseph', but it is likely that all four of these tribes had a direct relation to the Hyksos and were forced to leave Egypt after the Hyksos pharaohs had been driven out.

Another group of Amorite tribes that joined the Israelite alliance possibly consisted of Issahar, Zebulun, Gad, and Asher. The Bible describes these as part of the tribal hierarchy of southern tribes and traces their genealogy to Jacob's eldest wife, Leah, and to her slave girl, Zilpah. Most likely, the fate that befell these tribes in Egypt was similar to that of the 'house of Jacob'. Like the southern Hebrew tribes, they arrived in the Nile Delta later and, unlike the 'house of Joseph', had no connection with the Hyksos. They likewise were held back in Egypt and experienced all the woes of living in slavery to the pharaohs of the 19th Dynasty. These Amorite tribes left Egypt together with the southern Hebrew tribes, were with Moses at Mount Sinai, and after accepting his commandments, became part of the 'house of Jacob' and its family tree. But unlike their two southern fellow tribes, they refused to wander the desert for 40 years and left to join up with the 'house of Joseph'. The fact that the Bible does not in any way link their origins with Rachel and Bilhah, the matriarchs of the northern tribes, is evidence that they had a different genealogy from the latter. It is notable that the Book of Genesis, which contains ancient narratives from the epos of the southern and northern tribes, makes almost no mention of Naphtali, Dan, Issahar, Zebulun, Gad, and Asher during the pre-Egypt period. Probably, the convergence with these tribes occurred in

Egypt or following the departure from Egypt. Thus, in its final version the Israelite tribal confederation brought together three different groups of West Semitic tribes of Amorite origin, who returned to Canaan from Egypt at different times.

True unification of all 12 tribes occurred only during the period of the United Monarchy (late 11th century – 928 B.C.E.). Until then, the Israelite alliance existed either in incomplete form or purely nominally. This union was actually necessary only for the conquest of Canaan; and when Canaan had been conquered, even if incompletely, under Joshua, the leaders of the tribes began to feel unhappy at the diminishment of their power in favor of the common leader. From the point of view of the biblical writers, the Hebrew tribes were unified by three factors – tribal kinship, worship of Yahweh, and shared history. But the reality was somewhat different. The Hebrew tribes consisted not of one, but of three different West Semitic groups of Amorite origin, which made their alliance unstable. Worship of Yahweh was likewise not a uniting factor. It was the principal religion only in the case of the southern tribes and partly in the case of the Amorite tribes who had come out of Egypt together with Moses. Finally, until their departure for Egypt, and in Egypt itself too, these groups had different histories. In actual fact, the main thing that had united them earlier had been their status as Habiru/Apiru lacking a home and land, following their forced departure from Egypt. So the conquest of Canaan, even if it was only partial, disrupted the basis of their former unity. The second most important uniting factor was these tribes' dramatic memories of their stay in Egypt. However, with the passing of time and as they became increasingly Canaanized, this factor too became less influential. For this reason, the alliance's disintegration during the time of the judges was a natural and inevitable process. Chronologically, the period of the judges was a fairly short interval of time – between the middle of the 12th century and late 11th century B.C.E., although, according to the Bible, it should have been much longer. However, the biblical version was written only in the 6th century B.C.E., i.e. approximately 500-600 years after the time of the judges, when there was no longer any possibility of faithfully reproducing the chronological order of events and many facts had been distorted by the huge gap in time. As a result, the historical sequence of most episodes given in the Book of Judges was adversely affected. For instance, the story of Samson's fight against the Philistines, which is given at the end of the book, should actually be placed at its beginning. The same goes for the episodes with Micah's idol and the migration of the tribe of Dan to the north – events which should have been at the beginning of the book but that are actually at its end. Meanwhile, the story of the conflict with the tribe of Benjamin brings the Book of Judges to a close, although chronologically it took place under the rule of judge Othniel, which the authors of the book placed at its beginning. But the problem is not so much one of chronological order. The Book of Judges that we have today is a compilation of narratives taken from several different sources; it gives different versions of one and the same episodes of peaceful coexistence and confrontation with neighbors. Another thing that cannot be left out is that certain judges ruled not successively, one after the other, but simultaneously. Moreover, none of the judges – not even the best known, such as Gideon, Jephthah, Ehud, and Samson – ruled all of the tribes at once, but only some of them. Judge Samuel, for instance, according to the Bible, "appointed his sons as judges for Israel", but the text goes on to explain that "they served at Beersheba" (1 Samuel 8:1-3). It is likely that Samuel ruled the tribe of Judah, but appointed his sons to rule over the tribe of Simeon. Thus, in actual fact, he held power only over the two southern tribes, although his religious authority was recognized likewise among the northern tribes. However, even during attacks by enemies, only those tribes who were under direct threat came to the defense of their brothers; the others remained indifferent to their fate. The Song of Deborah, which tells of the war of the northern tribes against King of Hazor, condemns those tribes who did not come to the help of their brothers at a critical moment. The same happened when the Philistines pushed the tribe of Dan off its tribal land. After not receiving the help it was due from the other tribes, the tribe of Dan was forced to find itself new land in the very north of Canaan.

During the period of the judges, it was centrifugal rather than centripetal tendencies that dominated, so the Hebrew tribes did not so much unite with one another to fight the external enemy as they fought one another for land and political influence. While the tribe of Judah was the clear leader of the Southerners, the tribe of Ephraim attempted to occupy such a position of dominance among the Northerners. It not only refused to recognize the authority of judge Gideon, who was from the closely related tribe of Manasseh, but even threatened him with war. Relations between Ephraim and another judge, Jephthah of Gilead, ended even more sorrowfully. After starting a fratricidal war, the Ephraimites were surprised to suffer defeat at the hands of the Gileadites, and the latter took their revenge by butchering their opponents at a crossing of the Jordan River.

That the Israelite tribal league fell apart in clashes between the Hebrew tribes is confirmed by the conflict around the tribe of Benjamin. The background to this story is extraordinarily variegated and confused. It involves the insulting of a Levite, a crime in the spirit of Sodom and Gomorrah, intertribal quarrels, and fraternal concern for the future of this long-suffering Israelite tribe. Analysis of this episode leads us to think that it is not one but two intertribal conflicts that are intertwined here. The first was a clash between the neighboring tribes of Judah and Benjamin. The second was punishment of the tribe of Gad. The fact that the text mentions high priest Pinehas, son of Eleazar and grandson of Aaron, gives us reason to suppose that the story occurred during the rule of judge Othniel, from the tribe of Judah. Clearly, the amoral behavior of the inhabitants of the Benjamite city of Gibeah was merely a pretext for the war waged by Judah against Benjamin. The true cause of this conflict was likely the claims laid by both tribes to the land of the Hivites, with whom Joshua had previously concluded a peace agreement. The disintegration of the Israelite tribal league and the later arrival of the southern tribes in Canaan led to a re-division of the Hivite territory, which had still been independent in the time of Joshua. This conflict was exacerbated by the fact that both tribes laid claim to the land of yet another people, the Jebusites – including to the latter's principal city, Jebus (Jerusalem). The Book of Judges mentions that the tribe of Benjamin attempted – evidently prior to the arrival of the two southern tribes from the desert – to seize the territory of the Jebusites, but was unable to carry this attempt through to a successful conclusion: "The Benjamites, however, failed to dislodge the Jebusites, who were living in Jerusalem; to this day the Jebusites live there with the Benjamites" (Judges 1:21). However, even before leaving for Egypt, the tribe of Judah had regarded the Jebusites as their allies. Their worship of the Almighty God played an important role in the change in Abraham's religious views and in his renunciation of the old gods of Sumer. After the southern tribes returned to Canaan, their alliance with the Jebusites was renewed for some time. Rivalry for the land of the Hivites and Jebusites led the two tribes into military confrontation with one another. Possibly, Judah intervened as ally and protector of the Jebusites and Hivites. But, in spite of what the Bible says, it is likely that the northern tribes refrained from close involvement in this conflict. Otherwise, it would be impossible to understand how the military divisions of 11 tribes could have suffered defeat and for a long time been unable to overcome one of the smallest Israelite tribes – that of Benjamin. Probably, the refusal of the northern tribes to support the tribe of Benjamin in the latter's war with the southern tribe of Judah had its explanation in Benjamin's violation of the traditional peace between the 'house of Joseph' and the Hivite cities. Later, Othniel sought reconciliation with the tribe of Benjamin, compensating the latter with plunder from his resounding defeat of the tribe of Gad. One cannot help being surprised at the extremely severe punishment given to the inhabitants of Jabesh-Gilead (Gad), given that in the Song of Deborah those who refused to help their brother tribes were requited with nothing more than censure. It cannot be ruled out that the slaughter of the inhabitants of Gilead was revenge for their attempt to enter into an alliance with the Arameans or Ammonites, with whom Othniel was then at war. It is likewise possible that the reason for the severity of this punishment was Othniel's attempt to revive the Israelite alliance in the form in which it had existed under Joshua.

The Hebrew tribes who returned to Canaan composed approximately between a quarter and a third of the entire population of the country. In the south, where the population was not so dense, they possibly formed a larger percentage of the total and in the north a smaller percentage. Despite the fact that in any case they amounted to less than half the total population of Canaan, they together outnumbered any of the local peoples, and this gave them a decisive advantage over their opponents. Given that non-Israelite Palestine was always a conglomerate of mutually hostile city-states or semi-nomadic groups (in Transjordan, for instance), the likelihood of the potential opponents of the Hebrew tribes uniting was extremely small. For about two and a half centuries, the advance of the northern (Israelite) tribes was kept in check by Egyptian rule over Canaan. But when the Egyptians left and the second wave of returning Hebrew tribes arrived, the fate of Canaan was settled: it inevitably passed into the hands of the Hebrews. Although the disintegration of the Israelite tribal alliance during the time of the judges considerably weakened the Israelites' advance, this could not bring the conquest of Canaan to a halt. Henceforth, Canaan was conquered not so much by military means as by assimilation of the Hebrew tribes with the local peoples. This process began in the 15ᵗʰ century B.C.E., when several northern tribes returned from Egypt to Canaan. It was then that the 'house of Joseph' drew very close to the Hivites of central Palestine, particularly in Shechem. It is no coincidence that the recently identified Israelites on the bas reliefs of Pharaoh Merneptah are almost indistinguishable in looks and dress from traditional Canaanites. Their neighbors and relatives – the Shasu nomads (Edomites, Moabites, and Ammonites) – looked different. The intermarrying of Hebrews and the Canaanite and Amorite peoples was considerably facilitated by their possession of shared West Semitic origins and a common language. The extraordinary ease with which this intermixing took place is indicated by, for instance, the case of the Israelite hero and judge Samson, who took a fancy to a Philistine girl. In spite of their different ethnic origins, different faiths, and, even more importantly, the hostility between the two peoples, Samson was able without any difficulty at all to marry the girl of his choice. If marriage between circumcised Israelites and their uncircumcised enemies the Philistines was so easy to arrange, then one can imagine how things stood when it came to the closely related West Semitic peoples – the Canaanites and Amorites. In time, the latter became completely intermixed with the Hebrew tribes. The frequent mentions in the Pentateuch and the Book of Joshua of the necessity of driving out the Canaanite peoples seem like a mockery of the real situation. The biblical writers were in fact calling for the expulsion or destruction of those who had long since become an integral part of their people. The Song of Deborah contains yet another striking example of assimilation. Listing all those who had given help to their brothers, the authors name: "some [...] from Ephraim, whose roots were in Amalek" (Judges 5:14).

Thus Ephraim, which was the most important northern tribe in the 'house of Joseph', contained a clan or clans deriving from Amalek, the bitter enemy of the 'house of Jacob'. The memory of these people was preserved in the name of one of the mountains on the tribal land of Ephraim. This mountain – Mount Amalek – is specially mentioned by the Book of Judges as being the place where the Israelite judge Abdon, son of Hillel, a Pirathonite, was buried (Judges 12:15).

The Levites were in a special position. Unlike the other Hebrew tribes, they split in two: the majority went with Moses and the Northerners, while the minority remained with Judah and Simeon in the desert. Thus, the Levites were dispersed between the northern and southern tribes. This fact makes it easier to understand why they did not receive land of their own in Canaan and why, unlike the other tribes, they were not initially counted – and were subsequently counted in a special way and nevertheless turned out to be fewer in number than the other tribes.

The priestly clan of the Aaronites found themselves no better off. This clan was likewise split between the two southern tribes, who remained in the desert, and the tribes who left to join the 'house of Joseph'. High priest Eleazar, who was head of the Aaronites, and his son Phinehas joined the Northerners and their leader Joshua. This throws light on why Eleazar was buried in the mountains of Ephraim, nearly Shechem, and not in the south, on the territory of his kinsmen from the tribe of Judah. In time, however, deprived of the support they traditionally had from the southern tribes, the Aaronites were forced to cede leadership to the Levite dynasty, which derived from the sons of Moses. It was the Levites who created the religious center in Shiloh and managed it both before it was destroyed by the Philistines and afterwards. Pinehas was probably the last high priest of the northern tribes to come from the kin of Aaron. Deteriorating relations with the Levites forced Aaron's descendants to move to the territory of the Judahites, where the Aaronites continued to play the leading role in the worship of Yahweh. Thus two centers of worship of Yahweh sprang up – one in the north under the management of the Levites and the other in the south, under the Aaronites. This helps us understand both the ways in which the cult of Yahweh spread among the northern tribes, and the traditional rivalry between the priests of Shiloh (northern Levites) and the priests of the Jerusalem Temple (Aaronites). It cannot be ruled out that the mysterious death of Aaron's two sons in the desert happened not because they came too close to the Ark of the Covenant, but because they conflicted with the Levites over the right to conduct religious services.

Moses's spiritual descendants became those northern Levites who were led by Eleazar and his son Pinehas, and not those who remained with the southern tribes in the desert. Among the Judahites, the Levites had to be content with a secondary role as assistants to the Aaronites. Later, the followers of Yahweh from the northern and southern tribes closed ranks so as to fight rival, pagan cults, but the deep rift in relations between them remained right up to the destruction of the First Temple. At the same time, pursuing its own goals, each group had an interest in creating a common history and genealogy, as can be seen in the biblical version. When the Levites split and dispersed among the Hebrew tribes, this turned them into the main centripetal force in the Israelite tribal alliance, and it was they who became the main spreaders of the cult of Yahweh among the northern tribes. Admittedly, given the traditional influence of the supreme Canaanite god El among them, worship of Yahweh in the Northern Kingdom (Israel) spread more in the form of worship of El: all the characteristics of Yahweh were transferred to the familiar El and the latter's name was used to signify the one and Almighty God of the southern tribes.

The tribe of Dan: West Semitic or Indo-European?

Of all the tribes that joined the Israelite alliance the most enigmatic was Dan. As already said, there is absolutely no mention of
this tribe in the pre-Egypt period when the Hebrews were living
in Canaan. The only exception is the official genealogy, which
names the tribe's forefather, Dan, as the son of Jacob/Israel –
and, moreover, the son not by one of Jacob's wives, but by the
slave girl Bilhah. The second mention comes only in the list of
all members of the family of the forefather Jacob/Israel who had
left for Egypt. But the mention of Dan in the official genealogy
does not prove very much, given that this genealogy was drawn
up much later, in the time of the United Monarchy, and on the
basis of the political considerations of that period. Much more
important are episodes in the lives of the forefathers of the tribes
in the pre-Egypt period; and this is something that is completely
lacking in the case of the tribe of Dan. The first information, even
if completely trivial, on the tribe of Dan appears only during the
time of the wandering in the desert after the exodus from Egypt.
Oholiab, son of Ahisamach from the tribe of Dan, is named as
the master craftsman who helped build and embellish the Ark of
the Covenant (Exodus 35: 34-35). Another, more important episode, tells of the son of an Egyptian man and an Israelite woman
from the tribe of Dan who insulted and cursed the name of God,
for which he was stoned to death (Leviticus 24:10-11). This
gives us indirect proof that the tribe of Dan came out of Egypt
not with the 'house of Joseph' in the 15th century B.C.E., but with
the 'house of Jacob', together with Moses, at the beginning of the
12th century B.C.E. However, unlike the other four tribes that
joined Moses (Issahar, Zebulun, Gad, and Asher), the tribe of
Dan was not named as one of the sons of Jacob by Jacob's eldest
wife Leah and her slave girl Zilpah. The official genealogy makes
Dan the son of Bilhah, the slave girl of Rachel, which is to say a
member of the 'house of Joseph'. Why, then, were the Amorite

tribes of Issahar, Zebulun, Gad, and Asher closer to the group of southern tribes than was the tribe of Dan? Probably, the answer to this is given by that same extraordinarily important episode in which the son of the Egyptian and the Israelite woman from the tribe of Dan insulted the name of the Lord. In the Bible, nothing is accidental; even the most seemingly irrelevant episode in real life carries a certain historical and philosophical significance and reflects real facts, and any distortions merely concern the time at which events occurred or their evaluation. In the Pentateuch, the biblical writers never mentioned the ordinary tribe-members, but only those who were leaders or belonged to the tribal aristocracy. For this reason, the son of the Israelite woman, who is called by name, was evidently the son of the leader of the tribe of Dan. It is notable that his father is described as an Egyptian. But it was traditional at that time for only women, not men, to be given to other families and tribes. For instance, an Egyptian woman – the daughter of the influential priest Potipherah – was given to Joseph, and not the other way around. Thus the man whom the Bible calls an Egyptian, i.e. a foreigner and follower of a different faith, was in fact the true leader of the tribe of Dan who took a noble Israelite woman as his wife. It is not surprising that this foreign leader and his tribe did not adopt the cult of Yahweh even following the giving of the Sinai commandments. Clearly, this tribe, unlike the other Western Semites that had joined the alliance, found the cult of Yahweh utterly alien. Subsequently, Dan, together with the four Amorite tribes and two southern Hebrew tribes (Reuben and Levi), joined the 'house of Joseph' instead of wandering for 40 years in the desert in the company of Judah and Simeon. It is likely that Dan's foreign origins, rejection of the Lord of the Southerners, and subsequent alliance with the Northerners, forced the biblical authors to find a place for this tribe in the 'house of Joseph' as the latter's junior partner. Thus, the tribe of Dan remained a member of the family of Jacob/Israel, but was reduced in status to the very bottom of the tribal hierarchy.

Another important thing that characterizes the tribe of Dan is the story of its leader Samson and his uncompromising fight against the Philistines during the time of the judges. For some reason, not a single Hebrew tribe – and, above all, Judah and Benjamin, closest neighbors of the Philistines – was as hostile to the Philistines or fought against them as fiercely as the tribe of Dan, although these other tribes suffered no less at the hands of the Philistines. It is notable that after settling in southwestern Canaan, the Philistines did not destroy or drive out the local population – the Canaanites and the Rephaim (or Avvim, as they were called in that region), who were a more ancient people. So the Semitic and pre-Semitic population remained untouched, as the Bible makes perfectly clear. Why, then, did the tribe of Dan have to leave its allotted land, which bordered the lands of the Philistines? And was it really mere chance that made the Danites choose a place for themselves next to the Philistines? Does not the reason for the intense hostility between the Philistines and the tribe of Dan lie in the latter's Indo-European or Aegean origins? As history shows, related peoples often conflict with one another more fiercely than with foreigners. It is quite possible that the name Samson (Hebrew: Shimshon) and the names of Samson's parents had been Semitized in the same way as Moses's Egyptian name. And Samson's fight against the Philistines resembles the feats of Achaean heroes more than it does the kind of wars waged by the Israelite judges. Finally, the triumphal Song of Deborah contains an episode that throws light on the true origin of the tribe of Dan. While condemning those Israelite tribes that refused to help their brothers in the battle with Sisera, the military commander under King Jabin of Hazor, the Song of Deborah names the tribe of Dan and asks: "And Dan, why did he linger by the ships?" (Judges 5:17). This is a question that could have any specialist on ancient Jewish history stumped for an answer. How is it that an Israelite tribe of former semi-nomads who had recently settled on the land now suddenly comprised sailors? At that time, it was only the Phoenicians and the 'Sea Peoples' who 'lingered by the ships'. The former were West Semitic people, like the Israelites, while the latter were Indo-European tribes from the Aegean and Asia Minor. However, any suggestion that the tribe of Dan was of Phoenician origin can be dismissed immediately since this tribe came to Canaan from the Nile Delta. More probable is the idea that Dan originally came from Asia Minor or, rather, the Aegean. Incidentally, a 'Sea People' by the name of 'danuna' or 'da'anu' is first mentioned in Egyptian sources during the rule of pharaohs Amenhotep III and Akhenaten in the 14th century B.C.E. In the reign of Ramesses II, mercenaries from the 'Sea Peoples' fought on the side of the Egyptians against the Hittites at the famous battle of Kadesh. But these peoples' first attack on Egypt occurred only at the end of the 13th century B.C.E. during the reign of Merneptah. Considerably later, during the rule of Ramesses III (in the eighth year of the latter's reign), a 'Sea People' called 'Danyen' was named among those who attacked the Egyptian army near the Nile Delta. Possibly, this is the same people to which Hittite sources gave the slightly different name of 'Daniya-wana'. Finally, Homer talks of the Danaeans (another name for the Achaeans) who lived in Argolis and Argos on the Peloponnese in the south of Greece. If all these similar names are not a simple coincidence and the Israelite tribe of Dan was indeed part of this Aegean people, then this tribe probably appeared in the Nile Delta in the second half or at the end of the 13th century B.C.E., at the time when the 'Sea Peoples' began moving en masse to the east and southeast. If the Danites were directly related to the legendary Danaeans of Argolis, then they were close neighbors of the Mycenaeans, who are thought by archaeologists to have comprised a considerable part of the Philistine population. It is difficult to say how the inhabitants of ancient Argos came to Egypt. Were they mercenaries and military colonizers in the service of the Pharaoh, or captives who had been taken into slavery along with their families? At any rate, the ancient Egyptian sources confirm the existence of a large number of mercenaries and military colonizers from the 'Sea Peoples' in the Nile Delta during the rule of Ramesses II and Merneptah. Later, even more captives from among these peoples appeared in the region. Whatever the case was, during the time of troubles, when Egypt was in the grip of civil war just before Pharaoh Setnakht came to power, this 'Sea People' could have left Egypt in the same way as the Hebrew tribes of Moses. It might have been part of that same large 'rabble' mentioned by the Bible that caused Moses so much trouble and unpleasantness. If this was true, then in their search of a place for themselves in Canaan, the Danites joined the Israelite alliance that had been created by the northern tribes. The memory of their stay in Egypt and their forced homelessness in Canaan were factors that were stronger than ethnic kinship; it was this that united this group of Indo-Europeans with the Western Semites. Unlike the 'house of Joseph' and the 'house of Jacob', the tribe of Dan – like the four Amorite tribes that had joined the alliance (Issahar, Zebulun, Asher, and Gad) – likely did not practice circumcision and only agreed to undergo this ritual in Gilgal in order to become proper members of the Israelite tribal confederation. In those days the circumcision rite was not regarded as the exclusive attribute of the cult of Yahweh, but as a ceremony for solemnizing alliances with divinities or people. Thus began the process of Israelization for the Danites. Their main enemies were their old neighbors and opponents from their former motherland, the Philistines, who refused to give them access to the shore of the Mediterranean. Unable to live by arable agriculture and cattle-rearing alone, the former sailors left for the north of Canaan, where they seized the Canaanite city of Laish (Leshem), renamed it 'Dan', and settled. The northern shore of Canaan was controlled by the Phoenicians and the Tjeker, a people of Aegean origin, with both of whom the tribe of Dan quickly established mutual understanding. Subsequently, all the 'Sea Peoples' who had settled in Canaan – the Danites, Tjeker, and the Philistines themselves – merged with the Western Semites. Interestingly, the biblical story regarding Dan's move from the south to the north of Canaan does not mention any of the Danites by name – not even the leaders – even though it mentions Micah, the head of the Ephraimite clan who gave them temporary refuge. The episode of the Danites' move makes clear that among them there was not a single Levite priest; this was yet another difference between the Danites and the other Hebrew tribes. True, the southern Levite who was later invited to serve as a priest began practicing the cult of Yahweh in their midst, but – and this is very notable – it was in the old pagan form that Moses had condemned.

There is another point that casts doubt on whether the tribe of Dan could have had Israelite origins. The deathbed prophecy of patriarch Jacob contains an extremely interesting phrase: "Dan will provide justice for his people as one of the tribes of Israel" (Genesis 49:16); this implies that Dan would come to be like all the Hebrew tribes. Interestingly, nothing similar was said of any other Hebrew tribe. Why was emphasis put on Dan's becoming like all the other tribes; was this not a self-evident fact? Probably not. And this underlines the significance of other words in Jacob's prophecy about Dan: "I look for your deliverance, o Lord" (Genesis 49:18). The latter was especially important, since the incident in the Desert of Sinai showed how difficult it was for the leaders of the tribe of Dan to accept the God of Moses.

Of course, one may dispute whether the tribe of Dan was Semitic or Indo-European, but it cannot be denied that it was a

tribe which, prior to departure from Egypt, had no direct connection with either the 'house of Jacob' or the 'house of Joseph',
and had joined the Hebrews at a later date.

The Philistine threat

After the conquests made by Joshua, the Hebrew tribes became
the dominant ethnic group in Canaan, and total possession of
this country was, it seemed, only a matter of time. But in real life,
things rarely happen as smoothly as in theory. The Philistines,
an Indo-European people that had made its appearance in the
southwest of Canaan at the beginning of the 12th century B.C.E.,
had a considerable impact on the situation in this country during
the two centuries that followed. Although the Philistines could
hardly have outnumbered the Canaanite peoples, they possessed
two important advantages. First, they were militarily much better organized and had incomparable greater military experience,
both as a result of the lengthy wars they had fought to keep hold
of their former motherland and due to their service as mercenaries in the armies of the Egyptian pharaohs and the Hittite
rulers. Secondly, they made extensive use of iron as a material
in the manufacture of weapons. It cannot be said that the West
Semitic peoples, including the Israelites, had no knowledge of
iron whatsoever. In fact, they had been familiar with it for many
hundreds of years before the Philistines arrived. But, unlike the
Philistines, they did not have any cheap method of manufactur-
ing it. So anything that they made from iron cost them more than
if it had been made from gold. Iron weaponry was much more
effective than bronze and its use in battle on a mass scale gave a
considerable advantage.

The Philistine threat had already been well known to both
Moses and Joshua. Moses, wishing to avoid military confrontation with the Philistines, had refused to lead his people by the
shortest route into Canaan (this route laid alongside the seashore

A Philistine warrior from the reliefs at Medinet Habu, Thebes.

through the lands of the Philistines). Joshua, as the Bible acknowledges, "was unable to drive them out". The first blow from the newcomers from overseas fell on the Israelite tribe of Dan, the Philistines' closest neighbors. Samson, the judge and leader of the Danites, devoted his life to repelling the Philistine aggression, but the tribe of Dan was unable to stand firm under pressure from its hostile neighbors and, relinquishing its tribal lands, was forced to find a new motherland in the north of Canaan. According to the Song of Deborah, recorded in writing during the second half of the 12th century B.C.E., the tribe of Dan had by this time already settled in north Galilee. The second serious collision with the Philistines occurred during the rule of judge Shamgar, son of Anat, who "struck down six hundred Philistines with an oxgoad" (Judges 3:31). However, this was merely a probing maneuver. The Philistines' main drive for expansion came later, in the 11th century B.C.E. From the story of high priest Eli, we know of the major battle fought with the Philistines at Eben-Ezer and Aphek, which ended with the defeat of the Israelites and the seizure of the Hebrews' shrine, the Ark of the Covenant. Judging by the directions taken by the Philistines' military campaigns, they had greatest impact on the southern tribes of Judah and Simeon and the northern tribes of Benjamin, Ephraim, and, partly, Manasseh. It was these tribes that found themselves in the most difficult position, under attack from the Philistines and, periodically, from Ammon and Moab, and the tribes of the desert (the Midianites and the Amalekites) from Transjordan. Under the last judge and high priest, Samuel, the situation became slightly more stable: the northern and southern tribes managed to successfully repel several attacks by the Philistines, although wars with the latter continued throughout the rule of Samuel. It is difficult to say what the greater cause of these temporary successes was – internal problems of some kind that afflicted the Philistines or the fact that the Israelites had struck an alliance with the other West Semitic peoples. On this subject the Bible contains the following short, but significant sentence: "And there was peace between Israel and the Amorites" (1 Samuel 7:14). It is likely that the conflict between the Hebrew tribes and the Amorite (and Canaanite) peoples over the land of Canaan came to an end and the West Semitic peoples united in order to fight the enemy that represented the greatest threat, the Philistines. Perhaps, it was a pooling of resources that enabled them temporarily to halt the expansion of the Philistines. However, the decisive battles for power over Canaan still remained to be fought.

Selected
Bibliography

Aharoni, Y. Nothing Early and Nothing Late. Re-writing Israel's Conquest. *Biblical Archaeologist* 39: 55-76.

Albright W.F., *The Biblical Period from Abraham to Ezra*, 1963.

Barns G.W., *The Ashmolean Ostracon of "Sinuhe"*, London, 1952.

Bar-Yosef, O., 'Prehistoric Palestine' in: *The Oxford Encyclopedia of Archaeology in the Near East*, ed. E.M. Meyers, 4.207-12, New York: Oxford University Press, 1997.

Ben-Tor D., 'The Historical Implications of Middle Kingdom Scarabs found in Palestine bearing Private Names and Titles of Officials' in *BASOR* 294 (1994), 7-22.

Ben-Tor, A. (ed.), *The Archaeology of Ancient Israel*. New Haven, 1992.

Bietak M., *Avaris: The Capital of the Hyksos*, London, 1996.

Boling, R.G. *Judges*. New York, 1975

Bourriau J., "The Second Intermediate Period," in *The Oxford History of Ancient Egypt*, ed. Shaw I., New York: Oxford University Press, 2000, pp.185-217.

Bright J., *A History of Israel*, 4th edition, New York: Oxford University Press, 2001.

Brinkman J.A., *A Political History of Post-Kassite Babylonia, 1158-722 B.C.E.* (1968).

Chevalier R., 'The Greco-Roman Conception of the North: from Pytheas to Tacitus', *Arctic* 37:4, December 1984, pp. 341-346.

Clayton P. A., *Chronicle of the Pharaohs. The Reign-By-Reign Record of the Rulers and Dynasties of Ancient Egypt*, New York: Thames & Hudson, 1994.

Coogan, M. D., ed. and trans. *Stories from Ancient Canaan*, Philadelphia: Westminster, 1978.

Cross, F. M., *Cananite Myth and Hebrew Epic: Essays in the History of the Religion of Israel*, Cambridge, Mass: Harvard University Press, 1973.

Dever W. G. "Archaeology and the Israelite 'Conquest'." *In Anchor Bible Dictionary*, ed. Freedman D.N., 3.545-58. New York: Doubleday, 1992.

Dever W.G., *Who were the early Israelites and where did they come from?*, Wm. B. Eerdmans Publishing Co., Cambridge, 2003.

Diakonov I.M. (ed.), *Ancient Mesopotamia: Socio-Economic History*, 1981.

Diakonov, I.M, 'Starovavilonskiy period v Dvurechye' in: *Istoriya Drevnego Vostoka*, ed. I.M. Diakonov, Moscow: Glavnaya redaktsiya vostochnoy literatury, 1983.

Dothan T., *The Philistines and Their Material Culture*. New Haven: Yale University Press, 1982.

Dothan, T., and Dothan M., *Peoples of the Sea*. New York: Macmillan, 1992.

Eichler, B. L, 'Nuzi and the Bible: A Retrospective' in: *Dumu-e-dubba-a: Studies in Honor of Ake W. Sjoberg*, ed. H. Behrens, D. Loding, and M. T. Roth, pp. 107-19, Philadelphia: University Museum, 1989.

Finkelstein I, Mazar A. and Schmidt B.B., *The Quest for the Historical Israel. Debating Archaeology and the History of Early Israel*. Society of Biblical Literature: Atlanta, 2007.

Finkelstein I. and Silberman N.A., *The Bible Unearthed: Archaeology's New Vision of Ancient Israel and the Origin of its Sacred Texts*, New York: Free Press, 2001.

Finkelstein, I. and Naaman, N. (editors). *From Nomadism to Monarchy: Archaeological and Historical Aspects of Early Israel*. Jerusalem, 1994.

Finkelstein, I. *The Archaeology of the Israelite Settlement*. Jerusalem: Israel Exploration Society, 1988.

Freedman D.N. and Graf D.F., eds., *Palestine in Transition*, Sheffield, 1983.

Frerichs, E. S., and Lesko L.H., eds. *Exodus: The Egyptian Evidence.* Winona Lake, Ind.:Eisenbrauns, 1997.

Friedman R.E., *Who Wrote the Bible?*, New York: HarperCollins Publishers, 1997.

Gernot W., *The Hurrians*, 1989.

Gitin, S., Mazar, A. and Stern, E. *Mediterranean Peoples in Transition: Thirteenth To Early Tenth Centuries B.C.E.* Jerusalem, 1998.

Giveon R., *The Impact of Egypt on Canaan*, Gottingen, 1978.

Gottwald N.K., *The Tribes of Yahweh: A Sociology of the Religion of Liberated Israel 1250-1050 B.C.E.* Maryknoll, N.Y.: Orbis, 1979.

Grabbe L.L., *Ancient Israel.* New York: T & T Clark, 2007.

Greenberg M., *The Hab/piru*, New Haven, Conn., 1955.

Gurney O.R, *The Hittites*, revised edition, New York: Penguin, 1990.

Hayes W.C., *A Papyrus of the Late Middle Kingdom in the Brooklyn Museum*, Brooklyn, 1955.

Hazel M.G., 'Israel in the Merneptah Stela', *BASOR* 296 (1994), pp. 45-61.

Helck W., *Die Beziehungen Ägyptens zur Vorderasien*, Wiesbaden, 1972.

Hoffmeier, J.K. *Israel in Egypt: The Evidence for the Authentisity of the Exodus Tradition.* New York: Oxford University Press, 1997.

Isserlin B.S. J., *The Israelites.* Minneapolis: Fortress Press, 2001.

Jordanes, *The Origin and Deeds of the Goths* (3.12).

Josephus Flavius, *Against Apion*, Book 1, Section 73 (P., 1912).

Julius Caesar, *War in Gaul*, 4.16-18.

Kenyon K. M., *Archaeology in the Holy Land*, 4th ed, 1985.

Killebrew, A.E., *Biblical Peoples and Ethnicity.* Atlanta: Society of Biblical Literature, 2005.

Klengel, H., *Syria: 3000 to 300 B.C.E.: A Handbook of Political History*, Berlin: Akademie, 1992.

Krauss R., *Das Ende der Amarna-Zeit* (Hildesheim, 1976).

Kuhne C., *Die Chronologie der internazionalen Correspondenz von El-Amarna* Neu-Kirchen-Vluyn, 1973.

Kuhrt A., *The Ancient Near East c. 3000-330 B.C.E.*, 2 vols, London: Rutledge, 1995.

Lemche N.P., *Die Vorgeschichte Israels. Von den Änfangen bis zum Ausgang des 13. Jahrhunderts v. Chr.*, Stuttgart, 1996.

Leonard, A., Jr, 'Archaeological Sources for the History of Palestine: The Late Bronze Age', *Biblical Archaeologist 52*, 1989, 4-39.

Lloyd S., *The Archaeology of Mesopotamia: from the Old Stone to the Persian Conquest*, 1984.

Loretz O., *Habiru-Hebräer: Eine sozial-ling. Studie*, Berlin, 1984.

Machinist, P. "Outsiders or Insiders: The Biblical View of Emergent Israel and Its Contexts." In The Other in Jewish Thought and History: Consructions of Jewish Culture and Identity, eds. L. J. Silberstein and R. L. Cohn, 35-60. New York: New York University Press, 1994.

Manassa C., *The Great Karnak Inscription of Merneptah: Grand Strategy in the 13ᵗʰ Century B.C.*, Yale Egyptological Studies 5, New Haven: Yale Egyptological Seminar, 2003.

Manetho, *Aegyptiaca*, frag. 42, 1.75-79.2.

Mazar A., *Archaeology of the Land of the Bible, 10,000-586 B.C.E.E*, New York: Doubleday, 1992, p. 38.

McGovern P., *The Foreign Relations of the 'Hyksos'. A neutron activation study of Middle Bronze Age pottery from the Eastern Mediterranean*, Oxford, 2000.

Metzger, B.M., and Coogan M.D., eds, *The Oxford Companion to the Bible*, New York: Oxford University Press, 1993.

Moran W.L., *The Amarna Letters*, Baltimore: Johns Hopkins University Press, 1992.

Murnane W., *Texts from the Amarna Period in Egypt*, Atlanta, 1995.

Na'aman N., 'Habiru and Hebrews: The Transfer of a Social Term to the Literary Sphere', *JNES* 45, No. 4 (1986), pp. 271-88.

Na'aman, N. "The 'Conquest of Canaan' in the Book of Joshua and in History." In *From Nomadism to Monarchy: Archaeological and Historical Aspects of Early Israel*, Jerusalem, 1994. ed. I. Finkelstein and N. Na'aman, 218-81. Washington, D.C.: Biblical Archaeology Society, 1994.

Nelson, R.D. *Joshua: A Commentary.* Louisville, 1997.

Nicholson, E. W. *Exodus and Sinai in History and Tradition* (Oxford: Blackwell), 1973.

O'Donnell J., *Cassiodorus*, Berkeley: University of California Press, 1979.

Oren E., ed., *The Sea Peoples and Their World: A Reassessment*. Philadelphia: University of Pennsylvania, 2000.

Oren E.D. (ed.), *The Hyksos: New Historical and Archaeological Perspectives*, Philadelphia, 1997.

Orni, E., and Ephrat E., *Geography of Israel*. 4th ed., Jerusalem: Israel Universities Press, 1980.

Parrot A., *Abraham and His Times*, 1968.

Pliny the Elder, *Natural History* (4.100).

Pomponius Mela, *Description of the World* (III.3.31).

Postgate N., *The First Empires*, 1977.

Potts, D.T, *Mesopotamian Civilization: The Material Foundations*, Ithaca, NY: Cornell University Press, 1997.

Pritchard J.B., ed., *Ancient Near Eastern Texts Relating to the Old Testament*, Princeton: Princeton University Press, 1969.

Provan I., Long V.P., and Longman T. III, *A Biblical History of Israel*, Louisville, Kentucky: Westminster John Knox Press, 2003.

Quirke S., *The Administration of Egypt in the Late Middle Kingdom*, New Malden, 1990.

Rainey A.F., "Israel in Merenptah's Inscription and Reliefs", *IEJ* 5, pp.57-75.

Rainey, A. F. (ed.) *Egypt, Israel, Sinai: Archaeological and Historical Relationships in the Biblical Period*. Tel Aviv: Tel-Aviv University, 1987.

Redford D.B., *Egypt, Canaan and Israel in Ancient Times*, Princeton: Princeton University Press, 1993.

Redford, in the bibliography to chapter 3.

Riabinin A.I. and Kravets V.N., *Sovremennoe sostoyanie serovodorodnoy zony Chernogo moria: 1960-1986 gody*, 1989.

Roaf M., *Cultural Atlas of Mesopotamia and the Ancient Near East*, 1990.

Ryholt K., *The Political Situation in Egypt during the Second Intermediate Period*, Copenhagen, 1997.

Sandars, N.K., *The Sea Peoples: Warriors of the Ancient Mediterranean 1250-1150 B.C.E.* Rev.ed. New York: Thames and Hudson, 1985.

Sarna, N.M., *Exploring Exodus*, New York: Schocken Books, 1996.

Shanks H., ed., *Ancient Israel: From Abraham to the Roman Destruction of the Temple.* 2nd rev. ed. Washington: Biblical Archaeology Society, 1999.

Singer, I., 'A Concise History of Amurru', appendix in Sh. Izre'el, *Amurru Akkadian: A Linguistic Study,* 2, pp. 135-94, Harvard Semitic Studies, 41, Atlanta: Scholars Press, 1991.

Smith H.S. and Smith A., 'A Reconsideration of the Kamose Texts', *ZAS* 103 (1976), 48-76.

Smith M.S., *The Early History of God. Yahweh and the Other Deities in Ancient Israel.* 2nd ed. Dearborn, Michigan: Dove Booksellers, 2002.

Snell, D.C., *Life in the Ancient Near East, 3100-332 B.C.E.E,* New Haven, Conn: Yale University Press, 1997.

Stager L.E., 'Forging an Identity: The Emergence of Ancient Israel' in *The Oxford History of the Biblical World,* ed. D. Coogan. Oxford University Press: New York, 2001, pp.100-102.

Stiebing, W. H., *Out of the Desert? Archaeology and the Exodus/Conquest Narratives,* Buffalo, New York: Prometheus, 1989.

Tacitus, *Germania,* Part II.

The Book of Jubilees or the Little Genesis, trans. R.H. Charles and G.H. Box, Kessinger Publishing, LLC, 2006.

Tolmazin D., 'Changing Coastal Oceanography of the Black Sea', *Progress in Oceanography,* 15(4):pp. 217-316, 1985.

Vaux R. de, *Ancient Israel: Its Life and Institutions,* 2nd ed., 1973.

Wiener M.C.and Allen J., 'Separate Lives: the Ahmose Tempest Stela and the Theban eruption', *JNES* 57/1 (1998), 1-28.

Yurco, F. J. "3,200-Year-Old Picture of Israelites Found in Egypt." *Biblical Archaeology Review* 16, no. 5 (September-October 1990): 20-38. idem, 'Merenptah's Canaanite Campaign and Israel's Origins', in *Exodus: The Egyptian Evidence,* pp. 27-55.

Index

9 780578 536309